Barcode in Back

D0435499

REGULATING FLEXIBILITY

Regulating Flexibility

The Political Economy of Employment Standards

MARK P. THOMAS

McGill-Queen's University Press

Montreal & Kingston · London · Ithaca

© McGill-Queen's University Press 2009
ISBN-978-0-7735-3516-9

Legal deposit second quarter 2009
Bibliothèque nationale du Québec

Printed in Canada on acid-free paper that is 100% ancient forest free
(100% post-consumer recycled), processed chlorine free.

This book has been published with the help of a grant from the
Canadian Federation for the Humanities and Social Sciences, through
the Aid to Scholarly Publications Programme, using funds provided by
the Social Sciences and Humanities Research Council of Canada.

McGill-Queen's University Press acknowledges the support of the Canada
Council for the Arts for our publishing program. We also acknowledge
the financial support of the Government of Canada through the Book
Publishing Industry Development Program (BPIDP) for our publishing
activities.

National Library of Canada Cataloguing in Publication
Thomas, Mark P. (Mark Preston), 1969-
    Regulating flexibility: the political economy of employment standards /
    Mark P. Thomas.
    Includes bibliographical references and index.
    ISBN 978-0-7735-3516-9
    1. Labor laws and legislation – Canada. 2. Labor laws and legislation –
    Social aspects – Canada. 3. Manpower policy – Canada. I. Title.
    KE3247.T48 2009   344.7101   C2009-901259-6

Typeset in New Baskerville 10.5/13
by Infoscan Collette, Quebec City

Contents

Tables

Acknowledgments

The original framework for this project was conceived while I walked a picket line during a seventy-eight-day strike undertaken by teaching assistants, contract faculty, and graduate assistants (CUPE Local 3903) at York University, a strike that began on 26 October 2000 and ended in early January 2001. Writing is a much more solitary process than walking a picket line, of course, and while I constructed the outline of the project during picket shifts and in between strike support duties, the actual research and writing for this book took place over the course of a number of years following the resolution of that strike. But, like participating in the strike, I found working on this project to be a collaborative process. I would like to take this opportunity to acknowledge the many people who directly and indirectly contributed to the development of this text.

Norene Pupo was an exceptional supervisor throughout my doctoral program and has been a supportive mentor and colleague in the years since. Pat Armstrong and David McNally provided much-needed input, guidance, and support as the project developed. Along with essential feedback at all stages of the project, all three also provided inspiring examples of the ways in which academic work can be made relevant to communities outside the university. I am very fortunate to have many other colleagues in the field of labour studies from whom I have drawn support, energy, and inspiration as the writing of this work progressed. Special thanks to David Camfield, Wayne Lewchuk, Robert O'Brien, Steve Tufts, Leah Vosko, Don Wells, Charlotte Yates, the members of the Toronto Labour Studies Group, and all the "new voices" in Canadian labour studies. I would also like to thank Robin Smith and Daphne Paszterko at the Centre for Research on Work and Society at York University for providing me with a home in the first years of my appointment at York, and all the graduate and undergraduate students who helped to create such an energetic environment in the centre. Sarah Rogers was an outstanding research assistant as I brought this project to completion.

I am deeply grateful to Philip Cercone at McGill-Queen's University Press for his steadfast support for this book. I am equally appreciative for all the assistance I received from the staff at the press who kept the project moving. My thanks to Joanne Pisano, Ligy Alakkattussery, and Joan McGilvray. Navigating the myriad of documents at the Archives of Ontario would not have been possible without the assistance of the many skilled archivists who accommodated my research requests. I would particularly like to thank Mary Akenson, Judith Emory, and Susan Maclure in this regard. I also wish to thank the anonymous reviewers of earlier drafts of the book for supportive and insightful comments. An abbreviated version of chapter 2 first appeared as "Setting the Minimum: Ontario's Employment Standards in the Postwar Years, 1944–1968," *Labour/Le Travail: Journal of Canadian Labour Studies* 54 (2004): 49–82.

My sincerest thanks to all those who took time to participate in the project. Many organizations provided me with documents that illustrated their involvement in the employment standards policy-making process. I would like to pay special thanks to the members of the Employment Standards Work Group who participated in the project for all the information and assistance they provided. I would also like to thank all those who participated in the interviews. They all took time away from very busy schedules to patiently answer my questions, share their experiences and insights, and offer their enthusiasm for the project. For reasons of confidentiality, they must remain anonymous.

Finally, my family has been a source of constant and unequivocal support. I would like to thank my parents, Mary and Pat Thomas, for their encouragement through all the years of my university education and in the years since I began working at York University. And my deepest thanks to Alina Chatterjee, whose love and support carried me through the completion of the manuscript.

REGULATING FLEXIBILITY

Introduction

The social organization of employment has undergone profound changes within advanced capitalist economies in recent decades. Downsizing strategies and lean production techniques have reorganized workplaces and labour processes, while the growth in non-standard and precarious forms of employment has altered the structure of labour markets. At the same time, labour forces have experienced dramatic demographic shifts, driven by patterns of feminization and immigration. Overarching all of these developments have been processes of economic "globalization": the geographic reorganization of manufacturing production, the growing power and mobility of transnational corporations, the spread of neoliberal social and economic policies, and new forms of cultural interpenetration and commodification.

In *The Brave New World of Work*, European sociologist Ulrich Beck (2000) defines this current conjuncture as a "political economy of insecurity." Key characteristics of this contemporary social context include the collapse of welfare states, an increased individualization of economic risks, and growing precariousness in job tenure. Similarly, a recent report from the International Labour Organization (ILO) states that "in most countries, alongside basic rights at work, there is widespread concern about matters pertaining to employment, wages, skills and poverty alleviation, related directly or indirectly to trade and globalization" (ILO 2002, 165).

Transformations in the organization of work contribute directly to conditions of insecurity, which are reflected quite clearly in reports of working conditions in the Canadian labour market. Recent surveys of work experiences in Canada include findings of job insecurity, job stress, and growing levels of work-life conflict owing to long hours and a lack of control over working time.[1] There are also reports of increased levels of income disparity and economic insecurity, as the changing labour market includes growing numbers of the working poor.[2] Labour market policies have supported and exacerbated this trajectory.[3] As concerns about work quality and labour market insecurity grow, so too do policy debates regarding the appropriate labour market institutions and regulatory strategies to improve working conditions and workplace protections. Employment standards – legally established minimum standards that apply to most employers and employees – constitute a key element in these debates.

STUDYING EMPLOYMENT STANDARDS

In a very general sense, employment standards can be defined as "any governmentally established procedure, term or condition of employment, or employer requirement that has as its purpose the protection of employees from treatment at the workplace that society considers unfair or unjust" (Block and Roberts 2000, 277). In Canada, employment standards include legislated standards in the areas of minimum wages, hours of work, overtime, leaves, and paid vacations and holidays. These standards are largely regulated at the provincial level, although some employees fall under the jurisdiction of the federally regulated Canada Labour Code. Because the legal implementation of employment standards occurs at national and sub-national levels, there is little uniformity in either the adoption of specific standards or the levels of minimum protections, either within or between nation-states. At the international level, employment standards are captured in a more general set of labour rights defined as international labour standards, which also include broader principles relating to freedom of association, protections against discrimination, prohibitions on child labour and forced labour, and health and safety rights.

Employment standards are a central component in a system of labour market regulation. Understanding their dynamics reveals much about the social organization of labour markets, as they both reflect and play an important role in shaping broader norms of employment. Since they establish minimum standards, they regulate the employment rights of the most vulnerable workers, primarily those engaged in non-unionized jobs in secondary labour markets (Fairey 2007). They thus establish the "socially acceptable" minimum that sets the basic framework of working conditions within a labour market, including the base for collective bargaining (Mitchell 2003): this base includes fundamental principles regarding wages, working time, and time away from work. Examining the development and regulation of employment standards makes it possible to investigate the normative framework that shapes the social organization of employment.

Employment standards also provide an important indicator of change in contemporary labour markets. In the context of tendencies towards labour market "flexibility," in particular tendencies created through forms of nonstandard and precarious employment, an analysis of employment standards indicates the character of labour flexibility; it directs attention to the legal framework that establishes the basic standards for "flexible" employment and the role of the state in its regulation. Further, as tendencies towards flexibility have marginalized women workers and workers of colour, in particular (Cranford et al. 2003; Gabriel 1999; Galabuzi 2006), the study of employment standards also provides an important indicator of the gendered and racialized dimensions of employment rights and economic restructuring.

Finally, employment standards (generally defined as labour standards in the international context) are a key site for new forms of labour regulation in the contemporary global economy. Corporate mobility and corporate power, facilitated through transnational trade agreements and international financial institutions, both increase competitive pressures between nation-states and challenge nationally based regulatory systems. These processes have combined to promote forms of "labour flexibility" that are associated with downward pressure on employment and labour standards. In this context, new transnational strategies to regulate labour/employment standards have emerged as both alternatives and supplements to nationally based regulatory systems. Key examples are developed through the actions of and interactions between non-state actors, including labour organizations and labour rights NGOs, as these organizations attempt to create regulatory systems that reflect the transnational character of the global economy. Studying the changing dynamics of the regulation of employment standards facilitates an understanding of key dimensions of the processes known as economic globalization.

THE POLITICAL ECONOMY
OF EMPLOYMENT STANDARDS

This book is a study of the political economy of employment standards in the Canadian labour market, with a particular emphasis on the relationship between employment standards legislation and "labour flexibility." The book uses a case study approach focusing primarily on the regulation of employment standards in the province of Ontario, which provides the means to develop a highly detailed analysis of the processes of policy development and their impacts. The detailed case study makes it possible to examine the ways in which broader social relations and processes – neoliberalism or globalization, for example – are implemented in very localized social contexts, and conversely, the ways in which localized phenomenon may reflect and shape these broader social relations and processes.

This book examines the development of employment standards legislation through several distinct historical periods, showing how legislative developments were enmeshed in wider sets of social relations in each period. Ontario provides a leading-edge example of the development of standards in Canada at two key historical points: first, in early efforts to regulate labour market vulnerability in the late nineteenth century and, second, in the drive towards neoliberal "labour flexibility" at the end of the twentieth. Although the book outlines the historical background to employment standards legislation, it is the shift to neoliberalism and its particular forms of labour flexibility that constitute the central problematic of the book. Moving beyond the specific case of Ontario, the book argues that neoliberal reforms normalized increased levels of both employer-oriented flexibility and labour market insecurity for many groups of workers.

The time frame begins in 1884 and ends in 2004 and is divided into three historical periods: 1884 to 1939, 1940 to 1968, and 1968 to 2004. During the first period, employment standards were gender-specific and were designed to protect only the most vulnerable – who at the time were understood to be women and children – from excessive hours of work. The post–World War II period began with the generalization of hours of work standards to male workers and culminated with the enactment of the Ontario Employment Standards Act (ESA) in 1968. Employment standards during this period were officially gender neutral but nonetheless supported the highly gendered norms of the "standard employment relationship." In the third time frame, employment standards reforms were undertaken as part of wider shifts towards neoliberal labour flexibility.

While these three periods constitute the formal, historical boundaries of the study, a fourth period is implied in the final chapters of the book: that of a possible future for the re-regulation of employment standards based on the need to provide improved labour protection in the contemporary global economy. The analysis is based on data collected from archival records, publications from government and non-governmental organizations, key informant interviews, and quantitative labour market data (see appendix 1).

The analysis is based in a political economy perspective that encompasses "the complex of institutions and relations that constitute not only what are conventionally referred to as the political and economic systems but also the social, physical, ideological, and cultural systems" (Armstrong and Armstrong 1996, 5). Wallace Clement (1997) outlines the key assumptions. First, social relations are shaped by relations of economic production and social reproduction. Second, the organization of production and reproduction are not just economic relations but are fundamentally social, cultural, and political relations as well. Third, social relations are historical and dynamic. Fourth, tensions and contradictions within society produce resistance to the social order. And finally, human agency plays an important role in shaping social, political, and economic relations.

From this perspective, the state and the labour market are interrelated: changes in the labour market are not independent from labour and employment policies; similarly, changes in state policies may have an impact on the labour market. One does not merely follow the other; instead, the interrelationship creates a dynamic of both reproduction and social change. Moreover, the social organization of labour markets and the development of labour and employment policies are not natural, self-guiding phenomena. They are produced within specific social and historical contexts and through relations of conflict and contradiction. From this perspective, employment standards exist in a complex relationship with the labour market, not only by imposing standards on workplaces but also by contributing to the overall structure of the labour market and to changes in its social organization. Further, employment standards are a product of specific historical conditions and must be investigated as such.

While class relations are central to political economy, class cannot be abstracted from other social, cultural, and political relations (Acker 2006; Adib and Guerrier 2003; Bannerji 1995; Cook and Roberts 2000; Sudbury 1998). Political economy points social analysis towards understanding inequalities, power relationships, and tensions between intersecting social relations of class, gender, race, ethnicity, and immigration status, for example (Armstrong and Armstrong 1996). This method of analysis does not simply add together separately conceived social relations; rather, it recognizes differences in social experience (different class experiences depending on gender, for example) and builds a recognition of these differences into sociological research (Clement and Miles 1994). It sees the interconnections between relations of class, race, and gender while recognizing their historically and socially situated character. The concept of social reproduction, with its emphasis on the interconnected nature of the labour market and the domestic sphere, is central to this methodology, particularly in examining the gendered dimensions of policy development (Bezanson and Luxton 2006). From this perspective, then, employment standards must be examined as the product of an interconnected set of social, political, and economic relationships that are based in the class relations of capitalism, relations that are themselves simultaneously gendered and racialized and that are constructed through interconnections between states, markets, and households (O'Conner et al. 1999).

Finally, the central concept of social agency requires that employment standards be investigated as the product of complex interactions between human agents. While not always successful in securing specific goals, labour, business, and women's and community organizations have acted as some of the primary sources of pressure directed at the state to develop legislated standards. Their ideals and actions illustrate the dynamics of social agency in the process of policy development. By focusing on these organizations, this study also attempts to direct attention to the social forces that may promote new approaches to the regulation of employment standards and to alternative models of labour flexibility that may be able to counter conditions of labour market vulnerability and insecurity.

OUTLINE OF THE STUDY

The book begins with the analytic framework that is used throughout the study. Chapter 1 develops an analytic framework that brings together several bodies of scholarly research, including state theory and labour market segmentation theory, and connects these to the theme of labour flexibility. Building on political economy that is grounded in intersectional analysis, the chapter integrates the concepts of feminization and racialization into this approach. It argues for the need to integrate the analysis of labour market institutions (the state, unions, employer associations) with the study of the wider sets of social relations between states, markets, and households.

This framework forms a backdrop for the study of employment standards legislation in Ontario presented in chapters 2 to 4. Chapter 2 explores the early origins of employment standards by outlining legislative developments in pre– and post–World War II time frames. The Ontario Factories Act of 1884, with its legislated maximum hours of work for women and children, was the first attempt by the state to regulate hours of work. Minimum wage laws for women workers were also introduced during this period, just after the First World War. The chapter argues that these early examples of employment standards legislation established patterns that remained consistent in key ways throughout the twentieth century, both in their efforts to minimize their impact on business interests and in their gendered approach to labour market policy. Postwar employment standards legislation is situated in the context of the postwar settlement that included the enactment of certification and collective bargaining legislation that facilitated unionization in mass production industries. The gendered differentiation that was formally integrated into hours of work and minimum wage policies in the pre–World War II period was to a large extent eliminated over the course of the postwar years. Employment standards, nonetheless, remained implicitly gendered and also racialized. Thus, the state's regulation of employment standards contributed to patterns of segmentation within the postwar labour market. The chapter concludes by outlining the constellation of factors that shaped the development of the Ontario Employment Standards Act, which was enacted in 1968.

By the early 1970s, the Keynesian paradigm that had shaped policy development in the postwar years was challenged by corporate interests intent on restructuring workplaces, labour markets, and labour policies. Chapter 3 examines the processes of labour market restructuring that began in the early 1970s, including shifts towards particular forms of labour flexibility. The chapter situates reforms to employment standards in the 1970s, 1980s, and early 1990s in a context of multiple recessions and dramatic labour market change. While several provincial governments investigated a variety of legislative reforms, and implemented a few, these reforms were not sufficient to counter the heightened conditions of insecurity that were building in the labour market at the time. Ultimately, the reforms undertaken in this period ensured that employment standards remained a secondary set of employment rights, encouraging rather than challenging the emerging neoliberal model of labour flexibility. Key to this were the many exemptions in the legislation, as well as a system of insufficient enforcement.

Chapter 3 also examines the regulatory practices embedded within employment standards legislation to more fully uncover these tendencies. Through a detailed examination of legislative coverage, enforcement, and dispute resolution practices, the chapter argues that these regulatory practices further exacerbated experiences of labour market vulnerability. It is through this discussion that the implications of the gendered and racialized dimensions of employment standards become the clearest.

Following the defeat of the New Democratic provincial government of the early 1990s, Ontario's politics took a sharp neoliberal turn. Chapter 4 focuses on employment standards reforms undertaken by the neoliberal government of Ontario at the end of the twentieth century. The chapter situates these reforms in the context of broader policy shifts oriented towards promoting market-based, privatized, and individualized social relations. The chapter argues that the policy reforms introduced through the Employment Standards Act 2000 reduced direct government involvement in the regulation of workplace standards, promoted increased employer control over work time, facilitated the normalization of nonstandard employment relationships, and increased the vulnerability of workers in non-unionized workplaces. While it claimed to promote "flexibility and fairness" for workers and employers, the new employment standards legislation actually promoted a one-sided model of labour flexibility that contributed to the normalization of the experiences of insecure employment. The chapter concludes by arguing that the restructuring of employment standards is a central component of a much broader process of labour market and workplace reorganization.

Finally, chapter 5 shifts the focus to the level of the global economy. Processes of economic globalization, including the geographic fragmentation of production, growing corporate power, and the predominance of neoliberal policies, have challenged and undermined traditional methods of labour market regulation. As mentioned above, new forms of regulation have emerged in this context. While employment standards are primarily regulated through national and sub-national (provincial, state) legislation, international and transnational institutions and agreements, such as the International Labour Organization and the North American Agreement on Labor Cooperation, have formed to work with and through nation states to regulate labour standards at international and transnational levels. Additionally, privatized forms of transnational labour regulation, such as corporate codes of conduct, have also emerged as non-state regulatory alternatives. The chapter therefore explores the ability of these institutions and mechanisms to develop and implement meaningful and effective labour standards in the contemporary global economy. While the chapter focuses on *supra*-national and non-state forms of regulation, it is connected to the case study developed in the rest of the book by examining the relationship between these mechanisms and localized, legislative-based models. A key determinant of the effectiveness of transnational strategies lies in the ways in which they are implemented and enforced at the local level. The chapter ends by making the case for a project of labour market re-regulation that works from the bottom up, beginning with strong localized legislation.

The book concludes on this theme by arguing that to address growing conditions of labour market insecurity and precariousness, we need a new approach to the regulation of employment standards. Re-regulating the labour market from the bottom up begins by raising the floor for the most vulnerable workers. Rather than treating minimum employment standards as a secondary form of protection, we must understand them as a cornerstone in a progressive project of labour market re-regulation.

1

"Labour Flexibility" and the Political Economy of Employment Standards

An economic downturn in the advanced capitalist economies beginning in the early 1970s initiated a widespread shift in the social organization of employment. "Labour flexibility" became a catchword to justify and promote the reorganization of production processes, employment relationships, and labour market policies. The need for more flexible systems of labour market regulation was widely promoted in corporate, government, and academic reports, including the highly influential 1994 OECD *Jobs Study* (Stanford 2000; Rubery and Grimshaw 2003). Developing labour flexibility was presented as a means to increase productivity, overcome unemployment, and reduce labour costs. The emphasis on particular forms of flexibility held profound implications for the regulation of employment standards.

This book aims to develop an integrated analysis of the political economy of employment standards. What role does employment standards legislation play in processes of labour market regulation? What are the social processes, relations, and forces that shape the regulation of employment standards? In what ways have employment standards been implicated in shifts to labour flexibility? In what ways are existing models of employment standards connected to conditions of labour market vulnerability and precariousness, and in what ways might alternative approaches to employment standards be capable of addressing such conditions? While subsequent chapters address the above questions in detail, this chapter aims to develop the theoretical framework that is used throughout this book to analyze the political economy of employment standards.

Building on the political economy methodology outlined in the introduction, this chapter establishes a framework that directs attention to the social processes and relations that shape the development of employment standards. It includes an analysis of labour market institutions, in particular governments and trade unions. It also suggests that while focusing on the state as a key actor, the analysis must also explore the larger sets of social relations of which employment standards are a part.

DEFINING "LABOUR FLEXIBILITY": INTRODUCTORY REMARKS

Within the scholarly literature on labour market regulation, the term "flexibility" is used – sometimes interchangeably and sometimes without conceptual clarity or distinction – in relation to a number of different concepts that characterize contemporary employment relationships, concepts such as nonstandard, contingent, precarious, and deregulated employment (Felstead and Jewson 1999). Given the wide range of usage, the term "labour flexibility" has taken on multiple meanings within the research literature, which has identified numerous forms of flexibility, including flexible employment relationships, flexible production strategies, flexible technologies, and flexible forms of labour market regulation (Burchell et al. 2002; Cook and Roberts 2000; Harvey 1990; Kalleberg 2001a; Salais 1992).

"Flexibility" has been used to refer to the "degree of adaptability of productive organizations," the "ability of workers to move from one job to another," the "laxity of legal constraints governing the contract of employment," the "adaptability of wages," and the "possibility for companies to relieve themselves of some of their social and fiscal payments" (Boyer 1988, 223–6). "Flexibility" may refer to policy strategies undertaken by nation-states to reverse trends of unemployment and labour market rigidity or to organizational strategies that alter the distribution of work tasks and the size of the labour force (Kalleberg 2001b; Standing 1999). Flexibility is also associated with employee empowerment and so-called family-friendly approaches to work time (Rosenfeld 2001). In uncritical accounts, labour flexibility is widely heralded as providing the keys to both productivity and work quality, as "newly skilled, continually learning, empowered and engaged workers, aided by entrepreneurial managers, strive to relax and flatten rigid bureaucracies, trim excessive use of organizational resources ... and use their experiential knowledge to improve the way they produce goods or serve people" (Smith 1997, 315–16).

When analyzing the implementation of flexibility strategies, it is essential to assess the power relations that underlie flexible employment and to consider the question of flexibility for whom, as employer-oriented flexibility and employee-oriented flexibility may diverge (Clement 2007; Fudge 2001; Rosenberg 1989). While the former prioritizes the reduction of labour costs, the removal of legal regulations, and the elimination of union-negotiated work rules and benefits, the latter seeks flexibility in work arrangements to better balance paid work with other, particularly household, responsibilities. Guy Standing (1992), for example, differentiates between "subordinated flexibility," which increases economic insecurity and labour market polarization, and "cooperative flexibility," which is premised on the need to improve labour security and collective regulations through new forms of unionism, new approaches to leaves and retirements, cooperative employment ventures, and income transfers. Similarly, Wallace Clement (2001, 80) has noted that "flexibility" can be "a euphemism for low-paid, available-on-demand, disposable workers or work that adapts to the variety of demands to which people are subject," such as family responsibilities, education, and other interests. In other words, labour flexibility is inherently shaped by the social relations and social conflicts of the workplace. In order to understand the social dynamics of labour flexibility, it is necessary to contextualize flexibility strategies within the dynamics of capitalist employment relations.

In the current period of labour market transformation, in which flexibility strategies have been popularized, flexibility is most often associated with the predominance of employer-oriented initiatives. Workplace flexibility strategies initiated in the 1980s produced a growth in insecure forms of employment, increased labour market and income polarization, and eroded collective agreements and regulatory protections, thereby promoting, overall, a "low road" to economic growth (Harrison 1994). These trends continued into the 1990s, as flexibility strategies continued to produce employment instability, as well as new forms of labour control and work intensification (Smith 1997). These shifts have generated wide-ranging employee concerns, in particular fears of employment and income insecurity (Hudson 2002). In this context, it is not difficult to see why many commentators argue that it is workers who have born the costs of flexibility (Drache 1992; Johnson et al. 1994). As Graham Lowe (2000, 80) suggests, while "flexibility" was "an economic catchword" in the 1990s, "in practice it has contributed little to improving the quality of work."

At the policy level, labour flexibility is often associated with the u.s. model of market deregulation (Stanford and Vosko 2004). Certainly, deregulation is a key principle of neoliberal strategies, as proponents advocate a deregulation of labour markets, reductions in state spending on employment and income security policies (e.g., unemployment insurance), and increased cross-border free trade (Brodie 1996a; McBride and Shields 1997). Policy in this political context is often shifted away from the provision of social security towards the promotion of individual entrepreneurialism (Peck 1996, 2001). Neoliberal deregulation may occur in forms that are either explicit, through strategies such as privatization or contracting out, or implicit, through a lack of enforcement of existing legislation (Bakker 1996).

Proponents of this model suggest that it is a recipe for employment growth and economic prosperity. Yet flexibility based on deregulation has produced rising inequality in both pay and employment prospects in North American labour markets (Rubery and Grimshaw 2003).[1] The u.s. model of flexibility has also tended to result in greater worker discipline, rather than improved quality of work or greater employee control over working time. In an examination of the general shift towards the workfare state, Jamie Peck (1996, 74) suggests that flexible labour policies attempt to "discipline the unemployed with the economic whip of market forces while further weakening labour unions and breaking up institutional structures used by labour (and employers) in defense against the market." Rather than a growth strategy, flexibility in this form is better understood as a strategy for employers to secure concessions or to construct a workforce that is easier to control.

Furthermore, the simple equation of flexibility with "deregulation" may in fact present a misleading picture of the social organization of contemporary labour markets. Beginning with the assertion that "there is no such thing as an unregulated or deregulated labour market," Guy Standing (1999, 39) argues that strategies of policy reform that are commonly described as deregulation should more accurately be described as promoting "market regulation," since they use legislation and policy to "maximize reliance on market forces" and to "weaken protective regulations, restrict collective institutions and strengthen pro-individualistic regulations" (42). When examined in this light, policies promoting labour flexibility may be better understood as *re*-regulating labour markets in ways that increase workers' exposure to market forces.[2]

FROM WELFARE STATES TO WORKFARE STATES

The market regulation model of labour flexibility developed in the context of broader political shifts from Keynesian to neoliberal state forms. The Keynesian welfare state (KWS) – the predominant form among the capitalist democracies from 1945 to 1975 – maintained policy goals of employment security and stability in order to promote economic growth. The general characteristics of the KWS included social policy oriented towards universal welfare rights, social needs, and economic redistribution; a system of labour market regulation based on extensive state involvement in the social reproduction of labour power and the goal of full male employment; macroeconomic policy based on interventionist measures supporting economies of scale; state discourses emphasizing productivity and planning; wage relations premised on the acceptance of collective bargaining and the promotion of norms of mass consumption; and highly regulated international relations (Peck 1996).[3]

This policy framework sought to provide workers with some income protection against market forces through social security policies such as unemployment insurance and old-age pensions (Esping-Andersen 1990).[4] While the welfare state never eliminated the commodity status of labour power, Keynesian polices did buffer the impact of the free market.[5] Employment security was primarily constructed through policies that supported the standard employment relationship for male wage earners (Vosko 2000).

Post–World War II labour relations policies were central to the efforts of the KWS to promote labour stability. These policies sought to respond to demands both for improved working conditions (from workers and unions), and for restrictions on industrial disruption (from employers). In the context of the period, Fordist approaches to mass production, combined with Keynesian welfare state policies, led to systems of labour relations in industrialized economies that have been described as "post-war political-economic settlements" (Hyman 1994, 5). The specificities of such arrangements varied within national boundaries (Albo and Roberts 1998). Nonetheless, the principles were similar: unions gained organizational stability; union members gained regular wage increases and stable employment; and employers were ensured of "responsible" unionism through regular collective bargaining, thereby minimizing workplace disruption (Phillips 1997; Russell 1990). This form of state intervention created a "hegemonic regime" as it sought to secure workers' consent to capitalist control of production through forms of state intervention that provided social welfare, restricted management discretion, and allowed for the bureaucratic regulation of the workplace through high levels of unionization (Burawoy 1985).[6] The hegemonic character of postwar industrial relations was based on interconnected compromises made by unions and employers that limited the capacity of unionized workers to challenge the capitalist order but that at the same time met some of the demands of union members.

Along with a policy approach that promoted stability, the state itself also became a site of stable employment. During the postwar years, public sector employment expanded dramatically, coinciding with the feminization of the labour market during the postwar period, which led many women into paid employment in the public sector. Following the unionization of public sector workplaces, the postwar Canadian state became a "crucial site of 'good' jobs for women" (Sears 1999, 101).

While the KWS sought to limit flexibility, at least for a core segment of workers in the primary labour market, the transition away from welfare state models towards neoliberal or "workfare" states brought new approaches to labour market regulation. Neoliberal states have sought to introduce greater flexibility in labour markets and employment relationships as a response to the "rigidity" of Keynesian policies. Their policy orientation may be defined as "the promotion of … market innovation; the enhancement of the structural competitiveness of open economies mainly through supply-side intervention; and the subordination of social policy to the demands of labour market flexibility and structural competitiveness" (Jessop 1993, 9). This orientation includes strategies such as social policy driven by cost-saving concerns, labour market re-regulation to promote competition, macroeconomic policy oriented towards the promotion of flexible innovation, wage relations based on flexible wage systems and individual merit pay, and the deregulation of cross-border activities (Peck 1996). To the extent that the KWS sought to de-commodify labour power, neoliberal states have reversed this process through the elimination of programs and entitlements that reduce workers' absolute reliance on the market.

The hegemonic regimes of the postwar period were replaced by forms of "hegemonic despotism" as shifts to neoliberal labour flexibility took hold (Burawoy 1985). These patterns are clear in the Canadian state's approach to labour relations as, following a neoliberal paradigm, successive federal and provincial governments implemented legislative measures to restrict and eliminate the labour rights established in the postwar era. By the 1970s, the Canadian state had begun to develop a more coercive approach to labour relations, in particular by placing greater restrictions on strike activity and on workplace organizing (Haiven 1995; McBride 1995; Panitch and Swartz 2003).

Specific measures included federal and provincial wage controls, back-to-work legislation, and the amendment or rewriting of various labour laws (McBride and Shields 1997). The 1975–78 Anti-Inflation Program, the 1982–83 "six-and-five" program, and the 1991 federal budget all circumvented the collective bargaining process to restrict wage gains of unionized workers, primarily those in the public sector.[7] The 1993 Social Contract program of the Ontario NDP government and the 1995 labour law reforms of the subsequent Conservative government provide notable provincial examples.[8] Currently, the basic legislative mechanisms of the postwar system still exist; but recurring recessions, high unemployment, economic restructuring, and neoliberal politics have prompted significant shifts in the regulatory context towards neoliberal versions of labour flexibility.[9]

While the principles of neoliberalism call for a reduction of state intervention in the economy, neoliberal state policies are in fact oriented towards changing the way in which the state intervenes, rather than simply organizing its withdrawal from market activities. In practice this has meant that as states have implemented the neoliberal paradigm, they have adopted an "increasingly active role in restructuring the economy in the interests of capital" (Wood 1998, 13). As discussed, this approach may include increased hostility towards trade unionism and policies that attempt to discipline workers to satisfy the demands of the contemporary labour market. Building on the assumption that states may have new or changing (but not reduced) roles in this context, it becomes evident, as already mentioned, that neoliberalism, particularly when viewed in relation to patterns of labour flexibility, is more accurately understood as a re-regulation (rather than a deregulation) of employment relations (Murray et al. 2000). Public policy has been reconstructed to promote the goals of economic competitiveness, thereby creating new forms of state regulation oriented towards supporting and promoting shifts towards neoliberal forms of labour flexibility.

Building on the conception of market regulation, it can be argued that the shift towards this particular model of flexibility is, in fact, a shift towards an *increased* commodification of labour. As discussed above, one of the central goals of the Keynesian Welfare State was to facilitate the de-commodification of labour power by providing a buffer for workers against the absolute forces of the capitalist market, for example through income security and unemployment insurance programs and through the forms of labour and employment law developed during the period of the welfare state (Fudge and Tucker 2001): specifically legislation that facilitates collective organization or that otherwise reduces the impact of market forces on conditions of employment. In the current conjuncture, neoliberal states have increasingly acted to support capitalist power against the interests of workers, and in the name of labour flexibility, they have sought to reduce or re-regulate those buffers.

This shift did not occur in an economic vacuum but in the context of a broader restructuring of workplaces, employment relationships, and labour markets, processes examined in further detail in later chapters. Under the name of flexibility, processes of restructuring have sought to increase competitive pressures between workers while reducing their employment security, their social power vis-à-vis their employers, their control over work, and their capacities to act collectively.

THE SOCIAL ORGANIZATION OF LABOUR MARKETS: SEGMENTATION, FEMINIZATION, RACIALIZATION

The traditional approach to analyzing labour market regulation focuses primarily on the role of labour market institutions – the state, trade unions, and employer associations (Rubery and Grimshaw 2003). An institutionalist approach seeks to understand how these institutions shape nationally or regionally specific patterns or processes. Since employment standards legislation is developed by the state, the state necessarily occupies a central position in the analysis of employment standards constructed in the following chapters. Focusing solely on state institutions does not present a complete picture of the dynamics of labour market regulation, however; there remains the need to account for the broader social relations that may shape the social organization of labour markets, as well as the development of and interactions between various labour market institutions.[10] The concepts of labour market segmentation, feminization, and racialization are particularly useful in this task.

Neoclassical labour market theories suggest that capitalist labour markets operate according to the principles of free economic competition in a self-equilibrating manner, where all actors within a market are subject to the same set of rules (the rules of competition and rational self-interest). Labour market segmentation theory developed out of a critique of these assumptions, in an attempt to account for a wider range of social, institutional, economic, and technological forces that shape the social organization of labour markets (Peck 1996).

Further, segmentation theorists rejected the conception of a single labour market, suggesting instead that within any labour market there are multiple sub-markets, which may be characterized by significant differences in working conditions, employment rights, and regulatory processes. At the core of segmentation theory is the assertion of labour market "dualism" – the division of labour markets into primary and secondary sectors (Doeringer and Piore 1971; Wilkinson 1981).[11] Primary markets are characterized by high levels of employment security and remuneration, occupational mobility through internal labour markets, and control over work. Jobs within primary labour markets also require high levels of formal skills and rely on high levels of technological investment and development. In contrast, secondary markets are characterized by low wages, low job security, few formal skill requirements, little technological investment, and little worker autonomy and mobility.

Early segmentation theorists advanced monocausal explanations for patterns of segmentation, explaining patterns of dualism by differences in the levels of technological advancement or by the dynamics of capitalist control (Rubery and Wilkinson 1994).[12] In attempt to move beyond these approaches, multicausal approaches assumed that labour market segmentation is shaped by multiple social and institutional forces and broader patterns of social organization (Peck 1996; Rubery 1992). At a general level, segmentation may result from the conditions of labour demand (technical requirements of production, internal firm stability, labour control strategies), labour supply (social reproduction, the social marginalization of specific categories of workers), or the influences of institutions such as the state and trade unions (Fudge and Tucker 2000). Further, no single set of conditions is accorded priority, as segmentation is considered to be "multiply determined" by "the combined effects of these three sets of causal tendencies" (Rubery and Wilkinson 1994, 61).

Segmentation theorists have sought to analyse patterns of segmentation in relation to, in part, the ascribed characteristics of workers, most notably gender and race. For example, feminist analyses of labour market segmentation have identified gendered dimensions to the social organization of labour markets and have developed the concept of feminization to explain several interrelated patterns in the labour markets of industrialized capitalist economies. Beginning in the post–World War II period, these labour markets experienced growing levels of participation of women in certain forms of paid work – the feminization of the workforce. Replicating earlier gendered divisions in work, however, this occurred along with the simultaneous designation of specific forms of work (or work tasks) as "women's work" – the feminization of work (Armstrong and Armstrong 1994; Rubery and Grimshaw 2003).

While women's participation in the labour force increased dramatically in the years following the postwar period, increases in participation were not accompanied by increases in the diversity of employment opportunities, as women's employment was largely shaped by highly gendered divisions of labour. For example, in Canada between 1941 and 1991 women's participation in the labour market increased from 20 percent to 60 percent (Armstrong and Armstrong 1994). By 1996, 71 percent of women with a spouse and children were working outside the home (Ontario 1998b). However, women were more likely to be employed in the service sector, in public service occupations such as nursing and elementary teaching, and in private sector service occupations, working as retail salespersons, secretaries, and cashiers (Statistics Canada 1998).[13] Further, women were much more likely to be employed in lower-tier (retail and consumer) services than men, and in forms of nonstandard work (Statistics Canada 1999, 2001). In 1996, 85 percent of women in the labour market were employed in the service sector, with 32 percent of these employed in the "lower-tier" services. Feminization and segmentation are thus connected, in part, through the overrepresentation of women workers in particular occupations and sectors.

Feminization also explains shifting employment norms in the last several decades of the twentieth century. One of the characteristics of the postwar economy was the emergence of the standard employment relationship (SER) as the dominant normative model of male employment. The SER was itself characterized as "a lifelong, continuous, full-time employment relationship where the worker has one employer and normally works on the employer's premises or under his or her direct supervision" (Vosko 2000, 24). Included within the SER were provisions for job security, predictable and reasonable hours, and a wage rate calculated to provide a male breadwinner with an income sufficient to support his family. The SER constituted an ideal type, however, rather than a homogenous employment experience. Many workers, particularly those who were not male and not white, fell outside the bounds of the SER, as employment outside the core industrial sectors was characterized by a variety of nonstandard employment relationships (NSERs) (Fudge and Vosko 2001a). Nonetheless, the SER provided a normative frame around which the expectations of employment during the postwar years came to be built.

The normative shift in employment relationships away from the SER is connected to the feminization of employment relationships (Vosko 2000). Beginning in the mid-1970s, the SER began to lose its dominant position in favour of nonstandard employment, which includes part-time work, temporary or contingent work, own-account self-employment, and work by multiple job-holders (NSER) (Krahn et al. 2006; Rinehart 2006).[14] This normative shift was premised on the assumption that increased flexibility within employment relationships is a fundamental necessity of economic competitiveness. Because of the way in which flexibility is built into the nonstandard employment relationship, nonstandard employment has been described as the "human resources equivalent to a just-in-time inventory system" (Barker and Christensen 1998, 1).[15]

As the concept of feminization implies, nonstandard employment relationships are themselves gendered. During the postwar period, nonstandard employment served to supplement and uphold the model of the SER and to provide employers with a flexible workforce, through gendered divisions of labour both within the household and in the labour market (Armstrong and Armstrong 1994; Fudge and Vosko 2001a). While women's labour market participation increased in the postwar years, women continued to be overrepresented in NSERs. By the mid-1990s, 40 percent of women, as compared to 27 percent of men, held some form of nonstandard employment, and women of all age categories were more likely to be employed in some form of nonstandard work (Krahn et al. 2006). By that point, women comprised over 70 percent of the adult part-time workforce and through the 1990s the growth in women's self-employment was approximately three times that of men's (Duffy 1997; Krahn et al. 2006; Statistics Canada 1997).

As the conditions of nonstandard employment correspond with the conditions of employment experienced by women, the growth in nonstandard employment has meant that more jobs are taking on the conditions of jobs most commonly held by women (Armstrong 1996). The feminization of the labour market is thus a multi-dimensional concept that refers to the increased participation of women in paid employment, gendered divisions of labour, and the shift in employment norms experienced by many advanced capitalist labour markets beginning in the 1970s.

Patterns of labour market segmentation and processes of labour market regulation are also shaped through processes of racialization – the "process by which racial categories are constructed as different and unequal in ways that lead to negative social, economic and political impacts for some groups" (Galabuzi 2001, 7). Patterns of racialization are clearly present within the Canadian labour market and include the ways in which immigrant and migrant workers are incorporated into the labour market, the ideological association of specific forms of work with racialized groups, and the overrepresentation of members of racialized groups in forms of nonstandard and precarious employment.

For example, patterns of marginalization stem directly from the manner in which migrant and immigrant workers are incorporated into the dominant relations of production of the society they are entering. Vic Satzewich (1991) identifies four primary forms of incorporation of foreign-born labourers: free immigrant labour, unfree immigrant labour, free migrant labour, and unfree migrant labour. Each form of incorporation is defined by the intersection of two conditions: the ability of the workers to circulate in the labour market and the nature of their citizenship status. Limited access to citizenship may be tied to legislative mechanisms that prevent free movement of workers, for example in the case of agricultural workers and domestic workers (Basok 2002; Macklin 1994; Stasiulis and Bakan 2005). Thus, citizenship is used to define entitlement to rights and protections in the labour market, since it legitimizes processes premised upon the principle that "foreigners" should not have the same rights (economic, political, social) as nationals (Sharma 2006). In this way, citizenship is connected to the creation of groups of "highly exploitable and socially excluded workers" by shaping their incorporation into a labour market in clearly racialized and gendered forms (Baines and Sharma 2002, 76).

Patterns of segmentation are also created through racist ideologies that construct associations between racialized groups and categories of employment that are generally considered to be undesirable. For example, divisions of labour in auto plants in the postwar years were shaped by forms of racism that led to Black men being most likely to be placed on the hardest, hottest, and dirtiest jobs (Sugiman 2001). When Canada's foreign agricultural workers program was developed in the 1960s, racist discourses about who would constitute a "potential future citizen" justified a policy that denied Mexican and Caribbean workers in the program access to permanent residency. Identified as being physically well-suited to agricultural harvesting, the migrant workers were simply granted temporary work permits (Satzewich 1991). Similarly, the social organization of domestic employment is shaped through the intersection of ideologies of race and gender, whereby assumptions about the "natural" care-giving abilities of racialized women workers (Caribbean and Philippino women in the case of Canada's Live-In Caregiver Program) have produced forms of gendered racism to legitimate their employment in reproductive labour (Brand 1999; Glenn 2001). Patterns of racialization develop from ideologies of femininity and masculinity and produce labour market divisions whereby racialized workers occupy the most physically demanding and the lowest status jobs (Acker 2006; Adib and Guerrier 2003; Calliste 2000).

Finally, along with their gendered character, contemporary patterns of growth in nonstandard and precarious employment display a racialized dimension, indicating that shifts towards greater labour flexibility through growth in these forms of employment have disproportionately affected racialized groups (Gabriel 1999). In particular, their impact is manifested through an overrepresentation of racialized groups in low-income and temporary work, particularly in service sector occupations (Cheung 2005; Galabuzi 2006; Jackson 2005; Teelucksingh and Galabuzi 2005). For example, approximately one-third of recent immigrants to Canada are employed in sales and service occupations, as compared to one-quarter of all Canadians. While members of racialized groups comprise approximately 13 percent of the Canadian population, through the late 1990s and into the twenty-first century they have been disproportionately represented in low-income, low-security occupations such as those of light-duty cleaners (19 percent), food service counter attendants and food preparers (17 percent), kitchen and food service helpers (24 percent), harvesting labourers (40 percent), sewing, textile and fabric workers (40 percent), taxi and limo drivers (36 percent), and electronics assemblers (42 percent). Moreover, these employment patterns have led to an overrepresentation of racialized group members amongst low-income earners. By the late 1990s, approximately 37 percent of women and 35 percent of men from racialized groups were low-income earners (as compared to 19 percent and 16 percent of other Canadians, respectively). This racialized segmentation in the labour market is reflected in a double-digit income gap between racialized group members and the Canadian population as a whole. Overall, processes of neoliberal labour market restructuring have intensified racialized labour market inequalities.

SOCIAL REPRODUCTION: STATES, MARKETS, HOUSEHOLDS

The above discussion of segmentation remained focused on the labour market itself and did not consider social relations *outside* the realm of paid employment that may in fact shape and be shaped by what happens within the labour market. To consider these factors, feminist political economists have used the concept of "social reproduction" to construct a deeper analysis of the underlying dynamics of labour market regulation by examining the interconnections between the social organization of paid work in the labour market and paid and unpaid work in households (Fudge and Vosko 2003; Clement 2007).

Social reproduction may be defined as being comprised of "the activities required to ensure day-to-day and generational survival of the population" (Luxton and Corman 2001, 29). This concept captures the interdependent relationship between paid employment and unpaid reproductive labour. The connection is established through the role of unpaid labour in the household, which, in conjunction with the earnings secured through paid labour, is used to produce the means of subsistence for self and family, therefore reproducing "the capacity to work again." Moreover, social reproduction conceptualizes unpaid labour in the home as more than simply a private service for families that is peripheral to the formal labour market. Rather, it is "an important and socially indispensable labour that contributes to the production of the labouring population and its labour power" (ibid.).[16]

This division between paid and unpaid labour contributes directly to the gendered and racialized segmentation of the labour market discussed above. Gendered divisions of labour within the home have restricted women's access to full-time paid employment, as it is women who are primarily responsible for the unpaid domestic labour (Pupo 1997). Moreover, gendered assumptions about women's responsibilities in the home have shaped the types of occupations available to women workers and the levels of pay and employment security associated with those occupations (Creese 1999; Steedman 1997). Women are overrepresented in the secondary labour market and in nonstandard employment relationships because of their responsibilities for unpaid domestic labour and because of assumptions about the forms of work most suited to women workers. Similarly, racialized ideologies have contributed to the construction of domestic work as a key site of employment for women of colour (Arat-Koç 2006; Brand 1999; Calliste 2000). Thus, the concept of social reproduction highlights a central dimension of labour market segmentation. This indicates that an analysis of the social organization of the workplace and the labour market would be incomplete if it did not account for interconnections with social relations that occur outside paid work (Clement 2001).

Furthermore, an analysis of the state would itself be incomplete if it did not also address the concept of social reproduction. In the process of labour market regulation, the state not only shapes the social organization of paid employment but also builds social and economic policies around and through specific models of social reproduction. As Bezanson and Luxton (2006, 3) state, "social reproduction offers a basis for understanding how various institutions … interact and balance power so that the work involved in the daily and generational production and maintenance of people is maintained." Variants of these tendencies are present in the models of both the Keynesian welfare state and the neoliberal workfare state. During the period of Fordism-Keynesianism, employment and social security policies were premised upon the norm of the male bread-winner and explicitly and implicitly promoted a model of social reproduction that depended on women's unpaid labour in the home.[17] As will be discussed in chapter 2, this gendered employment norm was central to the development of early employment standards legislation, emerging as it did as a form of labour protection designed for those who were in employment assumed to be secondary or supplementary to the primary (male) wage earner.

Neoliberal policies of the contemporary period have also promoted a model of social reproduction premised on women's unpaid labour in the home, despite the dramatic increases in women's participation in paid employment since the early years of the Keynesian period. This has occurred, for example, through the privatization of social services and the lack of support for child care, which, in the context of persisting gendered divisions of labour in households, have placed increasing pressures on women in the workforce (Bezanson and Luxton 2006; McKeen and Porter 2003; Jenson et al. 2003). Moreover, a re-privatization of reproductive labour has occurred in conjunction with shifts towards neoliberal models of labour flexibility based on forms of non-standard employment.

More specifically, and as outlined in chapter 3, longstanding gendered divisions are reflected in the overrepresentation of women workers in growing forms of flexible labour (in particular, part-time employment), forms of work made more precarious through neoliberal reforms to employment standards legislation in the late 1990s and early 2000s. Such legislative reforms, detailed in chapter 4, contribute to the increasing pressures experienced by women workers as they attempt to balance paid and unpaid work in a broader neoliberal environment. Overall, rather than simply focusing on the regulation of paid work, the concept of social reproduction directs attention towards the nexus of relations that may exist between the state, the labour market, and reproductive labour within households (O'Conner et al. 1999; Porter 2003).

The frame of social reproduction also provides the means to construct alternative conceptions of labour flexibility. Alternatives to the neoliberal model can be achieved through employment practices that give workers greater control over their time and their work and that provide workers with the capacity to balance work and non-work interests and responsibilities.[18] Examples include flextime, job sharing, options for homework (telecommuting), reduced work time, and family/care-oriented leaves (Duxbury et al. 2003; Rosenfeld 2001). Other options include reduced employee workloads and job-related travel time, full compensation for overtime work, child and elder care policies and programs, and the general promotion of flexible work arrangements that benefit employees. These policies are beginning to emerge as alternatives to the "more with less" mindset that became predominant during the 1990s.

Such practices are still not widespread within the Canadian labour market, however, and those most in need of employee-oriented flexible work arrangements do not have adequate access to them (Duxbury and Higgins 2001).[19] The conditions of labour flexibility that have become most familiar – part-time work, more overtime and long hours, a lack of control over work time, and job insecurity – have had a negative effect on people's abilities to balance work and non-work responsibilities and activities (Shalla 2007).[20] Several dimensions of this work-life imbalance, or work-life conflict, are becoming common in today's labour market: "role overload (having too much to do); work-to-family interference, where work gets in the way of family; and family-to-work interference, where family demands (such as child or elder care) get in the way of work" (Duxbury and Higgins 2001, 2).

A comparison of data collected on the impacts of work-life conflict in 1991 and 2001 found that high levels of stress at work were twice as prevalent in 2001 as in 1991 and that absenteeism rates of those with high levels of work-life conflict were three times those of employees with low levels of work-life conflict. As the lack of balance increases, so too do levels of stress, which create a corresponding decrease in physical and mental health, job satisfaction, and overall life satisfaction. This pattern affects not only employees but also employers, as increased levels of stress, combined with declining job satisfaction, create problems in recruitment and retention, as well as increased levels of absenteeism.[21]

Assessing labour flexibility through the frame of social reproduction provides the capacity to explore the relationships between paid and unpaid work, and between states, markets, and households. And it adds further depth to the analysis of patterns of labour market segmentation. The concept also points to possible directions for alternative forms of labour market regulation. Focusing on relations of social reproduction makes it possible to develop strategies for labour market regulation that could address concerns related to both workplace equity and general quality of life.[22] This theme will be revisited in the final chapter of the book, when alternative models of labour market regulation are explored.

TOWARDS A POLITICAL ECONOMY OF EMPLOYMENT STANDARDS

This chapter has developed a framework that can be used to analyze the political economy of employment standards. Strategies of labour flexibility have been identified as forms of market regulation, or conditions of heightened commodification, that have exacerbated class, race, and gender-based inequalities. The themes raised here weave themselves through the account of the political economy of employment standards that follows. Thus far, these themes have been discussed in a fairly abstract manner. The next several chapters will provide the concrete details of the social relations, social actors, and ideologies that have shaped the political economy of employment standards in specific historical contexts, using a case study of the regulation of employment standards in Ontario.

2

The Origins of Flexible Employment Standards

Labour standards legislation attempts to deal with various aspects of poverty by raising wages, improving working conditions, and opening up employment opportunities. There is general recognition that most such standards are primarily relief and not cures for poverty problems. Nevertheless, the legislation is widely accepted as necessary for the maintenance of minimum levels of living among low paid workers.

Ontario Department of Labour, 1965[1]

The social and economic implications of minimum standards are inter-related, and must be largely determined by that which is economically practicable.

Labour Gazette, September 1967, 567

Contemporary forms of labour regulation are rooted in historical patterns and social relations (Edwards 1994). This chapter begins with early initiatives regulating the hours of work of women and child workers through the Ontario Factories Act in the 1880s and proceeds to early minimum wages laws for women workers in the 1920s and 1930s.[2] The chapter then traces the post–World War II developments that led to the enactment of the Ontario Employment Standards Act (ESA) in 1968. The ESA was an amalgamation of existing minimum standards legislation, along with some new standards, including a legislated overtime premium. But was the act capable of substantially improving the employment conditions of low-wage workers? While the Ontario Minister of Labour Dalton Bales expressed concerns about poverty, he also cautioned that "when it comes down to considering improvements in standards of employment, we must improve but also maintain a balance that will help us to keep industry and to attract new industries to the province."[3] In other words, the government's new labour code should not undermine economic prerogatives with legislated employment protections.

The chapter raises several significant questions. First, how did pre– and post–World War II governments situate themselves in relation to employers and workers in the development of minimum standards? Second, in what ways did early minimum standards legislation contribute to patterns of labour market segmentation, and in particular patterns of gendered and racialized segmentation? And finally, to what extent did social actors with an interest in employment standards – labour, women's, and employer organizations – influence the state in its policy development?

MAXIMUM HOURS AND MINIMUM WAGES

The system of labour law during late-nineteenth-century Canada has been described as a system of "liberal voluntarism," which is characterized by minimal regulation of the employment relationship (Fudge and Tucker 2001).[4] Within this period, the state was largely reluctant to interfere with the business imperatives of the emerging industrial capitalist economy and left most of the conditions of employment to individual employment contracts and the "free" operation of the labour market. Ultimately, labour and employment legislation that developed during the period had little impact on employer control over the organization of the workplace.

Within the system of liberal voluntarism, the Master and Servant Act (MSA) of 1847 established the common law contract of employment, which was based on the presumption of the free exchange of equal, individual actors – employers and employees – within the labour market. Despite this presumption of formal equality, in the context of workplace relations circumscribed by pre-existing power imbalances that were determined by the social relationships of the system of wage labour, the MSA in effect established "the legal subordination of the worker" to the employer through a system of penalties for employees who abandoned or disobeyed their employers (Fudge and Tucker 2000, 252; Palmer 1992). While the act was individualistic in its overt orientation, it also had implications for the regulation of collective action. Industrial employers in Toronto used the MSA frequently in the mid to late 1800s to restrain worker militancy and to combat the growing strength of trade unions by prosecuting employees for both disobedience and desertion of employment, particularly during points of increased union activism (Kealey 1980).

It was illegal for workers to form trade unions before 1872. However, in response both to growing pressure from workers for legislative reforms and to concerns over the ambiguity of existing legislation used to criminally prosecute members of trades unions, the Dominion government passed the Trade Unions Act in 1872 (Black and Silver 2001). The act legalized trade unionism and ensured that workers could not be prosecuted for conspiracy for attempting to collectively improve wages, hours of labour, or other conditions of work. However, at the same time the government also passed the Criminal Law Amendment Act, which criminalized many activities associated with the combination of workers (Palmer 1992). The very limited legal rights established for workers under the Trade Unions Act provided minimum protection for workers attempting to undertake collective action. While it did provide some protection against criminal conspiracy charges, it did not protect workers against conspiracy charges under civil law (Heron 1996).

The Ontario Factories Act

Legislation to regulate the length of the working day marked the first significant foray into what eventually became employment standards.[5] Attention to the negative effects of long working hours had been raised in the early 1870s by the Nine Hour Movement, a movement of working men who sought to reduce daily hours of labour from ten to nine (Battye 1979; Kealey 1980).[6] While the Nine-Hour Movement was not successful in achieving its goal for the first time in Canada, it did publicize and politicize the issue of the need for reduced working time.[7]

When the Ontario government took action to enact legislative restrictions on the length of the working day, however, it was not responding to the concerns of the Nine Hour Leagues about the need for working *men* to reduce their working time in order to combat work intensification or to further their own moral, social, and intellectual development. Rather, it was responding to concerns raised about the impact of industrialism on two other groups of workers: women workers and child workers. At the same time that the skilled crafts were being restructured through mechanization and industrial expansion, larger numbers of women and children were being drawn into the growing industrial workforce. For the industrial capitalists of the period, women and child workers were considered to be a source of inexpensive labour and were increasingly employed in the garment industry, particularly through subcontracting and homeworking arrangements. Many workers under the age of fourteen were entering the industrial factories. The earnings of these workers were needed to support low family incomes.

Labour conditions for both of these groups were characterized by excessively low wages, long hours, little health and safety protection, poor sanitary conditions, and high levels of employment insecurity. In the garment industry, intense competition pressured contractors to continually reduce their production costs, leading to the spread of the "sweating" system (McIntosh 1993). Women workers in this industry regularly earned wages below subsistence levels: in Toronto wages ranged from $1.50 to $3.00 per week. Workers in garment factories worked standard work weeks of sixty hours during periods of high production, and homeworkers could work sixteen-hour days. Because they could be paid at very low rates, children under the age of fourteen were often employed in both the garment industry and in industries such as basket making, broom and brush-making, bookbinding, cotton and woolen manufacturing, and glass works (Hurl 1988).

Owing to the exclusionary practices of the craft unions of the time, these workers did not have the benefit of a labour organization to enable them to bargain for better working conditions. The labour movement was not silent on the issue, however. As early as 1881, the first Canadian local of the Knights of Labour called for the abolition of employment of children under fourteen years of age in factories, as did the Trades and Labour Congress at its founding convention in 1883 (Hurl 1988; McIntosh 1993).[8] Middle-class reformers also pressured for protective legislation for the women and child workers. Their perspective was influenced by Victorian ideals premised on the need to protect women and children from the threats of the industrial workplace to both their physical health and their morality, and to ensure that women's primary role as caregivers was maintained (Tucker 1988; Ursel 1992).

These concerns were directly addressed by the first provincial attempt at the regulation of minimum standards. The Ontario Factories Act, which was enacted by the Ontario Liberal government in 1884, set minimum ages and maximum hours for women and children working in factories. Under the act, it was illegal to employ boys under the age of twelve and girls under the age of fourteen. The act set maximum hours of work at ten hours per day and sixty hours per week for women, girls (fourteen to eighteen), and boys (twelve to fourteen). Similar legislation was later extended to shops (1888), mines (1890), and bakeshops (1895) (*Labour Gazette*, March 1908). The working-time standards established by this act would remain in effect until the end of World War II.

The Factories Act was hardly a panacea for employment rights. In order to ensure that employers were able to meet their business needs, the act provided for overtime permits and extra hours of work in the event of emergencies, and other exemptions, such as the employment of children in the seasonal canning industry (*Labour Gazette*, March 1908). The regulation of child labour was complicated by difficulties in determining the age of workers owing to falsification or lack of birth registration, and misrepresentation from parents. In addition, all workplaces of fewer than twenty employees were excluded. The enforcement capacity of the factory inspectors was limited by a lack of sufficient resources, and it was conditioned by their bias towards education rather than prosecution (Tucker 1988). A report on factory inspection stated that even after the implementation of the Factories Act, excessive hours of work for women and children continued to be a problem in some industries (*Labour Gazette*, November 1904).

The implementation of the Factories Act marked the inception of several central tendencies in the regulation of minimum standards. The act signified a recognition on the part of the state that it should play a role in establishing basic workplace standards. However, the act also established a pattern of state intervention that attempted to regulate class conflict "through relatively minor legislative concessions that were administered compatibly with the industrial capitalist order" (Tucker 1988, 83–4). In other words, while the state accepted a role in regulating workplace standards, this role was very much circumscribed by the imperatives of capitalist profitability. One of the central ways in which this was established was through the incorporation of flexibility into the legislation through the system of overtime permits and the exclusion of small workplaces. Intervention along the lines of liberal voluntarism – with its implicit presumption of the desirability of employer-employee negotiation of workplace standards – in the context of workplaces structured by the power relations of the wage labour system meant that the legislation did little to alter existing levels of employer power.

The class dynamics of the Factories Act cannot be separated from its gendered character. Through the act, the state accepted and promoted a gendered division of labour that was premised on a model of social reproduction organized around a male breadwinner and women's unpaid labour in the household, with women's paid employment assumed to be supplementary. These aspects of the Factories Act marked the beginning of a pattern of gendered state intervention in the labour market that set the tone for subsequent employment standards legislation.

The Early-Twentieth-Century Labour Market in Canada

In the early 1900s, Canadian workers were confronted with a growing concentration of economic power through corporate mergers and consolidations and the restructuring of labour processes in ways that furthered the transition away from skilled craft production towards semi-skilled and deskilled industrial manufacturing (Palmer 1992). The industrial revolution of the early twentieth century brought about increased pressure from industrialists to break craft-workers' monopoly over skilled labour and to introduce new labour processes designed to both increase labour productivity and intensify management control. Alongside the existing skilled craft workers was an emerging and rapidly expanding industrial workforce that was subject to intense levels of workplace exploitation characterized by low wages, long hours, and poor safety and sanitary conditions. While the Dominion government was willing to investigate the working conditions of the emerging industrial economy through task forces such as the 1886 Royal Commission on the Relations of Labor and Capital, it remained unmoved to enact legislation that would "over-regulate" these conditions.[9] As the nineteenth century turned to the twentieth, the principles of voluntarism continued to prevail, and the regulation of working conditions continued to be defined largely through the private negotiations between employers and employees.

This emerging industrial labour force included large numbers of immigrant workers. The majority of immigrants arriving in Canada during the early twentieth century were from Britain and the United

States, but many were also from eastern, central, and southern Europe, and China, Japan, and India. Immigrant workers, particularly those of non-British origin, were employed in labour-intensive resource industries such as mining and logging and were also often incorporated into low-wage industrial and service employment. These workers were subjected to multiple forms of overt racism and discrimination both in the labour market and through immigration policies that restricted their mobility in Canada (Creese 2006; Iacovetta et al. 1996; Stasiulis 1997).

Along with growing ethnic diversity, women's participation in the Canadian workforce climbed steadily, largely owing to the combined factors of industrial expansion and the transformation of agricultural and home-based production into a factory-based system (Frances et al. 1996). These women were either single and self-supporting, or they were contributing to a "family-wage." Employment patterns varied substantially across regions, but gendered divisions of labour in various forms were constantly present. Women's employment outside the home tended to reflect the unpaid work they performed within the home (cleaning, caring, cooking), as women were most often employed as typists, sales clerks, domestic servants, teachers, waitresses, nurses, or cleaners. These jobs were often low-paid and generally accorded a low status in relation to men's employment (Steedman 1997).

Because of employer opposition and the exclusivity of the craft unions, most of these industrial workers did not initially have the benefit of union organization. In response to the new forms of labour exploitation experienced within industrial production, a more broad-based and militant form of unionism known as industrial unionism began to emerge, creating a "full-fledged alternative" to craft unionism by World War I (Heron 1996, 36). While this new form of unionism offered the opportunity to organize larger numbers of workers, unionization rates during this period remained at low levels. In 1911, only 4.9 percent of non-agricultural workers were unionized. This figure grew to 16 percent by 1921 (Krahn et al. 2006). While industrial unionism was more broad-based in its organizing strategies with respect to skill, many of the patriarchal assumptions regarding women's employment remained intact, and the labour movement "generally lacked strategies to organize women workers" (Francis et al. 1996, 77).

In this context, growing pressure was placed on the state to develop legislative solutions to long hours, low wages, and unsafe working conditions. In particular, the labour movement and the women's social-reform movement were instrumental in shaping the state's approach to future minimum standards legislation. The legislative roots of contemporary employment standards can be found not only in the structure of the capitalist labour market and the policy approaches of the state but also within the positions and strategies of the organizations that pressured for legislative reform.

Organized Labour and Minimum Standards

As the central institution for organized workers in Canada, the Trades and Labour Congress (TLC) regularly lobbied the federal and provincial governments for improvements to minimum standards legislation. In Ontario, this effort included calls for stronger enforcement of the Ontario Factories Act, the appointment of more inspectors, and an increase in the minimum age of employment for children. At the federal level, the TLC pressured for legislation to establish the eight-hour day, first for employees under federal jurisdiction and then for all employees (*Labour Gazette*, April 1902, October 1903). As the demand for the eight-hour day became an entrenched position within the labour movement, it was coupled with the demand that it be accompanied with "a reasonable living wage," in order to ensure that a reduction in work time would not lead to a reduction in earnings (*Labour Gazette*, October 1911, 346). Like the Nine Hour Movement, the TLC sought the eight-hour day in order both to increase employment opportunities for a larger number of workers and to provide increased leisure time.

Two primary concerns shaped the labour movement's position on minimum standards. First, while a general consensus had emerged from organized labour with respect to the need to reduce work time, the tactics through which this could be accomplished were subject to intense debate. While some within the movement favored lobbying to achieve general legislation, others argued for workplace action in order to secure the eight-hour day within collective agreements (*Labour Gazette*, August 1925a). Those favoring collective workplace action to secure improved standards expressed a concern that, should governments enact general minimum standards, those standards would either set the limits on what could be achieved (as in the case of the minimum wage), or that such legislation would serve to undermine the existence of labour organizations.

The second concern related to the labour movement's aim to protect white, male employment. As immigration from non-Anglo-Celtic regions of the world increased, Canadian unions and the TLC began to take a concerted position in opposition to federal immigration policies in order to "defend" the jobs of white workers (Francis et al. 1996; Goutor 2007; Iacovetta et al. 1996). This anti-immigration position was connected to the TLC's stance on minimum standards. For example, at the turn of the century the Congress lobbied the government to introduce a minimum wage as a means to prevent job loss amongst white workers owing to the employment of Chinese and Japanese workers at lower rates of pay (*Labour Gazette*, April 1902).

This position on minimum standards legislation was also influenced by gender politics. The TLC favored a highly gendered division of labour and maintained in its platform the principle that child and female labour should be abolished in order to "protect the working-class family and male wage levels" (Francis et al. 1996, 61). This concern was not only economic, but it was also constructed through a frame of moral protectionism. For example, the Congress called upon the Ontario government to revoke all extra-hours permits that allowed women and girls to work at night, as "such work is physically and morally injurious to those individuals" (*Labour Gazette*, April 1909,1120). Underlying both the moral and the economic concerns of the TLC were assumptions regarding the primacy of the male breadwinner model of social reproduction.

Support for the male breadwinner model prompted the TLC to promote different strategies to regulate standards for male and female workers. The TLC took up the call for a female minimum wage in order to ensure that the entrance of women into the labour market did not lead to a lowering of male wages (Frances et al. 1996). Legislation was needed for women workers, as they were not considered to be potential trade unionists, and many within the labour movement viewed women's employment as a temporary stage in an individual woman's life. Because they were considered unorganizable and because paid employment was likely to be short-term, male unionists considered minimum standards legislation as the appropriate solution for women workers. The labour movement thereby supported a gendered and segmented approach to the state regulation of employment, pressuring the state to enact policies that would support the male breadwinner model.

Women's Organizing

Despite the often existent gender bias within the unions during this period, many women workers were highly active in union and other forms of political organizing, forcing the unions to include women's struggles in their strategies and actions. Women workers, particularly in the textile and garment industry, were active in the short-lived Knights of Labour during the 1880s, pressuring for equal pay and equal treatment in the workplace (Palmer 1992). By the early twentieth century, women were also active in organizing drives in sectors dominated by women workers, such as the garment and clothing trades. Half of all strikes involving women workers were in the textile and garment trades in the first two decades of the twentieth century (Francis et al. 1996). Strikes in these industries became more common as more women workers organized against sweatshop labour conditions and pressured employers for better wages and restrictions on hours of work (Frager 1992; Steedman 1997).

Along with women's increased participation in the labour movement, the middle class women's social reform movement became more prominent during this period. While its primary concern was to pressure the government to grant women voting rights, this movement was also concerned about women's conditions of employment. As with early reformers, the middle-class social reform movement sought to address the impact of industrial employment on women's morality and reproductive capacities. The National Council of Women opposed the employment of married women and pressured for the provision of separate washrooms for women workers (Newton 1995), indicating a significant gap between the positions of the middle-class reformers and the working class women who directly experienced the conditions of sweatshop labour (Frager 1992; McIntosh 1993). Nonetheless, by 1917 the NCW was demanding more comprehensive regulations for the working conditions (hours, wages, holidays) of women and children. By 1920 it called for all provinces to establish minimum wage boards (McCallum 1986). Like the TLC, the middle-class social reformers did not consider women's paid employment to be a desirable permanent condition, however. These reformers called for legislation to protect women in what they assumed would be a temporary stage of employment that might precede taking up their primary role in the home.

Employer Opposition to Government Regulation

While women's and labour organizations pushed for better minimum standards, employers constituted a strong source of resistance to increasing or improving minimum standards protections, particularly with respect maximum hours of work. The Canadian Manufacturers' Association (CMA) generally favored minimal state regulation of employment relations. When legislation was developed at federal and provincial levels, it sought to maximize legislative flexibility by pressuring respective governments for exemptions and exceptions. Employer opposition to employment regulations clearly promoted the principles of voluntarism that shaped state policy during the period, indicating the close relationship between capital and the state.

There are many examples of these practices in the interwar years. During the first meeting of the International Labour Organization (ILO) in 1919 – an organization that formed to promote international labour standards following the First World War – representatives of Canadian employers were unanimously opposed to the adoption of an eight-hour day convention.[10] Their primary reason was that the United States did not have a similar law in place (*Labour Gazette*, August 1925b). They argued that an eight-hour law in Canada would create a significant competitive advantage for the U.S. market, stating that "if the 8-hour day recommendation was carried into legislation it would have disastrous consequences in an undeveloped country such as Canada to which new capital must be attracted" (*Labour Gazette*, August 1922, 845).

Shortly after the first ILO meeting, the Industrial Relations Committee of the CMA indicated its intention to "oppose vigorously" any federal or provincial legislation that would restrict working time to eight hours per day or forty-eight per week, as did the Retail Merchants' Association of Ontario (*Labour Gazette*, June 1921, 803, February 1922). In the early years of the Depression, the CMA encouraged its members to voluntarily reduce hours of work as a means to prevent the reduction in numbers of workers employed; however, even in the context of the unemployment crisis, the association continued to oppose legislative initiatives to regulate hours of work (*Labour Gazette*, June 1933).

When the federal government introduced legislation to restrict maximum hours of work on federal contracts in the early 1930s, the CMA pressured for, and secured, exceptions and exemptions to recognize the "special circumstances" of particular industries, a strategy that employer representatives had used at the ILO in regard to the convention on the eight-hour day (*Labour Gazette*, June 1931, June 1936). Similarly, when male minimum wage legislation was developed later in the decade (see below), the CMA pressured to ensure that any hours maximums contained within the minimum wage laws would refer only to the hours to which the weekly minimum could be applied and would not constitute an absolute weekly hours maximum. Employer associations asserted that private negotiations between employers and employees were the appropriate method to determine workplace standards.

Minimum Standards and Industrial Voluntarism

During this period, and in the context of these various pressures, policymakers began to take a more active interest in the regulation of the labour market, marking the beginning of the period of industrial voluntarism (Fudge and Tucker 2001).[11] The federal government initiated its first attempt to regulate wages through the 1900 House of Commons Policy on Fair Wages, which required that individuals on government contracts be paid wages equivalent to those of workers engaged in similar occupations in the same district. Hours of work were subject to the same standard. While the policy applied only to workers employed in public construction contracts, it served to introduce the principle of fairness in wages into public policy (Brennan 2000). A day's rest per week was provided through the federal Lord's Day Act of 1906.

While the federal government indicated that it was willing to consider a possible legislative response to the pressures from organized labour for a general eight-hour day, the Supreme Court confirmed in 1925 that the regulation of hours of work fell within provincial jurisdiction, with the exception of "servants of the Dominion Government" or "those parts of Canada which are not within the boundaries of the province" (*Labour Gazette*, July 1924; July 1925). This decision led Prime Minister Mackenzie King to advocate for uniform labour laws across the provinces, since "if there is not uniformity it very often happens that the particular province that has higher standards in labour ultimately loses in consequence of the lower standards that exist in other provinces" (*Labour Gazette*, April 1926, 305). As direct evidence of King's concerns, while approving in principle the eight-hour day or forty-eight-hour week in 1924, the Ontario government did not enact 8/48 legislation at the time, owing to concerns over economic competition from jurisdictions that did not have similar regulations (*Labour Gazette*, June 1924). Overall, the dictates of voluntarism continued to delineate the state's approach to labour market regulation during this period.

The Ontario Minimum Wage Act

While hours of work legislation was left largely untouched, many provinces began to establish some form of minimum wage legislation shortly following World War I. In Ontario, the 1920 Minimum Wage Act was the most significant intervention in the regulation of minimum standards in the province since the 1884 Factories Act. Following the gendered path set by the Factories Act, and consistent with the policy positions of the TLC and social reformers, the Minimum Wage Act established a regulatory framework for women's wages and created a provincial board to determine weekly minimums. The act covered most female employees, with the exception of domestic servants and farm workers (McCallum 1986). Rates were established by industry, rather than in a general manner, and were developed through consultations with both employers and employees in the given industry. The board was also given the authority to issue special permits for rates lower than the established minimums in cases of emergencies and for persons with disabilities, thereby providing some flexibility to industry minimums (*Labour Gazette*, August 1929). The rates were also to take into account regional differences in living costs (McCallum 1986). In 1922, the act was amended to permit the board to establish a maximum number of hours to which the minimum weekly wage could be applied and to establish overtime rates.

The gendered character of this legislation built on the principles of gendered segmentation established within the earlier hours of work legislation like the Factories Act. The state accepted the need for a women's minimum wage because of the predominance of women in low-wage industries and the low levels of women's union-ization. This was considered a threat to the wages of those (male) wage earners who were supporting their families. Further to this, it was assumed that women were not sole supporters of dependents but were, rather, earning a supplemental income or holding a tem-porary position. The official basis for the provision of a female minimum wage (as opposed to a general minimum applicable to both men and women) was presented as follows: "In the Canadian provinces, as in the American states, the minimum wage laws relate only to female employees, the reason for this distinction being that women are employed in low-wage industries, partly because of the comparatively short period during which a large number of them are at work, and the fact that they are not generally organized in unions for their own protection and, therefore, lack the bargaining power that unionism confers ... and partly because many of them are satisfied to add something to the family income, thus endanger-ing the wages of those wholly dependent on themselves" (*Labour Gazette*, July 1924, 556).

Accepting the assumption that women were less likely to join unions and were therefore in greater need of protective legislation than men, the provincial government sought to compensate for their lack of bargaining power through the Minimum Wage Board (Brennan 2000; Whittingham 1970). The cost-of-living budgets determined by the Minimum Wage Board cemented reliance on a male breadwinner, as they "made no allowance for the support of dependants, or for savings for retirement" (McCallum 1986, 55). Minimum wages were "designed only to cover the 'transitory anoma-lies' (that is, temporary, single female wage earners), which fell outside the scope of the patriarchal household" (Russell 1991, 85; see also Little 1998; Steedman 1997). Like the Factories Act before it, the Minimum Wage Act thereby premised its system of labour regulation on a model of social reproduction based on a highly gendered division of labour.

The Minimum Wage Act combined class and gender relations in a way that minimized its impact on employer power in the workplace. The Minimum Wage Board showed a tendency to be more coopera-tive with employers than with labour representatives, first, in a reluctance to prosecute employers who violated the act and, second, by developing wage rates primarily in consultation with employers. Further, the act relied primarily on an individualized complaints-based enforcement process, placing the responsibility to report minimum wage violations on individual workers (McIntosh 1993). Employers did not maintain a strong opposition to the principle of female minimum wage rates as "[c]ooperation in the creation of tripartite boards to establish a minimum wage for women was a small concession for a business order threatened by industrial unrest and widespread support for basic readjustments in the relations of labour and capital" (McCallum 1986, 39). Finally, many women workers were not covered by minimum wage orders in the years following the implementation of the Minimum Wage Act (McCallum 1986). Domestic workers and homeworkers were excluded, indicating the racialized dimensions of the act, as domestic work was a common form of employment for Black women (Brand 1991). Following the Factories Act, and setting the stage for future developments, the Minimum Wage Act displayed the exemptions and exclusions, ineffective enforcement, and individualized complaints-based process typical of minimum standards legislation.

Overall, the construction of minimum wage rates and their inability to fully address the problem of sub-standard wages can be explained through an intersection of the actions of the state, unions, and employers, and the prevailing ideological context. Women's activism placed pressure on employers and the state to improve women's wages. However, in the context of employer opposition to most state regulation, a male-dominated trade union movement, and an ideological climate shaped by the presumption that women's wage labour was either temporary or supplemental, the industry-based minimum wage codes for women were constructed in a manner that served to reinforce women's secondary status in the paid labour market. The 1920 Minimum Wage Act reflected a segmented approach to labour market regulation and played a central role in shaping patterns of gendered segmentation in the early-twentieth-century industrial capitalist labour market.

SETTING THE GROUNDWORK
FOR GENERAL STANDARDS

The years of the Great Depression prompted both the federal and the provincial governments to consider social and economic policy reforms to dampen the effects of free-market capitalism. Yet, while new regulatory strategies emerged during the years of the Great

Depression, intervention remained highly provisional. In terms of the regulation of employment standards, the minimal and explicitly gendered framework of the early twentieth century remained intact.

The years of the Depression were significant nonetheless. While comprehensive employment standards for male and female workers were not forthcoming, it was becoming apparent that a shift away from this formally gendered framework was emerging. Government workers fared somewhat better than those in the private sector in terms of legislated standards. The eight-hour day was legislated for workers under federal jurisdiction in 1930 with the Fair Wages and Eight-Hour Day Act (Brennan 2000). In 1935, this was replaced with the *Fair* Wages and Hours of Labour Act, which established the eight-hour day and forty-four-hour week for federal employees. That same year the federal Parliament ratified the International Labour Organization convention regarding a general eight-hour day and forty-eight-hour week. Federal legislation was not applicable to the majority of workers, however, as employment standards for all workers not employed under federal jurisdiction were clearly established by Supreme Court and Privy Council rulings to be the responsibility of the provinces.

In Ontario, Mitch Hepburn's Liberal government sought to address growing concerns about a "sweatshop crisis" characterized by increasing hours of work and declining wages (Klee 2000). Following the federal model, minimum standards for workers employed on Ontario government construction contracts were improved. The 1934 Fair Wages and Eight Hour Day Act set maximum hours for these workers at eight per day and required that "all employees shall be paid such wages as are generally accepted as current from time to time for competent workmen in the district in which the work is being performed ... provided that wages shall in all cases be such as are fair and reasonable."[12] The act applied to contracts of all departments of the Public Service, the Hydro Electric Power Commission, and all other provincial commissions "and like bodies."

General minimum standards were not extended to the private sector, however. As an alternative to legislated standards, the government implemented the Ontario Industrial Standards Act (ISA) in 1935. The ISA was enacted in an attempt to establish industry-wide employment standards, but it did not set minimum standards itself. Rather, it established a process though which employers and employees could negotiate such standards. According to Arthur Roebuck, the Ontario minister of labour at the time, "[w]ere the Government to attempt to legislate for industry by a general minimum wage or to set the hours that men can work in an arbitrary way, it would not be successful and it would probably do more harm that good."[13]

Industry-specific standards were to be established by the private parties. But by 1937, only 65,000 of the province's 650,000 non-agricultural wage labourers were covered by standards negotiated through the act, and 80 percent of the ISA schedules were in industries that had previously been unionized (Fudge and Tucker 2001).[14] The ISA offered little to workers who were not organized into trade unions. Even in sectors where its schedules had been negotiated, the state did not provide an effective enforcement regime. Thus, the limitations of the ISA were visible before the end of the 1930s (Klee 2000). Outside government workforces, the voluntaristic approach continued to prevail in Ontario.

During these years, calls for a male minimum wage began to grow from within organized labour and the political left. As early as 1926, J.S. Woodsworth had moved a resolution in federal Parliament calling for a minimum wage for men (*Labour Gazette*, July 1926). That year organized labour took up the call for provincial legislatures to "pass legislation to provide for a minimum wage for all male workers, 'such minima to be not less than that set out in the Labour Gazette as necessary to maintain a family in a decent standard of living, the wage to be based on an eight-hour day'" (*Labour Gazette*, October 1926, 971–2). Unlike the union support for a female minimum wage, this support for a male minimum wage was designed to take into account the needs of family dependents. Social pressure for a male minimum grew in the mid-1930s, as mayors of Ontario municipalities also called upon the provincial government to enact a male minimum wage.[15]

While it adopted convention resolutions that called for a male minimum wage, organized labour continued to have reservations about such a prospect, owing to concerns about the implications for men's wage levels. Specifically, the Congress feared that a male minimum wage could also become a maximum wage (*Labour Gazette*, February 1935a). In 1935, the TLC submitted to the government that if other legislative measures were taken, including the provision of maximum hours of work, uniformity of labour laws across the provinces, sufficient penalties for labour law violations, prohibition of exemptions from existing laws, recognition of the right to organize, and effective enforcement of existing legislation, then the need for a male minimum wage would be eliminated. Similarly, the Toronto District Labour Council expressed concern that a male minimum wage would prevent unions from negotiating wages higher than the minimum rate, urging that instead of a male minimum wage, the province enact legislation that would provide workers with "the legal right to organize into a Trade Union of their own choosing."[16]

Employers' associations, such as the Toronto Board of Trade, the Retail Merchant's Association, and the Ontario Restaurant Owners' Association, became more supportive of a male minimum wage in hopes that it would increase consumer spending power and combat competitive pressures that, without a legislated minimum, continued to drive wages to lower and lower levels.[17] However, employer support for the male minimum wage was premised on the assumption that minimum wage legislation would not become "fair wages" legislation and that the act would not establish the principle of paid holidays. Employers also sought assurances that any hours of work regulations attached to a male minimum wage would only establish maximums for the purpose of calculating wage rates (the maximum number of hours to which the weekly minimum wage could be applied) and would not constitute absolute weekly hours maximums. When it became clear that minimum wage legislation would not be used to establish absolute hours restrictions, even the CMA expressed tentative support for a legislated male minimum wage, stating, "the payment of unduly low wages may be more effectively restrained by minimum wage legislation than by the *Industrial Standards Act*."[18]

By 1937, of the 650,000 non-agricultural wage labourers in the province, 438,500 were male workers with no wage protection. Many were married, with dependents, and had an average wage of less than $12.50 per week, which was the rate set by the Minimum Wage Board for single women working in the city of Toronto. Further, the provincial government noted that these workers "have no degree of bargaining power with their employers, because there is an ample supply of labour of this type at the present time and there is no prospect that this reservoir will be drained in the future."[19]

In light of the growing concern over low male wages, and in response to growing public support for a male minimum wage, a new Minimum Wage Act was implemented in Ontario in 1937. The new Industry and Labour Board created by the act was empowered to set minimum wage rates for both men and women and to set rates across either industries or regional zones (*Labour Gazette*, March 1937). The government's position was that the legislation was intended not to establish minimum rates in highly unionized industries but rather to improve the living standards "of those who have found it impossible to bargain collectively or to organize for the purpose of improving their wages and working conditions."[20] However, while the board was able to set minimum wages for men, it issued only one order to that effect. For most male workers, voluntarism continued to prevail in the regulation of wages.

In summary, from the Factories Act of the late nineteenth century to the amended Minimum Wage Act of 1937, the Ontario government slowly responded to concerns from labour and social reformers by attempting to ameliorate some of the harshest conditions of industrial employment. However, interventions in the regulation of minimum standards always sought to maintain flexibility for employers and generally remained well within the boundaries of the principles of voluntarism. Any shift away from voluntarism was provisional, applying only to specific categories of workers, included regulations with gendered and racialized implications, and did little to alter the secondary status of non-organized workers.[21] Thus, the early regulation of minimum standards contributed to a labour market structure that was characterized by a relatively small group of workers in primary sector employment with the benefits of unionization and a larger group of workers in the secondary labour market (often women and recent immigrants) who were reliant on secondary standards.

CONSOLIDATING THE MINIMUM DURING THE POSTWAR YEARS

The post–World War II labour market was defined by the continued expansion of large-scale manufacturing, particularly through the implementation of Fordist "just-in-case" production systems (Rinehart 2006). It was within the primary labour market, which included the unionized mass production industries, with their largely white, male workforce, that the employment norm of the standard employment relationship became fixed, providing these workers with full-time, stable jobs. Outside unionized mass production, there existed a growing number of nonstandard employment relationships within the secondary labour market, characterized by job insecurity, part-time hours, low-pay, and little opportunity for advancement (Fudge and Vosko 2001).

Gendered and racialized diversification and segmentation within the labour market also increased dramatically during the postwar years. Between 1941 and 1971, women's labour force participation rate doubled from 20 to 40 percent (Armstrong and Armstrong 1994). Over two million immigrants arrived in Canada between the years of 1946 and 1961, accounting for a significant portion of labour market growth during this period (Palmer 1992). Many of these new immigrant workers were from Eastern and Southern Europe, rather than from Britain. These forms of labour force diversification intersected with early patterns of segmentation. Women's increased participation in paid work was characterized by a concentration in specific occupations (secretarial, service, health) that were associated with women's "natural" abilities (caring, cleaning, cooking). Non-Anglo immigrants were predominantly employed in low-wage labour. Rates of unionization for women and immigrant workers remained low relative to that of Anglo-Saxon, male workers. The entrenchment of the SER in the unionized mass production industries further contributed to patterns of gendered and racialized segmentation.

Labour market regulation during the postwar period was defined by the development of the welfare state. In Canada, the welfare state developed as a result of a range of social pressures, including labour unrest and the socialist-oriented policies of the Co-Operative Commonwealth Federation (CCF), and it was also influenced by the legacy of the Depression years, all of which encouraged the adoption of a Keynesian approach to social and economic policy (Heron 1996; McBride and Shields 1997). At the federal level, the Mackenzie King government announced a commitment to a number of measures of social security reform in the early 1940s.[22] Specifically, the federal government committed itself to developing policies that would promote full employment, provide some social security and social assistance, and ensure the recognition of the rights of trade unions to bargain collectively, while continuing to respect the primary interests of capital (McBride and Shields 1997). From this framework evolved policies and funding for unemployment insurance, family allowances, welfare and social assistance, old age pensions, job creation and job training programs, and public health care. The implementation of Keynesianism in Canada was limited in all of these areas, as the policy program of the postwar federal government was designed to ensure a political and economic climate ultimately favourable to the private interests of capital (McInnis 2002).[23]

The welfare state was joined to the system of Fordist mass production through postwar labour legislation that instituted the regime of industrial pluralism and secured the process of collective bargaining as the primary means through which organized workers could improve their workplace standards (Fudge and Tucker 2001). In 1944, the government introduced Privy Council Order 1003, which provided the basis for compulsory union recognition and the right to free collective bargaining. The legislation was in some ways modeled after the Wagner Act in the United States, as it provided basic acceptance of the rights to union recognition and collective bargaining and attempted to establish conciliatory processes for the resolution of labour disputes (McBride 1995). Unions received new responsibilities under the legislation as well, however, as strikes during the life of a contract were disallowed and grievance procedures were bureaucratized to remove the role of shopfloor disruptions in the resolution of grievances. These procedures were supported through the Rand Formula, which established the principle of mandatory union dues.[24] P.C. 1003, originally a wartime measure, was extended into the years following the war. It became a permanent framework for Canadian labour relations in 1948 as part of the Industrial Relations and Disputes Investigation Act (IRDIA), which itself provided a model for the provinces, as jurisdiction over labour relations returned to them in the late 1940s.[25]

P.C. 1003 and the Rand Formula are generally seen as the cornerstones of the postwar system of labour relations in Canada. They established key labour rights for Canadian workers in the areas of collective bargaining and union recognition. These rights, initially won by private sector workers, were later won by many, but not all, workers in the public sector.[26] This system supported unionization in large-scale, manufacturing employment, and thus its beneficiaries were largely white, male blue-collar workers employed in standard employment relationships (Fudge and Vosko 2001). Women workers in the public sector would benefit from the legislation once public sector workplaces began to unionize (Sears 1999). But in the private sector, many workers, particularly women and members of racialized groups, who were not employed in the core manufacturing sectors, did not secure unionization as a result of the postwar settlement.

These workers had to rely on employment standards legislation to set the basic standards in their workplaces.

Hours of Work, Minimum Wages, and Equal Pay in Postwar Ontario

It was in this context of the emerging postwar regime of industrial legality that the Ontario provincial government announced its plans for substantial changes to labour and employment legislation. In the summer of 1944, the province introduced the Hours of Work and Vacations with Pay Act (HWVPA). The act marked the most significant intervention in the regulation of minimum standards in Ontario since the 1884 Factories Act and the 1920 Minimum Wage Act. The act reduced maximum hours of work from ten per day and sixty per week for women to eight per day and forty-eight per week for all employees, including men, in all industrial undertakings. The act also introduced an annual paid vacation of one week per year, with holiday pay set at two percent of an employee's annual earnings (*Labour Gazette*, July 1944, September 1944). These standards were established at levels that were considered to reflect the prevailing industrial conditions at the time, as "the effect of this legislation has been to make permanent for everyone working in industry in Ontario the basic conditions which generally prevailed."[27] Further, the maximum hours provisions were introduced to "spread employment over a greater number of employees and also to prohibit an employer from requiring his [*sic*] employees to work excessive hours."[28] In addition, the act included the right to refuse overtime.

While expanding the scope of minimum standards, the provincial government also intended to respect the imperatives of private enterprise.[29] A number of exceptions and exemptions were built into the act to address the concerns of employers. Employers could exceed the maximum hours of work in the case of accidents, urgent repairs, or emergency work, and in cases where "the nature of the work or the perishable nature of the raw material being processed requires such extended daily or weekly working hours."[30] The Industry and Labour Board was empowered to authorize longer hours (daily or weekly) in cases where employers and employees (or their representatives) were in agreement. The eight-hour daily maximum could be exceeded if "an employer has by custom or practice established a working week of 48 hours or less ... but the daily hours are in excess of eight hours," for example, in cases where a forty-eight-hour work week was scheduled over fewer than six days.[31] Up to 120 hours of overtime per employee per year were permitted (the legislation did not set an overtime premium rate, however). As well, certain employee groups were exempted from the provisions, including managers, supervisors, and professionals (Ontario 1987a). Finally, as the legislation was enacted during wartime, all war industries were exempt at the time of its initial application.[32]

While the new maximum hours of work provisions represented a reduction in work time maximums, the act ensured that employers were granted flexibility in the organization of work time through the various exceptions, and exemptions, and system of special permits. As noted by the Ontario Task Force on Hours of Work and Overtime, "the greater stringency of the vastly extended coverage and the more stringent maximums at eight hours per day and 48 per week were offset, in part at least, by greater flexibility through extensive exemptions and by downplaying the 8-hour-per-day maximum where longer hours were the custom" (Ontario 1987, 25). Exemptions and exceptions to ensure flexibility – understood as relief from the legislated standards – were both a legacy of past minimum standards legislation and a central feature of the state's approach to the provision of minimum standards for the remainder of the twentieth century.

This approach to employment standards received strong criticism from organized labour. For example, the Ontario Federation of Labour complained that employers were able to "almost willy-nilly get permits to exceed the maximum" (*Labour Gazette*, February 1968, 68). The Industry and Labour Board focused most of its enforcement attention on the weekly, rather than the daily maximum, resulting in complaints from unions that daily maximums were exceeded without employee consent.[33] The ease with which permits were granted, combined with weak enforcement practices and a lack of reinstatement provisions for workers who were fired for refusing to work overtime, drastically reduced the impact of the maximum hours regulations.

In the years following the war, the provincial government also supported small business opposition to improvements to the HWVPA. In 1951, the CCF presented bills that were intended to reduce maximum hours of work from forty-eight to forty, preserve the eight-hour day with no reduction in take-home pay, establish an overtime

Table 1
Weekly Minimum Wage Rates, Women Workers, 1947 ($)

Zone	Experienced Workers	Inexperienced Workers
1	16.80	14.50 (1st 3 months)
		15.50 (2nd 3 months)
2	15.80	13.50 (1st 3 months)
		14.50 (2nd 3 months)
3	13.80	11.50 (1st 3 months)
		12.50 (2nd 3 months)

Source: AO RG 7-14, File 7-14-0-130, box 3. The Minimum Wage Act, Order No. 2, made by the Industry and Labour Board under the Act, 1947.

premium at time-and-a-half, and provide two weeks of vacation with pay at four percent of a worker's annual salary.[34] In opposing the CCF amendments, the minister of labour stated that "I think that [the CCF] have failed to give due consideration to the fact that there are many small businesses and many employers who employ one or two employees would could not sustain the burdens which this type of legislation seeks to impose."[35] While the new hours of work standards constituted a more general approach to minimum standards, the social goals of the legislation remained clearly circumscribed by the imperatives of business interests within the province.

The reformed postwar minimum standards framework also included changes to the regulation of minimum wages. In 1947, all old minimum wage orders were revoked and the province was divided into three minimum-wage zones, based on population size.[36] New minimum-wage orders based on a forty-eight-hour workweek were issued for women workers in each of these zones. The 1947 rates for each of the zones are provided in table 1. Even though the 1937 Minimum Wage Act allowed the Industry and Labour Board to set minimum wage rates for men, the new orders left men's rates unregulated (Whittingham 1970).

While the Minimum Wage Act set floors for women's wages, there was no general legislation to prevent women workers from receiving wages below the level of male workers when performing the same work. Following the war, pressure on the federal and provincial governments to address this disparity escalated. During the war, larger numbers of women had entered the wage labour force to replace men in jobs that had previously been virtually exclusively male jobs. Even though the jobs had previously been held by men and therefore had not been devalued in the same manner as jobs traditionally held by women, the wages for women remained below those of men doing the same job (*Labour Gazette*, November 1958). This "wage gap" became a concern for women's organizations such as the National Council of Women and the Federation of Business and Professional Women's Clubs, organizations that began to exert concerted pressure for equal pay legislation (*Labour Gazette*, November 1958). Within the labour movement, women activists called for legislative action not only for equal pay, but also for equal "opportunity of employment." In other words, they called for an end to gender discrimination in hiring and promotions (*Labour Gazette*, October 1952). Male unionists were also willing to support the principle of pay equity, partly fearing that lower wages for women could undermine both male employment (through the replacement of men with women), and "the wage rates and standards won by the trade unions over a long period of time" (*Labour Gazette*, September 1959, 904).[37] At the international level, the ILO adopted the Convention on Equal Remuneration for Work of Equal Value in 1951, adding further impetus to the growing campaign for equal pay.

Ontario was the first Canadian province to enact "equal pay" legislation. In 1951, the provincial government passed the Fair Remuneration to Female Employees Act, which came into effect on 1 January 1952. The act brought the principle of equal pay for equal work into legislation and was designed to "ensure that a woman who is doing the same job as a man is paid at the same wage rate" (*Labour Gazette*, November 1958, 1228). More specifically, employers were prohibited from discriminating between male and female employees by paying a lower rate to a woman for "the same work in the same establishment" (*Labour Gazette*, April 1951, 443).[38] Coverage of the act was extended to all employers. During the 1950s, similar legislation was enacted in Saskatchewan, British Columbia, Manitoba, Nova Scotia, and Alberta, and at the federal level.[39] By the end of the decade, equal pay laws covered approximately 67 percent of women in the Canadian labour force.[40]

An overview of the legislative developments of the immediate postwar period reveals the segmented approach to labour market regulation that developed in the era of industrial pluralism. The labour relations legislation of the postwar settlement secured the means by which unionized workers could improve their standards (through compulsory collective bargaining), while non-unionized workers relied on employment standards legislation (for example, in the areas of hours of work and minimum wages) for regulatory protection. Further, while the regulation of employment standards took on a more generalized (formally gender neutral) character, the broader policy approach developing within the postwar system of labour market regulation remained premised on the designation of employment standards as legislation primarily applicable to workers in supplemental and/or transitory forms of employment. As Judy Fudge and Leah Vosko (2001a) suggest, the implications of this segmented approach to postwar labour market regulation were profound. It contributed to the normalization of the standard employment relationship (full-time, continuous employment) within the unionized mass production industries, providing workers in those industries with full-time, stable, well-paying jobs, and thereby entrenched a distinct pattern of segmentation between primary and secondary labour markets. Employment relationships within the secondary labour market, those regulated by employment standards, were characterized by job insecurity, part-time hours, low pay, and little opportunity for advancement. The segmented nature of labour market regulation supported this segmented labour market structure.

The implementation of the postwar settlement not only facilitated the unionization of the mass production industries, with their largely male, blue-collar workforces, but also further channelled union activities towards seeking improvements to workplace standards through collective bargaining and did little to encourage the unionization of the secondary labour market. The effect of this was to further ingrain divisions between the working conditions of unionized workers and those in the secondary sector (McInnis 2002). Many workers, particularly women, as well as many workers of colour, including the growing numbers of non-British immigrant workers, did not secure unionization as a result of the postwar settlement. These workers were left with employment standards legislation to set the basic standards in their workplaces, a regulatory framework that did not construct standards comparable to those negotiated through collective bargaining (Heron 1996).

Despite the removal of explicitly gendered language through the 1937 amendments to the Minimum Wage Act and the 1944 Hours of Work and Vacations with Pay Act, there were clear gendered dimensions to this segmentation. The new legislation replaced the explicitly gendered application of minimum standards (to women

workers) with a more general provision of a "safety net" for those
with "limited bargaining power" (Ontario 1987a, 26). But owing to
connections to the patterns of labour market segmentation discussed
above (women were most likely to be employed in workplaces where
minimum standards applied), employment standards legislation
took on an implicitly gendered character. Joan Sangster (1995, 131)
thus describes Ontario's postwar employment and welfare policies
as grounded in a "dichotomous understanding of women (occasional
workers) and men (permanent workers)."

   Over the first two decades of the postwar period, the regulation
of minimum standards shifted from an explicit orientation towards
protecting women and young workers to a general commitment to
constructing a set of standards for all vulnerable (non-unionized)
workers, male and female. Employment standards legislation sought
to promote a degree of decommodification through general minimum standards that provided these workers with some protection
from market forces. As Judy Fudge and Eric Tucker (2000, 277)
note, however, "[m]inimum entitlement could not depart too mark-
edly from market norms." While the postwar state sought to buffer
the effects of the market, as in the pre–World War II years, the
manner in which minimum standards were regulated ensured that
employers had flexibility with respect to the legally established
minimums.

The Labour Movement and Postwar Standards

The framework of industrial pluralism directed unions towards
collective bargaining, thus further entrenching the segmented
approach to labour market regulation. Organized labour's response
to these tendencies was not homogenous, however. In the postwar
years, the labour movement engaged in intense debates over the
appropriate tactics to use in seeking improvements to minimum
employment standards. As in the pre–World War II period, this
debate revolved around the question of whether to directly pressure
employers to improve standards through collective bargaining or
whether to pressure the state to enact legislation. The divisions
within this debate were shaped by political and institutional differences within the labour movement. Older, more strongly entrenched
unions were in favour of using collective bargaining exclusively, while
the newer industrial unions were open to the use of a combination

of legislative and workplace strategies.[41] At its annual convention in 1947, the TLC resolved to follow a plan of action based on "the securing of concessions asked for by direct negotiation rather than legislation" (*Labour Gazette*, November 1947, 1574). Conversely, at the Canadian Congress of Labour (CCL)annual convention in 1947,[42] delegates called for uniformity of labour legislation across the country and the adoption of ILO conventions, both of which should be accomplished through regular federal and provincial conferences. Further, for the CCL the eight-hour day and the forty-hour work week were to be achieved "through legislation and collective bargaining" (ibid., 1581).

This debate played out at the provincial level. At the annual meeting of the Ontario Provincial Federation of Labour (AFL-TLC), delegates expressed concern about an over-reliance on legislation. One delegate captured this sentiment clearly, stating, "[i]f labor unions are going to continue to be recognized as a labor movement, let's get out on our own feet and get what we want, instead of depending on government."[43] Another delegate expressed concern that unions were "drifting altogether too far into the field of asking the government to do everything for them." These sentiments were reflected in a recommendation of non-concurrence on a resolution calling for a legislated five-day, forty-hour work week for motormen and conductors; they were also expressed in debates over the question of equal pay for women workers at the end of the 1950s. While some unionists favoured equal-pay legislation, others saw the unionization of women workers and the securing of equal pay through collective bargaining as a more effective solution (*Labour Gazette*, September 1959).

Union officials expressed opposition to minimum wages for male workers. Based on the experience of women workers, there was the concern that the legislated minimum would become the maximum wage rate for the industry. Moreover, union officials asserted that legislation would be of little value without unions present to enforce legislated standards. This assertion was based on the difficulties faced in securing enforcement of existing minimum wages legislation for women. In other words, non-unionized men should attempt to unionize to improve their wages, rather than look to the state for protection. This position was captured in a statement by an MP from East Hamilton, itself a highly unionized region: "[l]egislation will not take the place of trade unions."[44]

In Ontario, the provincial government was aware of these tensions within organized labour and used them as a rationale to oppose legislative improvements to existing minimum standards. For example, in response to the 1951 CCF proposals to reduce maximum hours of work from forty-eight to forty, preserve the eight-hour day with no reduction in take-home pay, establish an overtime premium at time-and-a-half, and provide two weeks of paid vacation at four percent of a worker's annual salary, the minister of labour stated, "I think that the members of this House will agree that the proposals contained in the various Bills offered by the members opposite to amend the *Hours of Work and Vacations with Pay Act* are the type which members of the Ontario Provincial Federation of Labour think should be left to collective bargaining."[45]

In 1956, the TLC and the CCL merged to form the Canadian Labour Congress (CLC), providing organized labour with the opportunity to construct a united political and economic front. Its initial Platform of Principles signified an end to the TLC's opposition to achieving improvements to minimum standards through legislation. The platform included proposals for uniform labour and social legislation across the country, equal pay for equal work, a national minimum wage of one dollar per hour for male and female workers, a national Forty Hour Week Act, and a national Vacation and Holiday Act with two weeks of paid vacation (*Labour Gazette*, June 1956). In its first meeting with the federal government, the CLC presented its legislative goals, which included: "uniform labour legislation covering all workers" (*Labour Gazette*, February 1957, 147–8). Soon after, it called upon the federal government to take the lead in minimum standards by adopting its proposals for federally regulated industries and by initiating a federal-provincial conference on labour standards to develop uniformity in standards across the country (*Labour Gazette*, November 1957).

In Ontario, delegates at the 1962 annual convention of the Ontario Federation of Labour committed the organization to directing "all its energies toward gaining a 30-hour work week and a public medical care plan for the province" (*Labour Gazette*, December 1962, 1355). Its affiliates were called upon to win the thirty-hour week through bargaining, while the demand to the provincial government was to establish a forty-hour work week through legislation.[46]

Elements within the labour movement that supported the further development of minimum standards legislation, combined with the general militancy of the 1940s, contributed to the increased social pressure placed on the state to improve the existing minimum standards legislation. Despite the desire for legislative improvements, however, organized labour continued to place primary emphasis on improving workplace standards through collective bargaining. This strategy had limited success. By the early 1960s, attempts to reduce work time below forty hours per week through collective bargaining had been successful in only a few industries, such as the printing industry and the women's garment industry. In most cases, demands for a shorter work week were generally dropped in final bargaining in favour of other benefits (*Labour Gazette*, March 1962).

Overall, the lack of strong, coordinated pressure limited the potential for legislative gains (Fudge and Tucker 2000). The effect of the divisions within organized labour was to reinforce the strategy of collective bargaining of unionized workers as the primary means through which working conditions would be improved. The hegemonic character of postwar labour relations legislation drew organized labour further away from those outside the bounds of industrial pluralism. During the 1950s, the lack of a strong, unified labour movement organizing around demands for improved minimum standards legislation further reinforced the state's segmented approach to labour market regulation.

Consolidating the Minimum in Ontario

The social context of the 1960s, including growing labour unrest, marked in particular by activism amongst young workers and militant and unionized elements within public sector workforces, set the stage for a shift to a comprehensive labour standards framework. In this context, the federal government embarked on a nation-wide "war on poverty," which included strategies to re-regulate minimum standards through new standards for workers in federally regulated industries. The federal Task Force on Industrial Relations called for stronger general labour standards to combat the poverty experienced by low-wage workers.[47]

Within the Ontario provincial government, Ministry of Labour officials were increasingly aware of the inadequacy of existing minimum standards legislation and of the need to develop a new solution to the continued economic marginalization of low-wage workers in the province, as "a portion of the labour force had difficulty in maintaining even a subsistence standard of living."[48] Thus, by the mid-1960s, the Ontario Department of Labour was in the process of developing a comprehensive labour standards code that would bring together existing legislation in the areas of minimum wages, hours of work, and equal pay.[49]

The processes of change began with a focus on the minimum wage. In 1960, a provincial government committee was appointed to explore the possibility of creating a legislated male minimum wage,[50] as "a portion of the labour force had difficulty in maintaining even a subsistence standard of living."[51] Concerns over the exploitation of unorganized workers, along with the general lack of minimum protection for male workers, were also raised at this time.[52] Combined, these facts provided the government with the rationale to develop a new approach to the regulation of minimum wages. As Minister of Labour H.L. Rowntree stated, "[w]hile, on the whole, earnings and income are at record levels and the vast majority of our people are better off than they ever have been before, there still exist pockets of low wages and of conditions which could only be described as bordering upon, if not actually, exploitative."[53]

While a coming shift was taking shape, internal debates within the provincial government over the minimum wage indicate that there was no clear consensus. In a memorandum to the minister of labour, the Industry and Labour Board expressed concern that the introduction of a male minimum wage could create economic and political problems within the province, stating that "[i]t may be difficult to establish a minimum wage rate for male workers which would be ... high enough to be compatible with existing wage rates throughout Ontario without facing possible danger of affecting unemployment as a result of employers reducing costs by employing less staff to meet any established legal requirement, and on the other hand a minimum wage rate in sufficient amount to offset general criticism from such a wage rate being ... too low."[54] After several meetings between December 1960 and February 1961, the committee concluded that a legislated weekly minimum wage for men was not necessary because the existing Minimum Wage Act permitted the establishment of male minimum wage rates through minimum wage orders. Further, the committee stated that it could not recommend a general minimum wage for men "without considerable further study of the impact which such a step would have on the economy of the Province."[55]

Nonetheless, union pressure for a general minimum wage, combined with the general concern within the government over the economic marginalization of low-wage workers, pushed forward a new approach to the regulation of minimum wages.[56] In disagreement with the minimum wage committee, the Ontario minister of labour took the position that a male minimum wage of $1.00 per hour would be both politically and economically feasible, even in the event of some short-term unemployment.[57] The practice of setting only a women's minimum wage was finally abandoned in 1963 (Ursel 1992). The solution was the adoption of a gradual approach that would phase in a general minimum wage across the province.

Under the 1963 amendments to the Minimum Wage Act, the Minimum Wage Board was empowered to establish minimum wages on an hourly basis for both men and women. New minimum wage orders were put into effect on 30 June 1963, setting the first general male minimum wage in the province. Once again, the rates were set not at a common level across the province but on a regional basis according to the three-zone system. The legislation was designed to phase in a common general minimum wage of $1.00 per hour across the province for both men and women ($1.25 for construction workers). This general minimum wage became province-wide on 27 December 1965.[58]

This new legislation followed the pattern set by other postwar minimum standards legislation by constructing a social safety net that provided both minimum standards as well as accommodations for business. In terms of flexibility, the phase-in approach was meant to take into account concern raised within the business community, which had indicated cautious support so long as the rates did not increase to the point where they could have a detrimental impact on marginal industries that employ large numbers of unskilled labourers.[59]

No such shift was immediately apparent in response to social pressure to improve hours of work and vacations standards, however. By the early 1960s, the forty-hour work week was standard in most industries. Other provincial jurisdictions, including Manitoba, Saskatchewan, Alberta, and British Columbia, had two weeks of paid vacation, as compared to one in Ontario.[60] In response to union and employee concerns about excessive overtime, the minister of labour raised the possibility of reducing the weekly maximum to forty-four, stating that the "maximum 48-hour week appears to be out of step with the times and a more appropriate maximum work week would probably be 44."[61] Yet the provincial government resisted reducing legislated working-time maximums, citing concerns over both labour shortages and inflationary pressures.[62]

The Canada Labour Standards Code

The lack of consensus within the Ontario government over the specifics of the minimum wage paled in comparison to the tensions that developed between the province and the federal Department of Labour over the issue of general labour standards. These tensions were apparent in the reactions of provincial officials to the development of the Canada Labour (Standards) Code, itself a product of the social context of labour militancy and the federal government's "war on poverty."

At a 1964 federal-provincial labour conference, the federal government indicated its intentions to enact comprehensive labour standards legislation for all industries under its jurisdiction. The proposal was considered to be a logical step in the development of postwar labour legislation that had begun almost twenty years earlier with the Industrial Relations and Disputes Investigation Act (IRDIA) in 1948. While some employees under federal jurisdiction were able to negotiate their standards through collective bargaining, it was recognized that employees who were not unionized were considered unlikely to become so. Thus, there was a need for legislation of this nature (*Labour Gazette*, April 1964).

The Canada Labour (Standards) Code came into effect in July 1965 and set labour standards for all industries under federal jurisdiction. The code established maximum hours of work of eight hours per day and forty per week, with an overtime rate of time-and-a-half for hours over forty. The code also set a minimum wage for both men and women at $1.25 per hour, two weeks of paid vacation per year, and eight statutory holidays for workers in the federal jurisdiction. In 1966, the Canada Labour (Safety) Code codified the regulation of health and safety standards for workers in the federal jurisdiction. In 1967, the Canada Labour Code consolidated these labour statutes with federal labour relations legislation (*Labour Gazette*, December 1964; HRDC 2000a).

While the new federal labour code established minimum standards for all federally regulated industries, it followed the pattern set by existing provincial minimum standards legislation, specifically by providing measures to ensure employer flexibility. For example, the code permitted the averaging of overtime hours over a period of multiple weeks as a means to avoid payment of time-and-a-half for extra hours worked in a week.[63] In addition to the overtime averaging provisions, an adjustment (deferment) period was provided for some industries with respect to the application of the wages and hours of work provisions (*Labour Gazette*, September 1967).

Both employers and the Ontario provincial government voiced opposition to the federal code. Employers, particularly those in the trucking industry, feared that the hours of work restrictions could have a detrimental impact on work scheduling.[64] Ontario minister of labour H.L. Rowntree agreed, arguing that the federal labour code could create an unequal level of competition, as some companies in gray-area jurisdictions (trucking and highway transport) were covered by the federal code, while others remained under provincial jurisdiction, with different hours-of-work regulations. In a more general sense, the new code was criticized in a memo produced by the Ontario Department of Labour for taking a leading-edge approach to legislated standards by exceeding standards set through collective bargaining. This leading-edge approach was very different from the one favored by the province of Ontario, where "[n]o attempt is made to remove these matters from the bargaining table or to establish fair or living wages."[65]

The Ontario government was particularly concerned about the federal government's desire to promote a harmonization of labour standards across the provinces. It made clear that such an initiative would not be supported in Ontario. In a letter to the Department of the Prime Minister, Labour Minister H.L. Rowntree stated that "it is unrealistic to expect all economic regions across Canada to be capable of supporting a minimum wage of $1.25 or a forty-hour week or many other of the Code's provisions."[66] Provincial opposition to the standards within the code indicated that the Ontario government intended to maintain provincial autonomy and was not prepared to meet the minimum standards set by the federal government in its own legislation.

Consolidating Standards at the Provincial Level

Nonetheless, by the mid-1960s the Ontario provincial government was facing growing pressure from the labour movement to enact stronger legislative protections for workers who did not have the benefit of unionization and to legislate reduced working time in order to protect against the threat of unemployment created by technological innovation. The government was also aware that its existing approach to the regulation of minimum standards – at that time several separate pieces of legislation that set standards for hours of work, vacations with pay, minimum wages, and equal pay for equal work – was increasingly insufficient, as the standards lagged behind those of other jurisdictions. As indicated in Department of Labour reports on both minimum wages and hours of work, there remained "pockets of exploitation" within the province's workforce that required stronger legislative protection.[67]

For its part, the Ontario Federation of Labour used the standards set by the federal labour code as a rationale to push for improvements to provincial labour standards legislation. The OFL's strategy reflected a growing conviction within the labour movement that unionization and collective bargaining needed to be supplemented with legislative action. This was particularly the case in light of the increasing economic shift towards a service economy, as these jobs were "the hardest to organize and are the lowest paid."[68] The new federal code, combined with the broader "war on poverty," provided the organization with an opportunity to push for stronger provincial standards. In the words of the federation, "[s]urely the highly industrial province of Ontario should at least conform to the Federal standards."[69] The OFL argued that reduced work time, through legislation, could create employment opportunities for larger numbers of workers. Further, an increase in the minimum wage from $1 to $2 per hour was a necessary first step to reducing poverty rates in the province, as "[i]t does not take an economist or a statistician to show that the take-home pay under the present minimum wage standards is far below the amount necessary to live above the poverty line."[70]

Women's organizations supported further improvements to the legislated standards as well. At its 1967 annual convention, the Congress of Canadian Women called for an increase in the provincial minimum wage from $1.00 to $2.00 per hour. Such a raise was needed to reflect the realities of women's wage labour in the 1960s. Paid employment was not a temporary phase in a woman's life, as many women workers remained in the labour force until retirement, and the existing minimum wage rate was insufficient to meet the needs of women who were the "sole breadwinners" of their families.[71] As women were receiving as little as 75 percent of the salary paid to men for comparable work, the Business and Professional Women's Clubs in Ontario sought amendments to the equal pay legislation through the 1960s, specifically that the legislation be amended to cover "work of a comparable character done in the same establishment."[72]

In direct contrast to these positions, both large and small employers expressed a preference for standards to be set through workplace-level bargaining.[73] The CMA pressured for exemptions for employers with unionized workforces so that minimum standards legislation would not directly affect collective bargaining. In response to potential changes to the regulation of hours of work, small businesses sought greater flexibility in the scheduling of hours of work and opposed proposals for a required half-hour break after five hours of work. Such legislation, it was claimed, would "create a very definite hardship" on workers employed in continuous shift operations, as well as on consumers and entire industries.[74] Instead of legislated standards, "mutually satisfactory working conditions" that are negotiated between employers and employees were deemed more appropriate, as they are "more conducive to good labour relations than legislated working conditions."

Within the provincial government, the prevailing ideology regarding the role of minimum standards was tied to the goal of developing a general safety net for all those with "limited bargaining power" (Ontario 1987a, 26). For example, a government report titled *Labour Standards and Poverty in Ontario* suggested that, as "a portion of the labour force had difficulty in maintaining even a subsistence standard of living," minimum labour standards could play an important role in addressing the poverty that may result from low wages, long hours, and unfair competition.[75] Similarly, a 1968 minimum wage regulation indicated that "[a]n appropriate Minimum Wage helps to prevent severe economic and social exploitation and serves as a pressure towards the elimination of unfair wage competition."[76]

In the area of hours of work, despite the legislated maximum of forty-eight hours and the fact that the majority of workers in the province worked a standard work week of forty hours or less, the government was aware that between 13 and 16 percent of employees were working hours in excess of the maximum.[77] The province was also aware that its legislated hours standards exceeded both the ILO conventions and legislated maximums in many other jurisdictions. For example, Ontario was one of few jurisdictions in North America that did not provide holiday pay or overtime pay. Further, by that time other provincial jurisdictions, including Manitoba, Saskatchewan, Alberta, and British Columbia, had two weeks of paid vacation, as compared to one in Ontario.[78] These sentiments within the government created internal support for a new labour code and also created a political space for those outside the state pushing for better standards.

Yet, the same report indicated that these considerations were to be accomplished without creating undue hardships for employers, who were concerned about the potential impacts of increased legislated standards.[79] A subsequent memorandum on minimum wages from the Department of Labour in 1968 expressed the government's cautious sentiment with respect to the legislated minimum, stating that minimum wages themselves were not considered to be a means to eliminate poverty; rather, they were to provide a "socially and economically acceptable" floor.[80] Consistent with previous minimum standards initiatives, any new minimum standards legislation should not be used to develop "leading-edge" standards that would exceed standards negotiated through collective bargaining. For example, in response to an OFL demand in 1968 to increase paid vacation to two weeks per year, Minister of Labour Dalton Bales claimed that as many collective agreements did not yet have two weeks paid vacation, "the law is going to be rather hard on the economies of some employers if it imposes the requirements."[81]

Further, the province was certainly not prepared to follow the federal standard of the forty-hour work week. In response to business concerns over the possibility of a legislated forty-hour work week in 1965, E.G. Gibb, a Department of Labour official, stated it was "doubtful if any amendment along this line would be introduced by the Government at this Session."[82] A memorandum in 1968 clarified this position, stating, "to limit hours to 40 would not only hobble industry, but would also limit workers' opportunities to earn overtime pay, which would reduce their incomes."[83] Rather than a reduction of hours of work, the introduction of overtime pay was considered a possibility, as it would discourage excess hours of work and provide protection for workers against unpaid overtime, while at the same time not prohibiting the scheduling of extra hours. A departmental memorandum from 1966 indicates that an overtime rate could be phased in, first to apply to hours over forty-eight, and then to be reduced to hours over forty-four. Premium pay for work on seven statutory holidays was also recommended.[84]

While it was considering alterations to hours of work standards, the department also began to consider increasing the minimum wage. The government was not prepared to move as high as the OFL's recommendations on a $2.00 minimum wage, as it claimed that the federation's rate could harm marginal industries.[85] However, an increase in the minimum wage was considered necessary owing to a 15 percent increase in prices and a 29 percent increase in hourly manufacturing earnings since 1963, and to the fact that income support programs were providing a comparable income for workers who earned a minimum wage. In 1968, the minimum wage of one dollar per hour was 38 percent of the average manufacturing earnings in the province, down from 49 percent in 1963. A 1967 industry survey found that approximately 65 percent of workers in hotels, restaurants, and taverns, 45 percent of launderers, cleaners, and pressers, and 29 percent of workers in retail trade earned less than $1.30 per hour. The majority of these workers were part-time and either students or women.[86] In addition, seven provinces – Manitoba, New Brunswick, Nova Scotia, Prince Edward Island, Quebec, Saskatchewan, and British Columbia – along with the federal jurisdiction, all had rates higher than the Ontario minimum wage. Thus, the government advanced a recommendation for a minimum wage of either $1.25 or $1.30 per hour.[87]

The Ontario Employment Standards Act

Ontario's comprehensive labour standards code – the Ontario Employment Standards Act (ESA) – came into effect on 1 January 1969.[88] As minimum standards legislation, the ESA was designed to both "safeguard workers against exploitation and to protect employers against unfair competition based on lower standards,"[89] and it was primarily designed for those without collective agreements, particularly those in low-income employment.[90]

The general minimum wage was increased to $1.30 for men and women workers.[91] Hours of work maximums remained consistent at eight hours per day and forty-eight hours per week. An overtime premium rate of time-and-a-half was introduced for work over forty-eight hours per week, and employees were granted the right to refuse overtime. Holiday pay was set at time-and-a-half for seven statutory holidays – New Year's Day, Good Friday, Victoria Day, Dominion Day, Labour Day, Thanksgiving Day, and Christmas Day. Annual paid vacation of two weeks was to be compensated at a rate of 4 percent of a worker's annual salary.[92] As well, the act established a new process for the collection of unpaid wages up to a thousand dollars (*Labour Gazette*, January 1969a; Ontario 1987a). A director of employment standards, who was to operate under the discretion of the minister of labour, was appointed to administer the act and was given responsibility for issuing extra hours permits and for enforcing the provisions of the act (*Labour Gazette*, January 1969b). Existing equal-pay legislation was also incorporated into the act and the director took over responsibility for its enforcement.

Consistent with the previously existing approach to minimum standards, the ESA was designed to provide socially acceptable minimum standards without creating undue interference with business interests in the province. As with previous minimum standards legislation, the act included exemptions and special provisions designed to provide employers with the capacity to operate outside its standards. For example, R.M. Warren, executive director of manpower services, described the overtime provisions as a "flexible deterrent to excessively long hours."[93] The overtime premium was to provide the deterrent, while flexibility was gained through the possibility to average overtime hours over multiple weeks, subject to the director's approval. Further, the right to refuse overtime did not apply in cases where an employer had established a normal work day in excess of eight hours in a work week of forty-eight hours or less. Hours in excess of the weekly maximum were permitted through a permits system, to a maximum of one hundred hours of overtime per year, and different hours of work maximums were established for certain industries. Specific employee groups were exempted from some or all of the standards contained in the act.[94]

Organized labour was highly critical of the new legislation. In a 1969 submission to the provincial government, the OFL claimed that "the new minimums will do very little to help the unorganized workers participate in the prosperity they help to create."[95] The forty-eight-hour work week was defined as unrealistic, as industry standards were moving towards a forty-hour work week. The minimum wage levels were well below the poverty line established by the Economic Council of Canada for a family of four in 1969.[96]

The OFL was also highly critical of the various exemptions contained in the legislation.

Despite the various provisions in the act that promoted employer-oriented flexibility, employer associations also registered a number of concerns with the new legislation.[97] While the CMA was consulted prior to the ESA receiving royal assent, the association stated that the concerns of employers had not been addressed in the drafting of the regulations and that the act created many practical problems.[98] In addition, the association feared that the scheduling and pay arrangements could result in extra costs and that the act would threaten "the stability of existing working arrangements."[99] For unionized workplaces, both the CMA and the Ontario Chamber of Commerce (OCC) argued that employment standards legislation should not apply to an employer with a collective agreement, as this would undermine the process of free collective bargaining. According to the OCC, "union representatives are quite capable of protecting the best interests of their members concerning wages, hours of work, overtime and vacations."[100]

Many employer associations also opposed the requirements for overtime and holiday premiums. The OCC requested that employees in service industries be exempted from the holiday pay provisions, as "there is little justification for providing legislative authority which requires that such continuous operations as hospitals, hotels and communications enterprises should be required to pay above normal rates for maintaining normal service."[101] Overall, employers continued to favour individual or collective bargaining over legislated standards.

The government's response to critics of the minimum wage levels illustrates its perception of the role of the minimum wage specifically and of minimum standards more generally. The government recognized the need for a minimum wage in order to address the social problem of extremely low wage work. In response to claims that the minimum wage was too low, however, the government stated that the minimum wage levels were assumed to be a general floor below which wage rates could not go, rather than a fair or living wage. This floor was assumed to have income-raising potential, as increases to the minimum rates would lead to general increases in wage rates across the province.[102] It was not considered reasonable to set the minimum wage at a level that would ensure an income above the poverty line, as employees' family responsibilities and marital status were not to be considered in the determination of wage rates. In addition, the minimum wage was itself only part of a package of income-raising devices that included collective bargaining, the Industrial Standards Act, fair wage schedules for government contracts, and premium pay for overtime and statutory holidays.

Finally, the standards also had to take business interests into account. The government was not prepared to meet demands from the OFL and the NDP for a minimum wage of $2.25 per hour, as this rate "probably would have too heavy an impact on low-wage industries."[103] Competitive pressures required that the minimum wage be kept at a level in line with economic realities, lest companies decide to relocate to lower-wage jurisdictions. While the government exhibited some autonomy from the business community in setting minimum standards, that autonomy was clearly delimited by the prerogative to support private enterprise by minimizing the impact of the legislated minimums.

CONCLUSION

Building on almost a century of slow progression towards a general legislative framework to regulate minimum employment standards, the Ontario Employment Standards Act was the result of a convergence of a range of social forces and social processes. Labour and women's movements pushed policy-makers towards the enactment of a legislative floor for workplace standards. Pressure from the business community, the ideologies of welfare state policy-makers, and conflict between federal and provincial jurisdictions all acted to ensure the presence of "flexibility" within the emerging regulatory regime. And despite upsurges in labour militancy in the 1940s and 1960s, organized labour failed to develop a strategy to exert concerted pressure on the state to fundamentally alter its approach to minimum standards. Instead, the focus on collective bargaining favoured by many within the labour movement reinforced existing patterns of segmentation within the labour market.

The explicitly gendered legacy of Ontario's early minimum standards legislation continued to shape the regulation of employment standards in the postwar years. Despite the removal of explicitly gendered provisions in the areas of minimum wages and maximum hours, the regulation of postwar employment standards nonetheless remained premised upon the norms of the male breadwinner model and were still much more likely to apply to women workers. This approach to minimum standards supported and reproduced patterns of not only gendered but also racialized segmentation, as workers of colour and recent immigrant workers of largely non-British origins were also more likely to be reliant on the legislated standards, which were clearly set below conditions that were established by collective bargaining.

The end result, the Ontario Employment Standards Act, indicates that social forces both internal and external to the state created pressure to enact comprehensive employment standards legislation to provide some statutory protection for the most vulnerable workers in the province. Yet the resulting ESA also indicates that the interests of capital accumulation – the "economically practicable" – clearly predominated. The state's approach to employment standards thereby ensured standards of a secondary status for workers with the least bargaining power and thus reinforced and reproduced patterns of segmentation within a labour market that was built around the norm of the standard employment relationship. Because of the ways in which the state negotiated the tensions associated with providing social protection for exploited workers, while at the same time mini-mizing interference in the market, the capacity for postwar employ-ment standards to provide protection for the "pockets of exploitation" for which they were intended was severely compromised.

3

Recessions, Reforms, and Labour Market Transformation, 1970s–1990s

Employment standards legislation has been described as the collective agreement of the unorganized or as anti-exploitation legislation providing minimum standards for those persons who, by reason of lack of education, skill or organization, do not have a strong bargaining position in the labour market.[1]

There are more than 134,000 employment units in Ontario and it is not possible for the staff in the Employment Standards Branch to inspect all of these and certainly not simultaneously, particularly bearing in mind that we have a staff of some 56 inspectors. More than this, I am sure that you appreciate that when statutes such as the *Employment Standards Act* and its predecessor statutes have been passed and wide publicity given to their provisions, it is incumbent upon the public and organizations to comply with them without an individual visit from the staff to advise them of public responsibility.[2]

The years following World War II constituted a period of unparalleled economic growth for the advanced capitalist economies. By the late 1960s, however, the global economy entered a long downturn, characterized by recurring recessions, rising unemployment, and reduced rates of profitability. These conditions, combined with rising inflation (stagflation) and brought on by factors including an over-accumulation of fixed capital, intensified global competitiveness, the destabilization of the international financial system, and monetary policies promoting low inflation through high interest rates, constitute perhaps the most familiar symptoms of the downturn (Brenner 1998; Harvey 1990; McBride and Shields 1997; McNally 1999; Moody 1997).[3] In this context, emerging government and corporate accounts of the downturn focused on rising labour costs, the social power of organized labour, the "inflexibility" of the Fordist system of mass production, and Keynesian policy frameworks. The downturn produced a political and economic conjuncture within which profound transformations in labour markets and public policy took place.

As the first of the above quotes indicates, employment standards were described within state discourses as the means by which unorganized workers would be provided with a minimum level of protection. They were the means by which those most vulnerable to the exploitation of the unregulated market would be accorded a "socially acceptable" minimum level of protection.[4] Yet, as the Canadian labour market began a transition out of the Fordist postwar economy, the growing crisis of profitability experienced across the advanced capitalist states created pressures for policy reform. Business interests intensified pressures for flexible models of labour market regulation. Conversely, in the face of increasing economic insecurity and growing levels of unemployment, organized labour called for improvements to minimum standards. In addition, growing pressures for equity-based labour market policies, particularly from the women's movement, added to these dynamics of change. These competing factors shaped the trajectory of employment standards policy-making in the final three decades of the twentieth century.

In Ontario, successive provincial governments from each major party – Progressive Conservative, Liberal, and New Democratic – all made commitments to review and reform employment standards legislation. Taking the employment standards reforms of this period as its focus, this chapter examines this period of transition, sitting as it does between the era of the Keynesian welfare state and the emerging neoliberal model. However, the standards as written in legislation do not provide the whole story. This chapter also examines the administration of employment standards, focusing on coverage, exemptions, enforcement, and disputes resolution practices. While employment standards established minimum protections for most workers, in practice these standards were neither as comprehensive nor as unconditional as official state discourses indicated. In the years following its enactment, flexibility was facilitated both through a system of exemptions that reduced the scope of legislative coverage and through forms of "implicit deregulation" created by ineffective enforcement and disputes resolution practices.[5]

LABOUR MARKET CHANGE, 1970S–1990S

By the early 1970s, the labour market was clearly undergoing a process of transformation that included increased levels of unemployment, pronounced growth in nonstandard employment relationships, a polarization of work hours, and growing levels of precariousness.

Within Canada, the unemployment rate was comparatively low during the postwar period, increasing from an average of 2 percent in the 1940s to 5 percent in the 1960s. During the 1970s, the average unemployment rate increased to 6.7 percent. Unemployment averaged 9.5 percent during the 1980s, with a peak of 11.9 percent during the recession in the early years of the decade. The rate increased further to an average of 10.1 percent in the early 1990s, reaching a high of 11 percent in 1992 and 1993 (Krahn et al. 2006). Economic growth in the late 1990s brought the rate down below 7 percent at the end of the decade (Jackson et al. 2000). The overall increase in unemployment rates since the early 1970s, particularly the double-digit rates experienced during the early 1980s and 1990s, can be explained by a combination of permanent plant closures, corporate downsizing and restructuring, and federal monetary policies that attempted to reduce inflation through high interest rates (Burman 1997). As unemployment increased, so too did labour market insecurity, with a "fear factor" effect paving the way for new forms of work organization (for example, lean production) and new employment norms defined by greater flexibility (Stanford 2000).

North American manufacturing employment was hit particularly hard during the recessions of the early 1980s and early 1990s. Production became more decentralized through a reduction in the concentration of manufacturing facilities in core areas of industrial production, such as the northeastern region of the United States, southern Ontario, and parts of Quebec. In the early to mid-1980s, manufacturing employment in Canada declined by 141,000 jobs (Luxton and Corman 2001), while during the recession of the early 1990s, approximately one in five manufacturing jobs were lost (Jackson 1999). Overall, between 1988 and 1996 manufacturing employment declined by 290,000 jobs. This decline did not produce a complete de-industrialization of Canada's workforce, as by 1997 total manufacturing employment had returned to 1988 levels in terms of numbers of jobs, and the manufacturing share of Canada's GDP remained almost constant. The significance of manufacturing job loss during the 1980s and early 1990s should not be understated, however. During this period, employment in manufacturing fell as a percentage of total employment, while employment in service industries continued to increase.

The expansion of the service sector, though a key trend during this period, was not a recent phenomenon. The Canadian economy experienced dramatic growth in the service sector over the course of the twentieth century as a whole. In 1951, the manufacturing sector employed 31 percent of the workforce, and the service sector, 47 percent. By 1996, the service sector accounted for 74 percent of the Canadian labour force, while employment in manufacturing and construction accounted for 21 percent, and employment in agriculture and resource-based production just over 5 percent (Krahn et al. 2006).

Along with service sector growth, this period was characterized by the increasing frequency of nonstandard employment relationships. As discussed in chapter 1, nonstandard employment relationships include part-time work (less than thirty hours per week), temporary or contingent work, own-account self-employment (without paid help), and multiple job-holders (Krahn 1995). Beginning in the 1970s growth in nonstandard employment relationships began to accelerate and grew from 33 percent in 1989 to 38 percent by 1997 (Saunders 2003; Vosko et al. 2003). While the levels of nonstandard employment have stabilized in recent years, the transition that took place constituted a shift in the normative model of employment away from the standard employment relationship (Vosko 2000). And as discussed in chapter 1, these trends were highly gendered and racialized, with women and workers from racialized groups over-represented in nonstandard employment.

Growth in part-time work was substantial in these years. Between 1978 and 1998, part-time employment grew from 15 percent to 22 percent of the Canadian workforce, an average annual rate of 4.5 percent, as compared to average growth in full-time employment of 1.2 percent per year (Statistics Canada 1999). Part-time work was particularly prevalent in the lower-tier service sector; by 1998 over 40 percent of employment in accommodation and food services and over 35 percent of employment in retail trade, was part-time (Duffy 1997; Statistics Canada 1999).

Nationally, the other three forms of nonstandard employment all increased through the 1990s (Krahn 1995; Statistics Canada 1997).

Growth in self-employment was particularly significant. From 1986 to 1996, self-employment grew by 39 percent, increasing the proportion of self-employed workers to 16 percent, while growth in paid employment grew by 10 percent. In 1996, self-employment was most common in agriculture (61 percent), construction (35 percent), and business services (32 percent) (Statistics Canada 1997). Of the four types of self-employment,[6] own-account self-employment grew at a rate of 117 percent, with particularly significant growth in child care provision, as well as janitorial and cleaning services (Statistics Canada 1997). The fastest-growing of these occupations included providers of child care and janitorial and cleaning services. Owing to its high growth rate, self-employment accounted for approximately 58 percent of the net change in total employment during the 1990s (Statistics Canada 2000).

Growth in service sector employment and nonstandard work arrangements was accompanied by a polarization of work hours, or growing tendencies towards both short (under thirty-five hours) and long (over forty hours) workweeks. The proportion of employees working the standard workweek of thirty-five to forty hours declined between 1976 and 1998, while the proportion of employees working both long and short workweeks grew. This polarization of hours was segmented by industry and occupation: long hours were more prevalent in goods-producing industries and managerial and professional occupations, and short hours were more common in service-producing industries, particularly accommodation and food services (Hall 1999). Trends in overtime hours further contributed to the polarization of hours. Data from 1997 indicate that 17 percent of employees worked overtime, averaging approximately nine additional hours of work per week (Duchesne 1997; Yalnizyan 1998). Overtime hours were most prevalent in managerial and professional occupations and teaching and least likely in service occupations. Further, of those working overtime, over half (53 percent) were not paid for overtime.

Like other aspects of gender divisions within the labour market, working time patterns displayed pronounced gender differences. Women's annual hours of work increased significantly and contributed to an overall increase in average annual working hours. By the mid-1990s, however, while only 7.1 percent of men worked fewer than thirty-five hours, approximately 30 percent of women worked shorter hours (Shields 2000). Conversely, 24 percent of men, as compared to 8.6 percent of women worked long hours. Overall, average hours of work were noticeably lower in industries where women were more predominant, such in as educational services, health care and social assistance, and accommodation and food services. Further, while male workers were more likely than female workers to work overtime hours, 62 percent of women were unpaid for their overtime, compared to 38 percent of men (Yalnizyan 1998). These gender differences reflected the intersection of gendered divisions in forms of employment (for example, over-representation in part-time work) and gendered divisions in responsibilities for social reproduction. While the labour market participation of women increased dramatically, equality in the distribution of working hours did not follow.

Coinciding with these developments was an increase in precarious employment, a condition experienced disproportionately amongst women and members of racialized groups (Cranford et al. 2003).[7] Incidents of low pay are a key indicator of precariousness. Growth in low-paying jobs is connected with broader patterns of labour market change, including service sector growth. The lowest-paying service industries – retail trade, food and accommodation, and personal services – account for the greatest number of workers in the service sector and three-quarters of all workers employed in the service sector have average weekly earnings below the average earnings of those employed in the goods-producing sector.

The growth in nonstandard employment also contributed to increases in low-paying jobs. In 1995, temporary workers had weekly earnings that were only 65 percent of those with permanent jobs, while in 1999 part-time workers earned an average hourly wage that was 74 percent of that of full-time workers. Further, gender gaps in earnings are more pronounced in forms of nonstandard work (Jackson et al. 2000). For example, of women employed in forms of contingent work, 80 percent earned less than $1,500 per month, as compared to 66.6 percent of men in similar employment relationships (de Wolff 2000). The prevalence of low-income jobs amongst nonstandard forms of employment can be explained by a combination of fewer hours (in the case of part-time work), the precarious nature of the employment (which reduces the capacity of employees to pressure for higher wages), and a lack of unionization and fringe benefits.

Another indicator of precariousness is unionization. Union coverage both within nonstandard forms of employment and within lower-tier private service sector employment more generally is much lower than union coverage of those within a standard employment relationship and in manufacturing industries. Workers in these areas of high employment growth are therefore much less likely to have the regulatory protection of a collective agreement, and they are much more likely to be directly reliant on minimum standards legislation to regulate their conditions of employment.

Union density in Canada peaked at 37.2 percent in 1984, declining to approximately one-third of the non-agricultural work-force in the 1990s.[8] In the context of the forms of labour market change documented above, unions have not successfully kept pace with service sector growth, particularly in areas of nonstandard employment. By the end of the 1990s, union coverage of part-time workers (18 percent) was much lower than that of full-time workers (30 percent). Manufacturing and public sector employees were more likely to be covered by a collective agreement (31 percent and 70 percent respectively) than those in lower-tier service sector industries, such as accommodation and food services (5.5 percent). And union coverage of women in the private sector was 14.4 percent, reflecting women's disproportionate rates of employment in sales and service occupations, which have low rates of unionization (Akyeampong 2000).

Overall, during this period there was a clear shift away from the postwar norm of the standard employment relationship, a shift that included significant growth in nonstandard and precarious forms of employment. These trends furthered patterns of labour market flexibility and contributed to a growing gap in income inequalities (Yalnizyan 1998). These labour market transformations set the backdrop for employment standards reforms in the 1970s, 1980s, and 1990s.

EMPLOYMENT STANDARDS REVIEW, 1970S–80S

As this situation began to unfold during the 1970s, only minor employment standards reforms were being considered.[9] For example, termination notice requirements were added in 1971. In 1972, a pregnancy leave provision was added that gave employees with at least one year of seniority in workplaces of twenty-five or more employees up to twelve weeks (six and six) of pre- and post-natal leave and entitlement to their former or a comparable position. In

1975, the overtime pay (time-and-one-half) threshold was reduced from forty-eight hours to forty-four, pregnancy leave provisions were expanded to cover up to seventeen weeks of leave, and provisions requiring equal benefits under pension, health, and group insurance plans "regardless of age, sex and marital status" were also introduced. In 1976, the province introduced a differential (lower) minimum wage rate for servers in the hospitality industry.

As discussed, the early 1980s were years of escalating unemployment, with levels reaching close to 12 percent (Krahn et al. 2006). As the recession took hold, an Employment Standards Review Committee (ESRC) was struck to consider further possible reforms. The committee identified the need to improve employment standards in the areas of public holidays, vacations with pay, equal pay for equal work, and pregnancy leave. The committee also recommended adding new provisions in the areas of unpaid adoption leave and unpaid paternity leave, and protections against unjust dismissal and employer use of lie detector tests. Proposals were also considered to add a weekly rest period, so that employee consent would have to be obtained in order for employers to schedule seven or more consecutive days of work. However, these potential areas of change were "not considered to be timely, given the state of the economy, the burden that would be imposed on many employers, and the need to preserve jobs." Rather, they were to be "kept under continuous review as circumstances change."[10]

While initially mandated to undertake a specific review of the act, the ESRC was given an on-going responsibility to examine the ESA and the possible need for further amendments. At the time, the government continued to articulate the desire to use the ESA as a means to provide standards for those workers with minimal bargaining power in the labour market. The Employment Standards Branch recognized the need to improve the ESA because of factors such as improved legislation in other jurisdictions in Canada, improvements in collective agreements, and public support for legislative protection.[11] Thus, according to the ESB, "[w]hile it is recognized that there is concern about increasing government regulation in the private sector, there must be at the same time consideration of providing a minimum level of protection to the working population." In light of these sentiments, the ESRC and the government explored possibilities for employment standards reform in some detail during the years of both recession and recovery in the 1980s. Key areas targeted for reform included wage protection, severance pay, equal pay, and working time.

In the 1970s, the province recognized that employees continued to be vulnerable to a loss of wages in the event of employer bankruptcies and insolvencies.[12] Beginning in the mid-1970s, both the federal government and the Ontario provincial government explored the possibility of developing a wage protection program to ensure that employees would be able to secure some compensation in the event of employer insolvency. Under the federal Bankruptcy Act, employees were entitled to claim up to five hundred dollars in unpaid wages. However, employee claims held a status lower than those of secured creditors, meaning that the Bankruptcy Act did not guarantee that employees would be able to secure compensation for lost wages.[13] In cases where the act did not apply, employees could receive up to two thousand dollars in unpaid wages through the ESA.[14] Like the Bankruptcy Act, however, the ESA gave employee wages a lower priority than assets owed to secured creditors. While the amount in unpaid wages employees could claim was higher than that allowed by the Bankruptcy Act, many individual claims exceeded this amount.[15] In addition, the lack of secured status meant that employee claims were often not met. Finally, recovery of unpaid wages was often subject to lengthy delays, meaning that employees would not receive the wages owed to them at the time of the bankruptcy or insolvency.[16]

Because of federal inaction on the issue, the Progressive Conservative Ontario government also considered developing a method to protect employee wages. Provincial proposals included increasing the statutory priority of wages, enacting a wage insurance fund, or creating a statutory trust, whereby an amount equivalent to owed wages could be separated out of employer assets.[17] The Employment Standards Branch also recommended raising the amount of unpaid wages that could be claimed by an employee from $2,000 to $4,000.[18] As the recession of the early 1980s led to increased incidences of employer bankruptcy and insolvency, pressure on the government to provide some form of wage protection also increased, including from the labour movement and in editorials in major newspapers.[19] However, while it continued to recognize the problem, the province did not seek to amend the ESA to improve employee protection in the event of bankruptcy or insolvency, citing a lack of clarity regarding potential jurisdictional conflicts with the federal bankruptcy legislation (Ontario 1985).

Instead of policy reform, the province struck a task force on Wage Protection in Insolvency Situations in 1983. The report of the task force, presented in 1985, recommended that if the federal government did not accept responsibility for wage protection in insolvency situations, wage claims should be protected through amendments to the ESA that would include the establishment of a wage protection fund (Ontario 1985). At the time, Minister of Labour William Wrye expressed a commitment to address the need for some form of wage protection, stating: "All too frequently, once such secured creditors as bankers and suppliers have been paid, there has not been enough money left to satisfy the legitimate wage claims of employees. More to the point, the only recourse in these situations has been through the courts. That remedy has proved to be expensive, time consuming and, often, ineffective."[20] Despite the recommendations of the Commission on Wage Protection in Insolvency Situations that the province develop wage protection measures within the ESA, however, no such policy changes were made during the 1980s.

On the other hand, in response to growing concerns over layoffs resulting from the recession of the early 1980s, severance pay provisions were introduced into the ESA in 1981.[21] They provided employees with a minimum of five years of service with one week's pay for each year worked up to a maximum of twenty-six weeks in cases of mass termination.[22] The provisions were amended by the provincial Liberal government in 1987, in order to require employers to provide termination notices one week in advance for any employee employed longer than three months, with an additional week's notice for each year of employment, up to a maximum of eight weeks.[23] Workers with five years of employment at a business with an annual payroll of at least $2.5 million became eligible for severance pay (Ontario 1987c,12). In addition, the new severance provisions were extended to workers whose temporary lay-off extended beyond thirty-five weeks in a fifty-two-week period. Overall, the amendments had the potential to increase the number of workers eligible for severance pay fivefold.[24] Further, in the case of mass layoffs, the legislation required that employers provide the Ministry of Labour with an explanation of the economic circumstances surrounding the termination, a summary of consultations with employees and the affected community, any proposed measures to help those laid off, and a statistical profile of affected workers.

Finally, by the mid-1970s the equal-pay provisions of the ESA began to receive widespread criticism from women's and human rights organizations, organized labour, and opposition political parties, all of which emphasized the need to recognize "work of equal value."[25] The specific provisions in the ESA at the time were criticized for not effectively combating pay differentials between male and female employees, specifically by limiting evaluation criteria to single establishments (and thereby not protecting against gender-segregation between establishments) and by evaluating skill, effort, and responsibility separately. Beginning in the mid-1970s, the province began to explore the possibility of improving the ESA's equal-pay provisions, including incorporating the concept of "equal value" into the ESA.

In January 1984, the NDP held public hearings on the issue of equal pay that garnered wide participation from women's organizations, organized labour, and many community groups, all of which pushed for the incorporation of the concept of "equal value" into the equal-pay provision.[26] The province, however, remained opposed to this measure.[27] Instead, the government recommended a composite test that only "slightly broadened" the existing legislation and did not include the concept of equal pay for work of equal value.[28] This approach was designed to use a composite measure of skills, effort, responsibility, and working conditions in jobs that were substantially the same in order to assess the need for equal pay.[29] Thus, when the composite approach was incorporated into the ESA, it rendered the equal-pay provisions applicable only to work that was substantially the same. The equal-value concept emerged in future legislative developments through the Pay Equity Act (Armstrong et al. 2003; Fudge 1996).[30]

The Hours of Work Task Force

The recession of the early 1980s drew growing attention to hours of work standards. At the time, there were growing concerns, raised largely by the Ontario labour movement, over the simultaneous existence of substantial amounts of overtime work and high levels of unemployment in the Ontario labour market.[31] While there was no broad-based consensus within the labour movement regarding a desire to restrict overtime in order to further job creation, there was pressure from some unions.[32] As well, the high levels of unemployment experienced in the early 1980s contributed to growing anxiety amongst the general public over joblessness.

In 1986, the Minister of Labour William Wrye struck the Task Force on Hours of Work and Overtime to examine the job creation potential of restrictions on hours of work and overtime. Following a period of public consultations and an analysis of written submissions and commissioned reports, the task force issued a report in 1987 entitled *Working Times* (Ontario 1987a). The report contained twenty-two recommendations that the task force claimed attempted to "strike a balance" between "emerging community standards, the job-creation effects of provincial legislation, and the need for the Ontario economy to remain competitive in the future."[33] The recommendations regarding hours of work and overtime included reducing the overtime hours requirement from 44 hours to 40; introducing an overtime block of 250 hours of overtime per employee; making all overtime in excess of 40 hours voluntary; limiting daily work hours to 12; making overtime work in excess of 12 hours per day voluntary; allowing special permits to exceed the 250 hours overtime block, to be issued in some situations; making the issuance of overtime permits subject to an appeals procedure; and allowing for time off in lieu of overtime pay.

The task force also made recommendations regarding the leave provisions in the ESA, including introducing an entitlement to unpaid leave and increasing the paid vacation time to three weeks after five years of service. Finally, the task force made a number of recommendations regarding the need for the Ministry of Labour to include hours of work considerations when designing health and safety regulations, to raise the public profile of hours of work and overtime issues, and to undertake regular reviews of the hours-of-work standards.

In defining the principles that shaped its mandate, the task force stated that it desired "to maintain a relatively flexible employment standards system" (Ontario 1987a, 4). For example, the 250-hour block of allowable overtime was designed so as to permit greater flexibility in the scheduling of overtime. Other recommendations meant to ensure flexibility included a phase-in period for the 250-hour block, accommodations for the scheduling of compressed work weeks, hours-averaging provisions, additional overtime permits beyond the 250-hour block, and the allowance of time off in lieu of overtime (Ontario 1987b).

The task force did not recommend reducing working time in order to address the problem of unemployment, however. Rather, it asserted that while some job creation did exist, it was not likely to be significant.[34] The report concluded its examination of this issue by stating that "it appears that there may be some job-creation potential in policies to reduce hours of work and overtime, but that this potential is severely limited, mainly because the cost increase associated with hours-of-work and overtime restrictions also reduces the demand for labour in general" (Ontario 1987a, 99). Yet, despite the attempts of the task force to ensure flexibility for the business community, the report did not instigate legislative reforms in any of these areas.

Overall, while the legacy of the 1970s and 1980s was mixed, the reforms of this period displayed many shortcomings for workers reliant on employment standards. The severance benefits represented a step forward, but the equal-pay amendments were clearly insufficient. And despite the recommendations of two major task forces on the key areas of working time and wage protection, employment standards in these areas remained unchanged.

SOCIAL DEMOCRACY AND THE ESA, 1990–1995

In 1990 the New Democratic Party, under the leadership of Bob Rae, was elected to provincial government. The NDP took office with the pledge to enact significant changes to labour and employment laws in Ontario. The party was elected just as the province was about to enter another major recession, however. This factor, combined with high levels of business opposition to its proposed labour and employment law reforms, as well as the government's own adoption of the principles of deficit reduction as a means to resolve recessionary economic problems, dampened its reform project (Panitch and Schwartz 2003).

Notable reforms to labour and employment legislation were contained in the NDP's Amendments to the Ontario Labour Relations Act in 1993 (Bill 40). The reforms included allowing for the "combining" of bargaining units of an employer and the same trade union; including full- and part-time units and clerical production units in the same or geographically separate workplace; imposing

Table 2
Minimum Wage Increases, Ontario, 1985–95 ($)

Year	General Rate
1985	4.00
1986	4.35
1987	4.55
1988	4.75
1989	5.00
1990	5.40
1991	6.00
1992	6.35
1993	NI
1994	6.70
1995	6.85

Source: AO RG 7-186. News releases, various years.

strict time limits for arbitration decisions; introducing trade union "successor rights" in the event of the sale of a business; putting some restrictions on the use of replacement workers; and instituting expedited hearings for complaints during organizing activities (Schenk 1995; Watson 1997). Bill 40 also included amendments that extended the right to unionize to previously excluded groups, including agricultural workers and domestic workers, thereby opening the possibility of unionization to workers who had previously had to rely only on the ESA for workplace regulation.

The NDP also made a commitment to raise the general minimum wage to a rate equivalent to 60 percent of the average wage by 1995.[35] The previous Liberal government had implemented a series of annual increases between 1986 and 1990 that raised the minimum wage by 8 percent over the increases in the consumer price index during the same period.[36] When the NDP took power, the minimum wage was 48 percent of the 1989 average wage. A series of regular increases that began in November 1991 increased the minimum wage by more than 25 percent over 1990 levels. Following the 1994 wage increase (which was announced in 1993), the minimum wage reached 52 percent of the average wage;[37] however, the goal of 60 percent of the general minimum wage not reached. Table 2 shows annual minimum wage rates from 1985 to 1995.

The most significant amendment made by the NDP to employment standards was in the area of wage protection.[38] In October 1990, Premier Rae announced the government's intention to establish a fund to ensure employees received unpaid wages in the event of business bankruptcy or insolvency.[39] The government would be responsible for recovering the monies owed by employers after the fact.[40] Legislation for the Employee Wage Protection Program was introduced in the spring of 1991 and given Royal Assent in the fall of that year.[41] The purpose of the program was threefold: first, to provide employees with compensation for unpaid wages, commissions, overtime wages, vacation pay, holiday pay, termination and severance pay and pay in lieu of notice, up to a maximum of five thousand dollars per employee; second, to provide for "enhanced enforcement of officers' and directors' liability for wages and other payments through the ESA"; and third, to provide for an expedited appeals process for employers and a new system for adjudicating employee appeals (Ontario 1991). The program, which was funded out of general provincial revenues, was administered through the Employment Standards Branch of the Minister of Labour, and Employment Standards officers were given the ability to order payments under the program. Upon payment of a claim, the government would attempt to recover funds from employers and businesses.

By introducing a wage protection program, the NDP acted on an issue that had been identified as a significant inadequacy for at least fifteen years. Overall, however, the NDP's reforms did not significantly alter the long-standing regulatory approach to established employment standards as a "secondary" form of labour market protection (as compared to workplace standards established through collective bargaining) for non-unionized workers. The minimum wage goals were not reached, and working-time reforms were not broached. Organizations that represented domestic workers claimed that rights to unionization would not be effective without further changes to the Labour Relations Act that would facilitate broader-based forms of collective bargaining.[42]

Overall, in the context of shifts towards greater labour market flexibility and insecurity, in particular shifts created through growth in nonstandard and precarious employment, Ontario provincial governments of the 1970s, 1980s, and early 1990s did not seek to alter the secondary status of employment standards. This meant that as larger numbers of workers were drawn into flexible forms of employment, the regulatory regime governing these employment relations was unable to counteract heightened tendencies of segmentation and insecurity.

MINIMUM STANDARDS WITH MANY EXCEPTIONS

The inability of employment standards to address tendencies towards segmentation and insecurity highlighted a key tension identified in chapter 2: that between the commitment to accomplish socially desirable goals (protecting workers with little bargaining power) and the need to do so within the context of the "economically practicable." As argued in chapter 2, this tension stemmed from a long-standing tradition within minimum standards legislation. The official discourse of social protectionism remained constant through the period of labour market transition discussed in this chapter, as the state regularly expressed its intention to "ensure that workers benefit from minimum acceptable conditions of employment and to actively promote the adoption of socially desirable terms and conditions of employment."[43] John R. Scott, director of the Employment Standards Branch during the 1970s, described the employment standards policy of the Ministry of Labour as being "to extend the minimum benefits of the legislation to the greatest possible number of employees in Ontario."[44]

Yet, along with this commitment to establish minimum standards for workers without collective agreements, the state also maintained an ideological commitment to respect the business prerogatives of the province's employers. As illustrated in chapter 2, when determining the nature and extent of policy coverage, the state often accorded social goals a secondary status to the "economically practicable." This was accomplished in part through the construction of employment standards as secondary rather than as "leading-edge" standards. This was also accomplished through administrative practices related to coverage and enforcement.

The system of exemptions underlines this contradictory approach to the regulation of employment standards. In order to develop a regulatory system that provided basic standards *and* recognized the needs of employers, it was deemed necessary to construct specific regulations to meet the needs of specific industries, thereby reducing the scope of legislated standards. While governments claimed that the ESA was intended to provide protection against exploitation for as many workers as possible, it was simultaneously stated that "universal application of all the basic standards is not seen as possible" as "variations in terms of employment, types of work, and characteristics of certain industries will always require some exceptions."[45] In other words, exemptions were developed to ensure that the legislation would maintain flexibility in application (Kinley 1987).

Aside from practical concerns regarding the need to account for a lack of uniformity in business practices in the province, there was a reluctance to regulate employment standards in a manner that would impinge upon negotiations between employers and employees. As stated in a report of the Hours of Work Task Force in the mid-1980s, "whatever the motive for legislating the limits in the first place, the government does not, in fact, wish to disrupt private contractual arrangements with respect to hours of work and overtime" (Dewees 1987, 7). The practice of exemptions provided a mechanism through which private contractual relationships could remain free from government interference. While the specifics of these provisions changed over time, the principle of maintaining flexibility through exemptions remained a constant.[46]

As the reasons for exemptions for specific categories of workers vary from group to group, it is instructive to examine a sample of these exemptions in some detail. In what follows, the coverage of three specific categories of workers is assessed: domestic workers, homeworkers in the garment industry, and seasonal agricultural workers. Because of the nature of the work they perform, these categories of workers have been identified as requiring special consideration within ESA regulations. What this has meant in terms of ESA policy and practice is that these workers have been subject to unequal coverage under the ESA in comparison to the workforce as a whole. As will be illustrated through these specific cases, the construction of "special consideration" is a highly gendered and racialized process.

When the ESA was enacted, live-in domestic workers who were employed by a householder were exempted from the act. They were extended coverage under the collection of provisions for wages, equal pay for equal work, equal benefits, pregnancy leave, and notice of termination in the mid-1970s but remained exempt from most of the key standards regulated by the act, including the minimum wage, hours of work, overtime pay, public holidays, and vacation pay. Various reasons have been presented by the Ministry of Labour to explain these exemptions, including the need to recognize the special relationship that arises because the workers are employed in the employer's home; the need to avoid increasing the cost of domestic labour (through the minimum wage); and the perceived difficulty in measuring and enforcing hours of work and overtime owing to the "lack of a sharp distinction between personal time and working hours."[47] In part, these rationales for the exemptions stem from an assumption that "state intervention in the private sphere is inappropriate" (Macklin 1994, 14).

There is a clearly gendered element to this determination. The labour performed by domestic workers has been undervalued because it has been characterized as work that is "naturally" women's work and because it is generally hidden from public view. This under-valuation has influenced the formulation of employment standards exemptions, as it has contributed to the construction of domestic labour as not constituting real work. As stated in a report from the labour ministry's Women's Bureau, "[t]hese attitudes toward domestic work have, in turn, led to an exclusion of such workers when labour legislation has been passed in almost all jurisdictions."[48] Further, these gendered determinations are also subject to processes of racialization, with most live-in domestic workers entering this form of employment as temporary workers from either the Caribbean or the Philippines. Specifically, a "natural" affinity for domestic labour has been attributed to women of these national origins (Brand 1999; Macklin 1994). Exemptions from legislated standards were constructed (whether explicitly or implicitly) in relation to these gendered and racialized ideological constructions.

Because of the conditions of extreme vulnerability created by this lack of regulation, community groups representing immigrant women working in domestic employment lobbied to expand the ESA coverage. Effective 1 January 1981, domestic workers were extended coverage under the minimum wage, weekly rest period, and vacation pay and public holidays provisions of the act.[49] However, they remained exempt from maximum hours of work and overtime pay provisions. This exemption was justified by the claim that "hours actually worked are difficult to determine, particularly in the case of live-ins." These regulations applied only to full-time, live-in domestics. Those who worked twenty-four hours or less for one employer or who were employed as companions (for the elderly or ill) or as babysitters were not covered. As well, the quality of the rooming conditions of the live-in workers continued to be unregulated. The weekly rest period provisions were amended in 1984 to increase time off per week to forty-eight hours, and minimum wage increases were announced to increase wages to four dollars by March 1985.[50]

Feeling continued pressure from community groups who were lobbying to expand the ESA coverage and facing concerns that the exemptions could be deemed to be in contravention of the recently enacted Charter of Rights and Freedoms,[51] the Ontario government introduced significant changes to the coverage of domestics in 1987. All full-time domestics and nannies were extended coverage under the overtime pay provisions (after forty-four hours per week). In addition, the option of weekly and monthly wage minimums was eliminated, and the provincial hourly minimum was set as the minimum rate for domestics. Despite the claim that "domestic workers have as much right as anyone else to free time, to adequate wages, and to extra compensation for extra effort," domestic workers remained exempt from the maximum hours of work provisions. Application of that protection was not considered "practical when applied to live-in domestics," and it was felt that "any attempt to enforce maximum hours could lead to tensions in some domestic and child-care situations."[52]

Homeworkers, the second group of workers in question, are defined as employees who work in their own home, most frequently in the garment industry. As in the case of domestic workers, these workers were/are most often women who are recent immigrants (Gabriel 1999; Yanz et al. 1999). As with domestic workers, the determination of exemptions for homeworkers from the legislated standards cannot be separated from the invisibility of the work (it is/was done in private homes) and its highly gendered and racialized character.

In addition to working out of their own homes, homeworkers are generally paid on a piecework basis. When the ESA was enacted, homeworkers were covered by the minimum wage, vacation pay, and wage collection provisions and excluded from the maximum hours of work, overtime pay, and statutory holidays provisions.[53] Widespread allegations of employer exploitation of homeworkers in the garment industry,[54] combined with pressure from unions, pushed the state to improve the protections for homeworkers under the ESA (INTERCEDE 1993). In 1993, the New Democratic provincial government announced a package of reforms to the ESA home-worker regulations that included coverage for homeworkers in the areas of hours of work, overtime, and holiday pay; a 10 percent premium to the minimum wage to cover overhead costs (heating, electricity, purchase of machinery); an employer requirement to provide a written summary of their conditions of employment; and an employer fee to obtain homework permits in order to finance the costs of additional enforcement.[55] As will be discussed below, however, expanded coverage did not guarantee protection of basic standards, particularly for workers who work in such individualized and isolated conditions.

Seasonal agricultural workers are a third group whose special circumstances of employment have produced another example of racialized substandard employment rights through the ESA. The prevalence of labour shortages in Canadian agriculture has historically placed pressure on the Canadian state to ensure an adequate supply of seasonal agricultural labour. Through much of the twentieth century, the problem persisted, owing to the tendency of agricultural workers to leave agricultural production in favour of industries that offered more permanent employment. As one solution, the state sought to make use of racialized immigrant and migrant labour (Basok 2002; Preibisch and Binford 2007; Sharma 2006). It did so with the Seasonal Agricultural Workers Program (SAWP) and the incorporation of workers from Mexico and the Caribbean as *unfree* migrant labour, that is, as workers who are "granted the right of only temporary entry to the country, who [are] not defined as potential future citizens and members of the imagined community, and who [face] political/legal restrictions over their ability to circulate in the Canadian labour market" (Satzewich 1991, 107).

Before World War II, the Canadian government undertook many initiatives to address labour shortages in Canadian agriculture, including "the placement of workers looking for jobs on farms through the federally coordinated provincial employment offices; the establishment and operation of agricultural schools and colleges; land settlement programs; the development of organized transfers of harvest labour to the Prairie Provinces; and the aiding in the placement of some immigrants in agriculture" (Haythorne 1960, 23). During the war years, the agricultural industry began to experience severe labour shortages. To resolve them, a more formalized government approach was required.

In 1942, the federal government instituted regulations restricting farmers and farm labourers to agricultural work. A year later, it postponed military service for agricultural labourers and offered to transport them free of charge to areas experiencing labour short- ages. As well, Canada and the United States signed a joint agreement to allow freedom of movement of farm labourers and grain harvest- ing machines across the border (Mysyk 1994). In 1943, the Federal- Provincial Farm Labour Program was developed. Coordinated by the National Selective Service, it was a joint program between the federal Department of Labour and the provincial departments of agriculture. The aim of the program was to mobilize local supplies of labour, organize transfers of workers to areas of labour shortage on a provincial, national, and international basis, encourage a more efficient use of farm manpower, and improve the living and working conditions of farm workers (Haythorne 1960). Under the program, Japanese Canadians (relocated as a result of the war), Aboriginal peoples, and prisoners of war were all incorporated into agricultural production in order to address labour shortages.

Following the war, the use of foreign labour became a primary means to compensate for shortages of domestic labour. Between 1946 and 1966, 89,680 immigrants, primarily from European coun- tries, many of whom were leaving Europe as a result of the war, entered Canada destined for seasonal agricultural production in Ontario (Satzewich 1991). Three of the major groups were Polish war veterans, displaced persons (as a result of the war), and Dutch farmers. Polish war veterans and displaced persons were both recruited by the Canadian state to fill employment vacancies in Ontario agriculture. Both groups were incorporated as unfree immi- grant labour having rights of permanent settlement but facing restrictions on their labour market mobility. While both "were con- sidered to be suitable as permanent settlers by most Canadian officials who dealt with immigration" and were thereby granted immigrant status, neither was granted the right to circulate freely in the Canadian employment market (Satzewich 1991, 330). Their entry and residency in Canada was contingent upon signing a con- tract that placed them under strict employment regulations concern- ing labour mobility.[56] While under contract, members of both groups were subject to deportation if they either quit or changed employment without permission from the Department of Labour.

Like the Polish war veterans and displaced persons, Dutch farmers were considered to be acceptable future citizens of Canada and were granted immigrant status, giving them permanent settlement rights

(Satzewich 1990). However, unlike the above two groups, Dutch farmers were not subject to restrictions in their ability to circulate in the Canadian labour market and thus were incorporated as free immigrant labour. Canadian officials preferred that they work for at least one season as agricultural labourers. However, they were not legally required to do so and were free to seek any form of employment they wished. Between 1947 and 1955, approximately 16,000 Dutch farmers and their families entered Canada, with the majority settling in Ontario.

Since members of all three groups incorporated as immigrant labour, all were accorded the right to apply for Canadian citizenship, which would grant them all the associated political rights and responsibilities, including the right to permanent residency. Dutch farmers were accorded immigrant status because they were identified by Canadian state officials as "desirable white settlers," who, because of their cultural and ethnic origin, were not only a source of farm labour but were also considered to be potential citizens of Canada (Satzewich 1990). Polish war veterans and displaced persons (generally of Eastern European origin) were also considered to be potential future citizens of Canada, although not before a process of "re-socialization."

While all three immigrant groups provided temporary relief to the employment shortages faced by agricultural growers, none of the three were potential permanent sources of seasonal agricultural labour, primarily because, once established, all three tended to seek forms of employment that would provide greater security and monetary benefits. Because all three groups were able to apply for citizenship, had the right to permanent residency, and were not permanently restricted to agricultural labour, there was no means to ensure that they would not seek other forms of employment. Agricultural employment was therefore most often viewed as a "stepping stone" to employment in other industries or to the establishment of one's own farm (Haythorne 1960, 56).

Despite attempts at improving the general living and working conditions of agricultural production, it was not possible to compete with the income or security offered by industrial or manufacturing employment. This meant that agricultural growers continued to be faced with uncertainty about whether or not there would be adequate labour to complete a harvest in any given year. The solution to this problem came in the form of the federal Seasonal Agricultural

Workers Program (SAWP), mentioned above, which facilitates the entry of foreign workers for temporary employment in the agricultural industry (Canada HRD 1996). In 1966, following intense lobbying pressure from growers, the federal government established an agreement with the Commonwealth Caribbean to import farm labourers on a seasonal basis. In its initial year, the program brought 264 Jamaican workers into Canada. In 1967, Trinidad-Tobago and Barbados became participants in the program as well. It expanded rapidly in ensuing years, and within a decade it was incorporating approximately 5,000 workers. In 1974, Mexico negotiated a similar agreement with the Canadian government that allowed Mexican workers into Canada on a temporary basis. In 1976, the program expanded again to facilitate entry of workers from Grenada, Antigua, Dominica, St Christopher-Nevis-Anguilla, St Lucia, St Vincent, and Monserrat. The program now brings in over 18,000 workers annually (Gibb 2006).

The workers' period of employment in Canada ranges from six to forty weeks, with a minimum of forty hours of work per week, though this can exceed sixty hours per week. Under the employment agreements that govern the program, farm labourers are paid an hourly wage just over Canadian minimum wage levels and are provided with health care coverage throughout their period of employment. Employers are responsible for covering transportation costs for their employees to and from their home country and for providing accommodations (Cecil and Ebanks 1992; Verma 2003). Essentially, the program facilitates the incorporation of workers as *unfree* migrant labour. Under the SAWP, workers are not permitted to seek employment outside their specified contract or to apply for permanent residence within Canada. Through these restrictions, the state is able to continually secure a seasonal labour force that is static in terms of upward mobility. Further, it secures a labour force that accepts the physically demanding and low-paying work and that is subject to labour standards exemptions and abuses without effective mechanisms of appeal (Sharma 2001; Suen 2000).[57]

Under the ESA, two primary categories of employees relate to the workers in the SAWP: farm workers and harvesters (Ontario 2007, 2). A farm worker is "a person employed on a farm whose work is directly related to the primary production of certain agricultural products," work that could include planting, cultivating, pruning, and caring for livestock. A harvester is someone who is employed to harvest crops of fruit, vegetables, or tobacco for marketing or storage. For both cases, there are exemptions from key standards in the ESA (Commission for Labor Cooperation 2002; Verma 2003).

Farm workers are exempt from the standards regulating hours of work, daily and weekly rest periods, eating periods, overtime pay, minimum wages, public holidays, and vacation pay. Harvesters are covered by minimum wage provisions and provisions for public holidays and vacation pay (if employed for thirteen weeks).[58] But like farm workers, harvesters are exempt from standards for hours of work, daily and weekly rest periods, eating periods, and overtime pay. These exemptions are justified with the argument that the application of the minimum standards would jeopardize the completion of the seasonal harvests. When viewed in relation to the processes of racialization previously discussed, the exemption of farm workers and harvesters from key standards of the ESA can be seen as yet another example of the ways in which labour flexibility through a lack of coverage by employment standards is connected to the racialization of labour-intensive, low-wage, low-status work.

Special Permits

Another form of flexibility that was integrated into ESA coverage lay in the system of extra-hours permits. The permit system was designed to regulate weekly hours of work, while at the same time enabling employers to meet the scheduling needs of their business operation. In effect, the system allowed a government to regulate the extent to which employers could exceed the weekly maximum hours of work protections. The rationale for the incorporation of the permit system into the ESA typifies the balancing act guiding the broader regulation of employment standards. While the need to provide minimum protections was articulated, in this case in the area of hours of work, so too was the need to avoid the imposition of hardship on employers. Thus, "[t]he objective of the approval and permit systems is to allow some flexibility with respect to maximum hours, thereby accounting for variations in types of work, characteristics of industries, economic and labour market conditions."[59] While the state expressed the desire to both regulate hours and provide employer flexibility, the potential for conflict between these two goals was recognized, as "in fulfilling the goals of flexibility, there is a danger of neglecting the goals of avoiding possible adverse effects of very long hours on workers."[60] Nevertheless, the permit system remained a central feature of employment standards legislation from the time of the enactment of the ESA through to the late 1990s.

The permit system was divided into four categories: "longer-days" permits that allowed employers to schedule regular work days longer than eight hours (but no more than twelve hours) (the gold category); excess-hours permits that entitled employers to schedule additional hours of overtime (up to one hundred hours) per employee per year (blue); extended excess-hours permits that allowed for hours in addition to those provided by the hundred-hour permits in special circumstances (green); and industry permits that applied to industries that were deemed to require hours flexibility beyond that provided by the standard legislation and the hundred-hour permits, for example service and construction-related industries (Ontario 1987a; 1998a). In all cases, a permit that allowed the scheduling of extra hours did not remove the employees' right to refuse hours of work beyond the regular daily and weekly maximums.

While most directly relevant to non-unionized workplaces, the permit system was frequently utilized by unionized employers. In the mid-1970s, 44 percent of all special permits were issued to the automotive, farm equipment, and electrical industries, which had high levels of unionization.[61] As well, the green permits were concentrated in large, unionized manufacturing establishments, particularly those in the transportation (automotive) equipment sector (Ontario 1987a). The use of the permit system in both unionized and non-unionized industries indicates that, while the ESA was generally considered to constitute a regulatory system for unorganized workers, the impact of the standards contained within the ESA was felt (directly or indirectly) across the Ontario labour market. Table 3 provides data on the number of permits issued each year from 1980–81 to 1994–95.

As indicated by permits data, the permits system increased the number of workers excluded from daily and weekly hours maximums established by the ESA, thereby providing another form of flexibility within the regulation of minimum standards that was highly favorable to employers. The impact of employer access to additional 100-hours permits was identified in a Ministry of Labour background report on the permits system, which stated that "the ease with which this permit can be obtained means that no direct control of weekly

Table 3
Extra Hours Permits, by Year, 1980–81 to 1994–95

Year	100 Hour (Blue)	Special (Green)	Total	Maximum Excess Hours Approved (Special Permits)
1980–81	229	263	492	NA
1981–82	211	293	504	357,960
1982–83	180	163	343	239,305
1983–84	294	274	568	875,950
1984–85	374	309	683	1,205,545
1985–86	435	161	596	956,280
1986–87	471	167	638	723,070
1987–88	373	197	570	878,717
1988–89	405	328	733	936,715
1989–90	303	347	650	2,007,650
1990–91	332	270	602	1,960,370
1991–92	380	197	577	1,706,800
1992–93	261	175	436	493,035
1993–94	317	137	454	1,953,525
1994–95	260	182	442	3,879,958

Source: Ontario Ministry of Labour, Employment Standards/Practices Branch, Fiscal Year Reports, 1981–82 to 1994–95.

hours is exercised up to the point where the 100 excess hours is exhausted."[62] Because the permits themselves were easily obtained, the Task Force on Hours of Work and Overtime raised concerns that the larger objectives of the ESA "may be traded off against the desires of any employer" (Dewees 1987, 15).

Overall, the system of exemptions and special permits constitutes a central means by which the state explicitly built employer-oriented flexibility into the administration of employment standards. Exemptions and special permits facilitated the avoidance of basic standards through various justifications that were constructed around the special nature of specific occupations, businesses, and industries. The effect of these special circumstances was to explicitly reduce the minimum-standards protections accorded to the specified categories of workers and to reduce the numbers and categories of workers covered by the employment standards legislation. Further, as indicated through the examples of domestic workers, homeworkers in the garment industry, and seasonal agricultural workers, the representation of special circumstances was constructed through gendered and racialized divisions of labour.

These various exceptions indicate that while employment standards legislation constructed a secondary set of standards for workers with little bargaining power generally, this secondary regulatory regime was itself further segmented, as it provided differential levels of standards amongst the workers who relied on the ESA. Overall, the policies of the ESA generally and the differential application of those policies produced a system of regulation that left specific groups of workers with little or no statutory protection from the social forces of the labour market.

Enforcement and Compliance

In addition to the legitimate ways to avoid minimum standards, a frequent lack of compliance with legislated standards has been cited as a key factor in creating conditions of labour market vulnerability (de Wolff 2000; Saunders 2003). The overall rate of compliance with minimum wage provisions in the late 1970s was estimated at 55 percent (Adams 1978). In the mid-1980s, the Ministry of Labour estimated that 35 percent of Ontario employers violated the provisions of the ESA.[63] Violations of the hours of work provisions were noted to be particularly prevalent, with estimates that for every extra hour allowed by a special permit, there were twenty-four extra hours worked (Dewees 1987). According to the Task Force on Hours of Work and Overtime, these findings suggest "the possibility of substantial non-compliance" with the ESA (Ontario 1987a, 50). Through the 1990s, the most common violations of the ESA were in the areas of vacation pay, unpaid wages, termination pay, and overtime, in that order.[64]

In 1996, a community-labour coalition known as the Employment Standards Work Group (ESWG) documented numerous ESA violations, based on case files from community legal clinics and reports to a "bad boss" telephone hotline set up by the ESWG and the Ontario Federation of Labour (ESWG 1996). Violations were reported across a wide range of occupations and industries, including garment production, construction, transportation, communication, retail, business services, personal services, and food and beverage services. They included unpaid wages and vacation pay, late and irregular pay, wages less than the minimum wage, unpaid overtime, denials for severance pay, layoffs without notice, illegitimate deductions from pay, hours of work in excess of the maximum allowable hours, work without scheduled breaks, employer intimidation, including sexual harassment and assault, and refusals for sick days and statutory holidays.

Workers also reported being required to work without pay during training periods, being held financially responsible for stolen inventory, being required to pay for work-related expenses, and being terminated just prior to three months of employment so that the ESA termination/severance provisions could be avoided. While the report was based on self-reported violations, rather than on a comprehensive study of Ontario's workplaces, the commonalities between the conditions reported by workers indicated the systemic nature of employment standards violations. This led the ESWG (1996, 1) to conclude that "[t]he cases are too widespread to be discounted as a few employers who are 'bad apples.'"[65]

Community legal workers who assist non-unionized employees in filing employment standards complaints further confirm these findings, indicating that employment standards violations continue to be prevalent, particularly in areas of low-wage employment: "We've had employers with huge, serious violations of the *Employment Standards Act*. They just basically got away with 'don't do that again.' In one particular case, I represented two workers ... the employer was cleaning the courthouses. In the cases of my clients, he didn't pay one of them for three weeks. The man was working 12 to 14 hours a day, six days a week. My other client worked for a month and a half, two months. One day she worked 18 hours straight. The employer kept no records. So the [Employment Practices] Branch said, 'well there are no records, so what can we do.'"[66]

Another tendency documented in the reports to the Bad Boss Hotline was the relationship between ESA violations and relations of race, gender, and immigration status. Many workers reliant on the ESA are women workers and members of racialized groups, including recent immigrants.[67] In commenting on this tendency, the ESWG (1996, 1) noted that "[w]omen, men and women who are immigrant workers, and visible minority workers face the greatest exploitation." Immigration status is particularly significant, as indicated by a lawyer from the Metro Chinese South-East Asian Legal Clinic, who stated that "in Toronto we understand that some employers pay according to your immigration status ... If you're a landed immigrant you get, say $4 an hour; if you're a refugee claimant with employment authorization, you get $3 an hour; if you don't have any status at all, you get $2" (quoted in Gabriel 1999,149).

A study of the working conditions of Chinese restaurant workers in Toronto in the late 1980s had similar findings. The report of the

Chinese Restaurant Workers Advisory Committee found "many instances of possible violations" in the areas of hours of work and minimum wage.[68] Work hours were found to be highly irregular, averaging over fifty hours per week, with no clear indication of whether or not workers were being paid overtime for extra hours. As in many similar cases, the low wages in the industry compelled workers to work longer hours, leaving them without time to undertake ESL or skills training. The report described the situation as a "cycle of vulnerability" where workers "remain locked in a job ghetto; trapped by their long hours, and afraid to rock the boat about their working conditions."[69] These workers failed to complain partly because they lacked information (from the Ministry of Labour) on employment standards in Chinese and therefore had little knowledge of existing standards and complaints procedures.[70]

These same problems were documented for both homeworkers in the garment industry and domestic workers, as both groups of workers are often required to work at substandard conditions.[71] In the early 1990s, wage rates for homeworkers were found to be highly variable, with many earning below the minimum wage, not receiving vacation pay, experiencing hours of work that exceeded the legally regulated maximum, and working overtime hours that were not compensated for at the overtime rate (INTERCEDE 1993). In addition, homeworkers reported having little or no control over either their rate of pay or the scheduling of their work. These conditions persisted throughout the 1990s, with wage rates ranging from $3 per hour to $12–13 per hour and average wages ranging between $6 and $8 per hour (Ng et al. 1999). Other problems reported with regard to payment of wages included employers not disclosing the piece rate until the work had been completed, late payment, payment for less than a negotiated rate, lack of overtime pay, and no vacation pay (Ng et al. 1999; Yanz et al. 1999). On the basis of their interviews with immigrant women working as homeworkers in the garment industry, Ng et al. (1999, 8) concluded that "most, if not all, employers [in this area of work] violate provincial labour standards legislation."

Similarly, in the early 1990s, despite a legal entitlement, only 33 percent of live-in domestic workers who regularly worked overtime hours received compensation at the overtime rate, and 43 percent of those who worked overtime received no compensation at all for their overtime hours (INTERCEDE 1993). The findings of the study led INTERCEDE (1993, 12), an organization that assists domestic workers with employment standards complaints, to assert that "[t]he claims submitted to the Ontario Ministry of Labour would only represent the tip of an iceberg of actual abuses perpetrated against domestic workers." A representative for INTERCEDE explains that these working conditions are created directly in relation to the immigration status of these workers:

> The working conditions of domestic workers who are in the temporary permit program, who have not yet become landed, are qualitatively different from those who have already landed ... Being on a temporary work status to begin with situates them in a "land of no rights." The common working conditions of women who are in the temporary status program, the Live-In Caregiver Program, are most ordinarily exploitative in terms of long working hours. That's the most ordinary, most common situation that they have. They may be paid the minimum wage. But if you count the number of hours that they work, where the employer does not formally recognize that they are working overtime, then ordinarily they are working up to 12 hours a day anyway ... The fact that they are on temporary status really lessens their capacity to enforce legal rights that are already existing.[72]

As these various reports and accounts illustrate, the problem of non-compliance with legislated employment standards faces many workers, particularly those in forms of low-wage employment, including women, members of racialized groups, and recent immigrants.

A common explanation for non-compliance is a lack of knowledge and/or understanding of the legislation. A report produced by the Canadian Federation of Independent Business references the findings of the Ontario Task Force on Hours of Work and Overtime, noting that "few people knew of or understood the workings of the 'blue' and 'green' permits, and the daily maximum hours provision was regularly ignored" (CFIB 2000, 3). The Ministry of Labour (MOL) has acknowledged that lack of employer knowledge of the ESA regulations has contributed to incidences of non-compliance. In the late 1970s, the MOL estimated that only 27 percent of employers were even informed of legislated minimum standards.[73]

But the MOL has also recognized that frequent non-compliance may not simply result from oversights or a lack of knowledge. A ministry brief in the mid-1970s acknowledged two reasons : "[e]ither the employer is not properly informed as to the requirements of an Act, and inadvertently violates an Act, or the violation is deliberate."[74] This recognition that some non-compliance is deliberate was expressed in a ministry discussion paper on employment standards reform issued over two decades later. In it, the MOL connected "widespread non-compliance" with the lack of correspondence between hours of work standards and "the needs of employers to run their businesses in a way that meets market pressures, new manufacturing processes or the intensive requirements of high technology industries" (Ontario 2000b, 8).

Other explanations focus on the enforcement and disputes resolutions practices of the legislation, as these practices have been identified as insufficient to address the problem (Fudge 1991). For example, a background report for the Task Force on Hours of Work and Overtime identified practices of "selective enforcement," which thereby ensured a level of non-compliance resulting from a failure to enforce certain provisions (Dewees 1987, 18).

An examination of employment standards enforcement practices supports this explanation. A program of routine, random workplace inspections provides a proactive method of detecting violations and also removes the onus of filing a complaint from an individual employee.[75] In the early 1980s, the Employment Standards Branch noted the effectiveness of the program and advocated inspections targeted at selected industries, stating that "[s]uch systematic, comprehensive patterns of enforcement have more long-term impact than remedial efforts, on an ad-hoc case-by-case basis."[76] The subsequent temporary program of inspections of selected industries found violation rates above 65 percent.[77] Despite the success of this approach, however, the number of inspections declined dramatically through the 1980s, from 1183 in 1981–82 to 85 in 1988–89, in part owing to inadequate budgets (Adams 1987). In the early 1990s, the branch reported that claim overloads further inhibited its capacity to undertake routine inspections, as they declined further to 21 by 1994–95.[78] As inspections declined, so too did the enforcement capacities of the ministry. Table 4 documents the number of inspections through the 1980s and early 1990s.

The Ministry of Labour's Employment Standards Branch identified insufficient staffing as a factor contributing to reduced inspections.[79] An examination of workload increases in relation to staffing levels

Table 4
Routine Inspections, by Year, 1980–81 to 1994–95

Year	Routine Inspections	Percentage in Violation
1980–81	1,304	NA
1981–82	1,183	NA
1982–83	936	43
1983–84	672	32
1984–85	321	26
1985–86	102	35
1986–87	234	44
1987–88	190	38
1988–89	85	38
1989–90	51	49
1990–91	40	NA
1991–92	24	25
1992–93	26	35
1993–94	31	58
1994–95	21	81

Source: Ontario Ministry of Labour, Employment Standards/Practices Branch, Fiscal Year Reports, 1981–82 to 1994–95.

within the branch between 1974 and 1981 illustrates this problem. During this period, substantial changes to the ESA led to an increased workload for employment standards inspectors. The changes included improvements to standards regarding public holidays (1974) and overtime pay and public holidays (1975), and the extension of the ESA coverage to harvest workers (1975) and domestic workers (1981). In addition, the labour Ontario labour force grew by 15 percent. During this period, the average workload per officer increased by 43 percent, while the branch experienced only an average yearly increase of 2.4 percent in its staffing. The result was an increased backlog of employment standards cases and a reduced capacity to conduct inspections.

While routine inspections constituted a central element of the ESA enforcement practices, the Ministry of Labour also continuously emphasized the need for employer-employee self-reliance in ensuring that the legislated standards were met.[80] Within the context of the ESA regulatory regime, self-reliance means worker self-reporting of violations through an individualized disputes resolution process.

This process begins with an employee either raising a concern with the employer or with the employee contacting the Ministry of Labour to register a complaint. Once a complaint has been filed, the disputes resolution process may go through several stages. First, employees will be encouraged by MOL staff to resolve the issue on their own through direct negotiations with their employer. If this step is not successful at bringing about a resolution of the complaint, the ministry will contact the employer to provide notification that a complaint has been filed and to "suggest that the employer take steps to resolve the situation" (Ontario 2001b). If the complaint remains unresolved, an employment standards officer will be assigned to the case to conduct an investigation, which may occur by telephone or by written correspondence, through a visit to the workplace or through a fact-finding meeting, where both employer and employee are given the opportunity to present information in support of their case. Following an investigation, the officer will decide whether or not the act has been contravened.[81] In the event that either the employer or the employee is unsatisfied with the assessment made by the employment standards officer, either may initiate an appeals procedure. Appeals must be filed within thirty days from the time that an officer's decision has been issued (Ontario 2001b). Employers and employees may appeal either the issue or the amount of compensation involved in the decision.

The employment standards complaints procedure was designed to mediate complaints so that they could be resolved without the issuance of a formal order or the use of a refereed hearing.[82] While employment standards officers can issue an order to compensate an employee for a violation of the act if an employer will not comply voluntarily, the primary emphasis within the disputes resolutions process is on the informal mediation of the dispute between an employer and employee, with the use of an officer only if necessary.

The emphasis on an individualized, privatized disputes resolution process exacerbated the problem of non-compliance by failing to account for the profoundly unequal power relationships that characterize many employer-employee relationships. Both the lack of anonymity in the complaints process and a fear of reprisal may inhibit an employee's likelihood of filing a complaint (Fudge 1991). Community legal workers report that fear of job loss is one of the primary factors making employees reluctant to file an ESA complaint.[83] As one union representative stated, "the reality is a lot of workers are scared to file a complaint."[84]

These claims are confirmed by findings that approximately 90 percent of complaints are filed by employees who no longer work for the employer in question (ESWG 1996; Kinley 1987). Without the ongoing protection of union representation, if they complain while they are still employed, employees are likely to face the prospect of dismissal.[85] This calls into question the ability of a process based on self-reliance to improve an ongoing employment relationship, and it highlights the ways in which it differs significantly from a grievance procedure under a collective agreement, which is designed to address a violation of the agreement in a manner that protects the aggrieved employee against job loss and attempts to ensure the ongoing stability of the employment relationship.

These tendencies are exacerbated by power imbalances in the workplace created through relations of race, class, gender, and immigration status, particularly in workplaces that employ visible minories or recent immigrants, as these workers face additional power imbalances in their workplaces resulting from language barriers, immigration status, and economic insecurity. Reports of employment standards violations experienced by Chinese workers in the 1980s led the Chinese National Council to send a letter to the Ontario Minister of Labour providing examples of factors that inhibited Chinese workers from filing ESA complaints:

> There are a number of reasons for not making complaints. Some workers are afraid that if they lodge complaints they might be singled out as trouble-makers. Others have little knowledge of the procedure of complaining, considering it as very troublesome, time consuming, and they don't know where and how to lodge the complaints. After all, language is considered a major factor, since most of the workers have difficulties to express in English and they believe that chances of getting an interpreter or meeting a Chinese speaking officer is very low … Regarding information on employment standards, there is no publication in Chinese and workers could not make telephone enquiries in Chinese. Information from the Ministry of Labour is totally cut off for those who do not know English or French.[86]

A community legal worker who deals largely with immigrant workers in downtown Toronto provides another illustration:

> All of the workers I represent are workers in service operations, cleaners, some factory workers, people who work in restaurants,

people who work in banquet halls. A large majority, about
80 percent of the ones that I work with, do not have permanent
status in Canada. These are people who are extremely vulnerable. They need that work. Even if they have made a refugee
claim and the refugee claim fails, they are not able to meet the
test to become a refugee, then many of them will take a human-
itarian/compassionate application. In order to succeed, you
have to prove establishment in Canada. A permanent job, and
having a letter of reference from your boss, is crucial. Even
those who are recent immigrants to Canada often have come
here on their own and their families are still abroad. So they
need a job, proof of stable employment, money to pay for the
tickets and the application. Immigration applications end up
costing about $1500 per person, adults … Major bucks.
So that's why people are really attached to their jobs, because
of that, and the economy.[87]

Overall, the individualized disputes resolution process privatizes the
regulation of employment standards and makes workers highly
susceptible to the many power imbalances in the workplace.

For those who do initiate the process, and even where violations
of the ESA are detected and penalties assessed, the regulatory system
does not guarantee that employees will receive the compensation
they are owed. Once initiated, the process itself can often be very
lengthy, involving significant delays in securing financial compensation for a violation. Throughout the 1980s, an average of approximately 14 percent of cases remained unresolved at year's end.[88] At
the end of the 1980s, the average settlement time for an employment standards complaint was six months.[89] In a letter to the minister of labour in 1988, a community legal worker complained that
"it takes approximately eight to ten weeks for the Ministry to complete a routine investigation, and several months or more if the
complaint is a difficult one."[90]

In addition, further difficulties may be experienced during the
collections process. Between 1981 and 1985, an average of 15 percent of employees did not receive the compensation they were owed.
Adams (1987) estimated that the collection rate for those working
under the minimum wage between 1981 and 1985 was less than
2 percent. Further, in the mid-1980s, only 37 percent of the actual
value of monetary awards assessed was collected (Ontario 1987). By

the mid-to-late 1990s, this figure increased only slightly to 38.5 percent.[91] During this time, employer insolvency was identified as a significant barrier to employees receiving payments (Fudge 1991b). By the early 1990s, informal insolvencies (cases where an employer closes or abandons an unprofitable business) and refusals to pay constituted 75 percent of employment standards wage claims.[92] The length of the process, combined with the clear possibility that a settlement, even if awarded, may never be received, constitutes another disincentive for employees to file complaints.

Overall, as this examination of administrative and enforcement practices demonstrates, the regulation of employment standards has been shaped by more than simply the process of policy development. Despite the emphasis on the need to establish minimum levels of protection for workers with little bargaining power, the administration of employment standards legislation has ensured that the standards could be evaded in several ways, both explicitly, through exemptions and special permits, and implicitly, through ineffective enforcement and disputes resolution processes. For those covered, these processes provided no guarantee that the legislated standards would be met. Like the policies themselves, the regulatory practices had highly gendered and racialized implications.

CONCLUSION

As the social organization of the labour market underwent a transformation driven by recessions, unemployment, and job growth in flexible forms of employment, processes that combined to promote increasing levels of polarization and insecurity, reforms to the regulatory framework that had been constructed to buffer the vulnerability of non-unionized workers were insufficient to counteract these tendencies. During the 1970s, 1980s, and 1990s, existing employment standards were amended and new standards were added, in particular in areas of equal pay for equal work, severance pay, and wage protection. As the labour market situation deteriorated, however, these reforms did not substantially alter the secondary status of employment standards. Thus, as larger numbers of workers were drawn into nonstandard and precarious forms of employment, the regulatory regime governing employment relations was not capable of counteracting growing labour market insecurity. Further, labour flexibility was also tied to regulatory practices that facilitated the avoidance of legislated standards. Overall, despite the official emphasis on the need to establish minimum levels of protection for workers with little bargaining power, the regulation of employment standards in the 1970s, 1980s, and 1990s did more to promote, rather than to counter, the emerging conditions of labour flexibility.

4

Back to the Sixty-Hour Work Week:
Flexible Employment Standards
for the "New Economy"

The workplaces and workers of Ontario are flexible, modern and adaptable. Employment standards legislation should be equally so.

Government of Ontario, *Time for Change*

When examining the government's proposed amendments it is important to evaluate who will benefit from the changes that the government proposes and who will lose.

Employment Standards Work Group, *Bad Boss Stories*

In 1999, the Ontario Progressive Conservative government, under the leadership of Premier Mike Harris, announced its intentions to dramatically reform – to "modernize" – the province's employment standards legislation. The government had been elected to its first mandate four years earlier on a platform that included promises to substantially re-write Ontario's labour and employment laws in order to make the province "open for business." In its platform, titled the Common Sense Revolution, it pledged to remove barriers to economic growth created by "ideologically-driven legislation and over-regulation" (PCPO 1995, 14). In an increasingly competitive global economy, businesses needed greater flexibility to respond to competitive pressures. To balance the competing demands of work and family, employees also needed greater flexibility and the ability to capitalize on "alternative" (i.e., nonstandard) scheduling arrangements. A comprehensive reform of employment standards, one that promoted both "fairness and flexibility," was the stated goal.

Shifts towards "labour flexibility" took place in the context of labour market change outlined in chapter 3 and involved both changing employment norms through the growth in nonstandard forms of employment, as well as movement away from welfare state models of labour market regulation and towards neoliberal approaches. In Ontario, neoliberalism was "brought down to earth" with the election of the Harris Conservative government in 1995 and its wide-ranging project of social and economic policy reform.[1] This chapter focuses on the reforms to employment standards legislation undertaken by this government (the most substantial reforms to the Employment Standards Act since its inception) and shows how "labour flexibility" and competitiveness were integrated into a process of labour market re-regulation that contributed directly to the normalization of a situation of heightened labour market vulnerability.

COMPETITIVENESS AND LABOUR MARKET RE-REGULATION

The modernization of Ontario's employment standards was premised on the need to adapt to the labour market change experienced between the mid-1970s and the late 1990s (Ontario 2000a). Employment standards legislation had not been fundamentally reformed since the Employment Standards Act was enacted in the late 1960s. Yet, as outlined in chapter 3, the labour market had changed considerably. In a document entitled *The Future of Work in Ontario*, released just months before the process of legislative reform began, the government outlined its interpretation of labour change, emphasizing an increase in the number of women working outside the home, the increasing importance of service sector occupations, and the emergence of alternative (nonstandard) forms of work. As well, the pressures of the "competitive global economy," which included "new trade rules, investment politics and technological change" were said to be creating the need for business flexibility. The government presented the report with the assertion that workplace and labour market change were requiring them to reconsider the "role the government should play in shaping the workplaces of the future" (Ontario 1998b, 6, 7). These assertions notwithstanding, the government's claims signified a broader neoliberal policy shift. Specifically, the need for the modernization of labour and employment laws was articulated through a discourse that tied ESA reform to the government's general economic commitment to "improve the province's competitive status as a place to invest" (Ontario 2000b, 4).

This emphasis on economic competitiveness, which is characteristic of the neoliberal policy paradigm, is a definitive element in the shift from the welfare state model to the workfare state (Jessop 1993; Johnson et al. 1994). Underlying this discourse is the assumption that regulatory interventions that run counter to the interests of short-term profitability will inhibit the competitiveness of markets. Thus, such forms of "red tape" must be eliminated. With respect to labour legislation, the discursive representation of competitive pressures has played a central role in shaping the re-regulation of labour relations by reconstructing the criteria through which public policy is evaluated (Murray et al. 2000). The project is one not only of reforming policy but also of reshaping workers' social expectations about employment (Peck 2001; Sears 1999).

The government's neoliberal policy orientation had increasingly taken hold in conjunction with the economic restructuring that began in the early 1970s.[2] As discussed in chapter 1, the neoliberal paradigm is grounded in an ideological attachment to the belief in the ability of the invisible hand of the market to correct all inefficiencies; it thereby favors market deregulation in place of state guidance. According to this paradigm, the relationship between states and markets should be formed along the following principles: "that institutions such as the state and the market should reflect the motivation of individual self-interest ... "that states provide a minimum of public goods along the lines of the nineteenth-century 'night watchman' state" ... [and] that the most efficient allocation of resources and maximization of utility occurs through markets" (Bakker 1996, 4). As discussed, this paradigm represents a fundamental shift away from the collectivist principles (however provisional) of the Keynesian welfare state towards an approach that emphasizes individualist and market-based mechanisms to address economic and social problems. More concretely, proponents of the neoliberal paradigm advocate a re-regulation of labour markets to promote flexibility, reductions in state spending on Keynesian-era policies (unemployment insurance), and increased cross-border free trade (Brodie 1996a; McBride and Shields 1997).

The changing political paradigm also promoted a shift in expectations concerning social security (Brodie 1996b). An ideological formulation of citizenship rights based on individualism and self-reliance, rather than on entitlement to basic levels of social welfare provided by the state, was part of this broader approach to public policy. Whereas the welfare state paradigm emphasized the collective character of social problems and the need for the state to place some limits on the unpredictability of market forces, the new conception of citizenship reflected the market-focused, individualist orientation of neoliberal public policy.

As Janine Brodie puts it (1996a, 19), the "new good citizen is one who recognizes the limits and liabilities of state provision and embraces the obligation to work longer and harder in order to become more self-reliant." And as Alan Sears (1999) argues, by creating a willingness to adapt to the pressures of the lean society – which includes longer work hours, reduced pay, user fees for previously subsidized services, and the incorporation of market discipline into the provision of public services – the neoliberal state has incorporated the principles of lean production into the conception of citizenship itself and is thereby attempting to foster the "lean person." This neoliberal conception has provided ideological justification for more insecure forms of employment (Johnson et al. 1994) and has helped to lower the expectations of Canadian workers with respect to employment rights.[3]

Within Canada, the neoliberal paradigm was promoted through the report of the Royal Commission on the Economic Union and Development Prospects for Canada issued in 1985 (Brodie 1996a). The ideology was incorporated into Canadian public policy at the federal level, first by the Mulroney Conservative governments that held office from 1984 to 1993 and then by the Chrétien Liberal governments beginning in 1993. Canadian neoliberalism was implemented along several fronts and included the restructuring of social programs developed during the postwar years (for example, Unemployment Insurance, Old Age Security, and Family Allowances); dramatic funding reductions in program spending in the areas of health, education, and social welfare; the privatization of public services; and fiscal policies geared towards the combined goals of tax and deficit reduction.[4] With respect to labour policies and labour relations, federal and provincial governments have sought to reduce or eliminate workers' rights established in the postwar era (Panitch and Swartz 2003).

Neoliberal attacks on unionized labour were met with opposition from the labour movement (Heron 1996; Palmer 1992). The CLC organized mass protests against wage controls in 1976 and monetarist policies in 1981. The militant Canadian Union of Postal Workers engaged in several bitter struggles over the reorganization of the postal services. Rather than adopt the concession bargaining approach of the United Auto Workers (UAW), the Canadian branch left that international union to form the Canadian Auto Workers union (CAW), establishing itself as one of Canada's most militant unions (Gindin 1995). Social movements and organized labour attempted to organize broad-based coalitions to oppose neoliberal provincial governments (Munro 1997; Palmer 1987; Turk 1997). Nonetheless, they were placed clearly on the defensive by successive recessions, workplace restructuring, increased corporate mobility, and the proliferation of neoliberal labour market polices. That policy framework was at the heart of the employment standards reform process that would unfold in the late 1990s.

Eliminating Red Tape

In the *Common Sense Revolution,* the Ontario government claimed that it would reduce the red tape regulating Ontario's businesses. To further this agenda, shortly after its election it struck the Red Tape Review Commission (RTRC) and gave it the mandate to review existing regulations that affected Ontario's businesses and related institutions, to make recommendations regarding the need to change or eliminate "inappropriate regulatory measures," and to develop review processes for proposed regulations (RTRC 1997, xii). The final report of the commission indicates the government's intended direction both with respect to public policy reform generally and employment standards reform specifically.

Within the report, the commission defined "red tape" as "those measures that diminish our economic competitiveness by adding unjustifiable requirements, costs or delays to the normal activities of business and institutions." This included "legislation, regulations, licenses, permits, approvals, standards, registration, filing and certification requirements, guidelines, procedures, paperwork, enforcement practices or other measures that are not truly needed to protect the health and safety of Ontarians or to maintain environmental quality" (RTRC 1997, 1). The report claimed that such unnecessary rules and regulations deterred job creation and reduced economic competitiveness by adding excessive costs to Ontario's businesses.

The commission produced numerous recommendations regarding the province's employment standards legislation, which was defined as "outdated" and unable to provide "the flexibility required to meet the needs of the modern workplace" (RTRC 1997, 92). The need to foster greater flexibility in employment relationships was central to the commission's recommendations, which dealt with hours of work and overtime, termination, and coverage. Specifically, the commission recommended that the maximum hours of work be increased from forty-eight to fifty, or to two hundred averaged over four weeks, that the permits system be significantly streamlined or eliminated, that coverage of the emergency exemptions be broadened, and that yearly hours limitations be "subject only to empirical evidence on health and safety risks associated with overtime hours worked" (96). It also recommended that employees be given the option of overtime compensation at either the premium hourly rate or through in-lieu time. Other ways in which the commission felt flexibility could be increased were through expanding the categories of employees exempt from the hours of work and overtime provisions and by providing employers with alternatives to existing severance pay requirements. It also recommended that employers, employees, and unions be given the capacity to "negotiate standards outside the confines" of the ESA, in order to reduce government-enforced regulation, leaving open the possibility that individual standards might fall below those of the ESA (95).

The wide-ranging recommendations supported and gave direction to the government's general intentions to re-regulate Ontario's labour market in ways that would encourage forms of labour flexibility that would primarily benefit employers. According to the commission, the role of government should be to foster this normative shift, as such a shift was needed to promote economic growth.

NEW EMPLOYMENT STANDARDS
FOR THE "NEW ECONOMY"

Following its election in 1995, the new government initially turned its attention to labour relations legislation, fulfilling a key election promise to its supporters in the business community. In its election platform, the Progressive Conservative party had claimed that the NDP's Bill 40 was a "proven job killer" and was impeding economic growth in the province (PCPO 1995, 15; Watson 1997). In October 1995, it introduced Bill 7, which repealed the Bill 40 amendments to the Labour Relations Act, changed certification procedures that had been in effect since 1950, and simplified decertification procedures (Schenk 1995; Watson 1997). Key amendments included replacing automatic certification following card signing with an election model using secret ballots; eliminating the prohibitions on the use of replacement workers; reducing the threshold to trigger a decertification vote from 45 percent to 40 percent; eliminating the requirement for the Ontario Labour Relations Board to dismiss a decertification application when the application was initiated by an employer or when an employer acted illegally with respect to the decertification process; introducing a requirement that a strike vote be taken within thirty days of the expiration of the collective agreement, or any time afterwards, for a legal strike mandate; and eliminating successor rights for government employees. Bill 7 also repealed the right of domestic workers and agricultural workers to unionize.

Further changes in the following years included the prevention of the unionization of participants in the provincial Workfare (work for welfare) program and the elimination of the ability of the Ontario Labour Relations Board to award bargaining rights to a union in cases where employers created a coercive atmosphere. These various legislative changes had a threefold effect on union organizing in the province (Yates 2000). First, they accelerated processes of labour market change, particularly with respect to the downsizing and reorganization of public sector employment. Second, they increased employer power vis-à-vis unionized employees, particularly through reduced threats of penalty for illegal activities in labour relations. Finally, they led to declines in union organizing successes.

While not immediately central, employment standards reform was nonetheless on the policy agenda. Bill 7 itself had implications for the ESA, as it phased out the Employee Wage Protection Program. The government also ended the annual increases to the minimum wage that had been occurring since the 1980s, freezing the general rate at $6.85.[5] The minimum wage freeze was a significant change in policy direction, as historically, minimum wage increases had been implemented regularly since the enactment of the ESA in order to protect the deterioration in wage rates of workers with little bargaining power.

In 1996, the government turned its attention directly to the Employment Standards Act, undertaking the first phase of a two-stage process of reform. Bill 49, the Employment Standards Improvement Act, reduced the time limit for workers to register formal complaints from two years to six months, and placed a $10,000 limit on monetary awards for ESA violations, regardless of the value of lost wages.[6] An employee would have to claim a larger amount through civil court but could not file a claim *and* take the employer to court for the same ESA violation, even if the claim exceeded $10,000. The act also introduced a provision preventing unionized employees from filing employment standards complaints with the Ministry of Labour, requiring them instead to resolve complaints through the grievance arbitration process, thereby placing the cost of administering complaints in the hands of unions, rather than the ministry. Bill 49 also privatized the collection of money owed to workers as a result of ESA violations.[7]

According to the provincial government, the amendments within Bill 49 were meant to encourage self-reliance between employers and employees in resolving ESA complaints.[8] As discussed in chapter 3, the practice of self-reliance reflects a privatization of the regulation of employment standards, by situating them in the context of direct negotiation between employers and employees, and thus reduces the effectiveness of the regulatory protections. Bill 49 accomplished this in several ways. First, by privatizing the collection of awards owed to workers and requiring that unions handle employment standards complaints through grievance procedures, the government directly reduced its role in the administration of employment standards. Second, the reduced time limit on filing ESA complaints and the ceiling on financial compensation restricted employees' abilities to secure protection from employment standards violations, indicating that underlying the stated goal of self-reliance lay the intention to curtail workers' rights.[9]

The amendments to the ESA contained in Bill 49 were highly favored by employer associations. The Retail Council of Canada (RCC) stated that "[t]he challenge of ESA reform is to facilitate ... diversity and flexibility in the best interests of both parties" and considered Bill 49 to be a "good first step" in this process (RCC 1996, 4). Similarly, the Canadian Federation of Independent Business (CFIB), a national association of small and medium-sized businesses, "commended the Ontario government for its resolve to undertake a two-stage overhaul of the ... ESA" and "supported Bill 49 ... as the first stage in that reform" (CFIB 2000,1). With its first stage of employment standards reforms, the government had given a clear indication of what it meant by "flexible, modern and adaptable" (Ontario 2000b, 4).

Time for Change

Following the enactment of Bill 49, and in order to initiate the second phase of the reforms, the government released a document entitled *The Future of Work in Ontario*, which both outlined its interpretation of labour market change and provided a justification for employment standards reform based on the need to respond to competitive pressures and the "new workplace" (Ontario 1998b). In choosing to highlight competitive pressures, rather than other aspects of labour market change such as unemployment and financial insecurity, *The Future of Work* framed the upcoming reforms in a manner that prioritized an employer-oriented strategy rather than employee-oriented social protection. This approach constituted a qualitative shift in the official discourse around employment standards. Whereas in previous eras social protection had been articulated in conjunction with "economic practicability," with the latter prevailing in the implementation process, now the promotion of economic competitiveness in the context of an increasingly competitive global economy was *the* central priority. For example, the document contained no discussion of the impact of the growth of nonstandard forms of work on job security, levels of compensation, or increased social polarization (OFL 1999).

In July 2000, the Ministry of Labour issued a consultation paper outlining its proposals to modernize Ontario's employment standards. The ESA was described as being "filled with language, concerns and approaches of an earlier era" and thus no longer relevant to the contemporary Ontario economy. In *Time for Change*, the government committed itself to modernizing the ESA so that it would "improve workplace flexibility" and thereby encourage growth and innovation (Ontario 2000b, 3).

Time for Change proposed a wide-ranging package of reforms in hours of work and overtime, vacation time, public holidays, family leave, coverage, administration, and enforcement. The hours of work and overtime proposals were perhaps the most controversial. The government proposed to eliminate the permit system for excess hours, to increase the maximum allowable hours of work per week to sixty (from forty-eight), to allow for this weekly maximum to be calculated over a three-week period, to allow for overtime (hours in excess of forty-four hours) to be averaged over a three-week period, and to require a rest period of twenty-four hours every seven days *or* forty-eight hours every fourteen days. Proposals on vacation pay and public holidays submitted that, subject to employer-employee agreement, vacations could be scheduled in daily increments, and employees could work public holidays with either additional pay or a substitute day off. A leave proposal was presented to provide those in workplaces of fifty or more employees with up to ten days of unpaid, job-protected leave in the event of family crises or illnesses. With respect to coverage, the government stated that it intended to re-evaluate existing exemptions and to take into account the need for new exemptions, including provisions that would recognize "*compelling economic or cost arguments that indicate an industry is placed in a serious competitive disadvantage by the application of a provision or provisions*" (Ontario 2000b, 15; emphasis added). As with Bill 49, *Time for Change* emphasized the need to encourage greater self-reliance on the part of employers and employees in the enforcement of standards. A series of escalating monetary penalties and an anti-reprisal provision that included giving ESA officers reinstatement powers were also proposed.

The proposals in *Time for Change* represented the most significant re-writing of employment standards legislation since the introduction of the ESA. Weekly maximum hours-of-work regulations had not been as high as 60 since before World War II. Further, if put into effect, the averaging of weekly hours could result in employees working even more than 60 hours in a given week, so long as the three-week total did not exceed 180 hours. Similarly, the averaging of overtime hours could result in employees working many hours in excess of 44 in a given week without regular overtime compensation (time-and-a-half), so long as the total hours worked for the three-week period did not exceed 132 hours. These proposals indicated that the government was willing to enhance the already-existing forms of employer-oriented flexibility contained within the ESA. Further, the government explicitly introduced the principle of competition into the regulation of employment standards by proposing that competitive disadvantage be taken into account when considering possible exemptions from minimum standards regulations. The proposed introduction of the principle of competition into the

ESA signified a clear shift away from the representation of employment standards as a necessary minimum safety net.

Time for Change solicited responses from all those concerned about employment standards. One month after the discussion paper was issued, the government undertook a consultation period where it received input from many employer, worker, and community organizations. The process took place in August and September of 2000 in five major cities across the province. Over fifty organizations submitted briefs during this period.

Once again, the proposed direction for ESA reform met with widespread support from employer associations. Their submissions to the MOL displayed a direct correspondence between their positions and that of the MOL. Employer associations emphasized strongly the need to introduce greater flexibility into the ESA in order to "recognize and accommodate the trend towards more varied work arrangements and allow greater choice in designing those arrangements" (CFIB 2000, 2). As well, a desire to minimize government regulation of minimum standards in favour of an approach that placed greater responsibility on workplace parties was generally articulated.[10]

For example, the Canadian Federation of Independent Businesses (CFIB) supported proposals to eliminate the excess hours permits, to increase the maximum weekly hours to sixty, to allow time off in lieu of overtime, to allow for hours averaging, and to allow for the scheduling of vacation time in daily increments (CFIB 2000). The Ontario Chamber of Commerce (OCC) supported a number of the proposals as well, including the proposals to eliminate the extra hours permits, to introduce greater flexibility into the scheduling of weekly rest periods and paid vacations, and to encourage greater self-reliance with respect to enforcement of the act (OCC 2000). The Toronto Board of Trade was "highly supportive" of the proposals to increase maximum weekly hours of work and to introduce hours averaging in the calculation of overtime pay.[11]

The support from employer associations was not unconditional however. The OCC expressed some concern that the proposals for overtime averaging "may still not provide enough flexibility to handle jobs in the emerging economies or sufficiently provide for two parties to arrange the most mutually convenient work relationship" (2000,1). As well, both the OCC and the CFIB raised concerns over the proposals to introduce family crisis leave, articulating the need for government to leave the negotiation of leaves to the discretion of workplace parties. The anti-reprisals and reinstatement provisions and the proposal for escalating monetary penalties were met with opposition as well. The general tendency of employer association opposition to these specific ESA proposals was to characterize them as either impractical and/or unnecessary (CFIB 2000; OCC 2000). Moreover, the proposal to expand the reinstatement provisions of the ESA was characterized as "a significant and unnecessary incursion by the government into the affairs of Ontario's workplaces" (OCC 2000, 9).

While the reactions of employer associations were favorable, though mixed, the proposed changes received across-the-board criticism from both organized labour and community organizations working with non-unionized workers. These organizations claimed that the proposed changes would benefit only employers and would lead to a reduction in workers' rights across the province.[12] In addition, both labour and community organizations expressed concern that the standards in the ESA were already insufficient and that the proposed changes would take employment standards back in time rather than forward.

For example, in a submission to the MOL, the Employment Standards Work Group (ESWG), a network of legal clinics, community centres, and organizations working with non-unionized workers in Toronto, stated: "A careful look at the proposals makes it clear that the Tories are not looking at the 21st century, rather they are looking back to the 19th century. When they talk about increasing flexibility, they mean that they propose to give employers greater power over working time ... When they talk about simplifying the *Employment Standards Act* and related legislation what they really mean is that they plan to get rid of workers' rights" (ESWG 2000, 5). The consultations process itself was viewed with skepticism because of its short notice and its limited scope.[13]

Labour and community organizations unanimously called for reduced, rather than increased, weekly hours maximums and for stronger enforcement mechanisms to improve the regulation of employment standards. They also called upon the government to amend the ESA family leave provisions to bring them in line with changes to the federal Employment Insurance program that provided parental and pregnancy leave benefits for up to fifty-two weeks. These calls framed a campaign undertaken to challenge the proposed reforms. The Employment Standards Work Group organized a campaign to oppose the Bill 147 amendments, focusing particularly on the sixty-hour workweek. The campaign included the distribution of leaflets, outreach and education, and several large demonstrations in downtown Toronto between December 2000 and July 2001. In April 2001, the campaign was connected to a global-justice demonstration, in order to highlight the connections between globalization, the restructuring of workplaces and labour laws, and the rise of precarious work.[14]

While the ESA 2000 campaign was not expected to stop the proclamation, it was designed to touch a nerve with the public about the ways in which the new act would lower the floor of workers' rights, in particular through the introduction of the sixty-hour work week. A member of the organization explains:

> The big victory for me in that campaign was that even though the government tried to deflect the attention away from the 60-hour work week, we were able to say that the important thing about this is having to work 60 hours. Anybody who talks about the new act talks about the 60 hours. After the fact, people started picking things up ... Even though the Minister kept on saying, and all the spin-doctors kept saying, no, this is not 60 hours, people were calling shows, people were asking questions about the 60 hours. I think that was the one message we managed to put through.[15]

The public attention notwithstanding, the campaign was not able to mobilize social pressure sufficiently to alter the government's plans, and the new employment standards legislation was passed in the following months.

THE RETURN OF THE SIXTY-HOUR WORK WEEK

With the proposals contained in *Time for Change* as a basis, new employment standards legislation was passed in December 2000 and proclaimed on 4 September 2001.[16] Key changes to the amended act are listed in table 5.

The final act did not differ greatly from the initial proposals. Increases to the weekly maximum hours of work (up to sixty) remained the same, although the proposal to allow for the averaging

Table 5
Bill 147: Changes to the Ontario Employment Standards Act

Hours of work	• Extension of the maximum hours of work per week to 60, with hours in excess of 48 subject to "employee consent" • Daily maximums can be increased beyond 8 to 13 • Employees still entitled to time and one-half for hours worked in excess of 44 per week, but overtime entitlements may be averaged over a period up to four weeks • Expansion of "exceptional circumstances" where hours maximums can be exceeded
Vacations and holidays	• Vacations (previously scheduled in one- or two-week blocks) may be scheduled in daily increments at the written request of an employee, subject to employer agreement • 24 hours of consecutive rest every 7 days or 48 hours every 14 days • Either time and one-half for hours worked on a public holiday, plus regular pay, or regular pay for the public holiday plus an alternative day off, with pay
Leaves	• Expanded parental and pregnancy leave provisions: 52 weeks leave for birth mothers and up to 37 weeks for new parents • New emergency leave up to 10 days of unpaid leave per year for family crisis, death, or personal or family illness for those in workplaces of 50 or more employees
Wages	• Payment by direct deposit now possible without employee consent • Time off in lieu of overtime pay possible, subject to employer agreement
Administration/ enforcement	• System of special permits for excess hours eliminated • Escalating fines for those in contravention of the act • Stronger anti-reprisal provisions for employees who are terminated or penalized for exercising their rights under the ESA • Employers required to post notices of employment standards in the workplace

Source: Employment Standards Act, S.O. 2000, C. 41; ESWG (2001), Fudge (2001), OFL (2001).

of weekly hours maximums over three weeks was dropped. The overtime averaging proposal was maintained and was increased to allow for averaging over a four-week period. Both of these provisions included the requirement of "employee consent" to alternative-hours arrangements. The new act also indirectly set a thirteen-hour limit on maximum daily hours. While no explicit limit was set, Bill 147 stipulated that an employee was to be entitled to eleven hours free from work each day (Fudge 2001). Proposals to introduce greater flexibility into the vacation and holiday provisions of the act were maintained. Despite the concerns raised by employer associations with respect to the proposals for new enforcement provisions (anti-reprisal protections and escalating fines) and family crisis leave, these proposals were also maintained in the final act. In addition, the government expanded the parental leave provisions of the act, to bring them in line with federal amendments to the Employment Insurance program, allowing for up to fifty-two weeks of unpaid, job-protected leave for birth mothers and up to thirty-seven weeks for new parents (generally fathers or adoptive parents).[17]

The government claimed that it sought to meet the needs of both employers and employees in its proposed legislation, citing the various forms of flexibility as benefiting both, and in particular identifying the anti-reprisals provisions and the new leave provisions as clearly beneficial to employees. Upon careful examination, however, it becomes apparent that the model of labour market regulation developed through the policy reforms process offered nothing to alleviate the situation of heightened labour market vulnerability experienced by workers in forms of precarious employment; rather, it supported the normalization of neoliberal labour flexibility. Specifically, the policy reforms introduced through the ESA 2000 reduced direct government involvement in the regulation of workplace standards, promoted increased employer control over work time, facilitated the normalization of nonstandard and low-wage employment relationships, and, overall, further entrenched a privatized model of the regulation of workplace standards (Fudge 2001; Mitchell 2003; Thomas 2002).

The reduction of government regulation of workplace standards and the increased capacity of employers to control working time stemmed from the transition from a permits-based system for extra hours to a system based on "employee consent" in the increase in allowable weekly hours and the system of overtime averaging. By extending maximum hours of work from 48 to 60 per week, the act provided employers with the ability to increase the work time of those employees already working long hours. Overtime averaging arrangements permitted instances where employees could work over 44 hours without compensation at time-and-a-half for those hours, if the total hours of work for the four-week period were less than 176. This measure enables significant reductions in the cost of overtime labour, thereby further encouraging the use of overtime.

While the possibilities for hours of work beyond forty-eight and overtime averaging were not new, Bill 147 removed the requirement for government approval of extra hours and overtime averaging, making such arrangements subject to "employee consent." Combined, these provisions shifted the regulation of working time standards back to the private relations between employers and employees and implicitly created the means for employers to exert greater control over the scheduling of extra work hours. As described by a community legal worker who assists non-unionized workers with employment standards complaints, this constituted a shift from "government having a responsibility to providing a basic floor to employers and employees negotiating what that floor is going to be and what those terms are going to be."[18]

The reliance on employee consent presumes an equitable relationship between employees and employers, as it "pretends there is no power imbalance in the workplace and that workers are free agents."[19] But because power imbalances are in fact created through the nature of the employment relationship, these amendments contribute directly to the pressure placed on employees to agree to employers' scheduling requests. A representative from a community group that represents homeworkers in the garment industry explains:

> [The Minister of Labour] may think that the employer and the employee can have the same power. But, in fact, it's not. You cannot say that you don't want to work this long, these kind of hours. If you don't want to work for this kind of pay, then you can't talk with the employer and ask them for more, or talk to them and say that this is too long … The employer will say "you can stay, or you can go." If I am a worker and I am dependent on the money for my living, what can I do? Even though I know that I am being exploited … even though I know I am being taken advantage [of], it doesn't seem that I have any other choice. I have to stay there.[20]

In effect, by promoting a system of workplace regulation premised on privatized negotiation between workers and employers, Bill 147 legislated that "employers get a lot more control over workers' daily lives."[21]

The financial insecurity of low-income employees reinforced this enhanced employer power, as the minimum wage was frozen from 1995 until 2004.[22] Through the nine-year freeze, the reforms increased the economic insecurity of those already in precarious employment relationships. The freeze also had clear implications for conditions of racialized income inequality. Poverty rates amongst racialized groups continued to increase through the late 1990s into the early twenty-first century. For example, in the city of Toronto, poverty rates for racialized families increased by 361 percent between 1980 and 2000. Through the 1990s, while approximately 25 percent of Canadians earned under ten dollars an hour, 41 percent of new-comers were in this earnings category. The racialized labour market trends outlined in chapter 1 – an overrepresentation of racialized groups in low-wage, low-status occupations – meant that workers from racialized groups were among those most directly affected by the minimum wage freeze.[23]

The implications of the Bill 147 reforms for workers from racialized groups is further highlighted by the fact that these power differentials are exacerbated in situations where workers are not permanent residents of Canada. A representative from a community group that assists domestic workers employed through the Live-In Caregiver Program with employment-related concerns explains:

> the new law says the employee may or may not agree. The balance is very obviously imbalanced between the employer and employee, especially when the worker is temporarily in the country. The imbalance is just so obvious. I cannot imagine anybody saying "no, I don't want to take my vacation for two days" … The last thing they would like to have is bad relations with their employer, who they want to work with for 24 months so that they can smoothly go through the 24-month require-ment. A lot of the new law, which is supposed to have the will or the choice of the worker, a lot of that doesn't apply at all to domestic workers.[24]

For workers in Canada on temporary work permits such as those women from the Caribbean and the Philippines employed as domes-tic workers, the process of securing "consent" for extra hours of work is determined through the racialized inequalities of the employ-ment relationship.

Through these tendencies, the employment standards reforms supported the normalization of nonstandard employment relation-ships. The potential for increased hours of work and reduced overtime costs (through averaging arrangements) when needed discourages employers from hiring additional workers, as, even when overtime costs are taken into account, it is generally less costly to pay overtime than to take on additional employees. Thus, the ability to schedule longer hours of work encouraged trends towards a model of employment whereby core groups of workers take on longer hours and are supplemented by a contingent of contract and part-time employees working irregular hours and shorter work weeks. In this way, employers secure greater capacity to maintain lean staffing levels (which are supplemented by contract/temporary workers) and to construct flexible and nonstandard employment relationships characterized by a lack of stability in hours of work.

As argued in chapter 1, labour market regulation both shapes and is shaped by relations of social reproduction. In fact, addressing concerns about family needs in the scheduling of work hours was central to the employment standards reforms process that produced Bill 147. One of the key promotional claims the government made about the ESA 2000 was that it would provide families with the flexibility they needed to balance work and non-work responsibilities. If "family friendly flexibility" refers to the capacity for people to balance their work and non-work responsibilities, however, the ESA 2000 offered little in this regard. As the above discussion demonstrates, rather than promoting a balanced approach to working time, the employment standards reforms provided a policy mechanism to promote a more polarized distribution of work hours, both through provisions that extended the work week and through provisions that encouraged unpaid overtime.

Nor did the new legislation provide employees with greater capacity to control their work time, as requirements for employee consent placed greater power in an employer's hands (Thomas 2007). Further, while the ten days of unpaid emergency leave for family responsibilities constituted a positive development, small workplaces (those with fewer than fifty employees) were exempted, leaving many workers unable to access this benefit. The extended parental leave was also a positive development, although its implementation was more or less assured by the widespread adoption of similar policies in all provinces following the amendments to the federal Employment Insurance program. In effect, the ESA reforms enhanced a neoliberal working-time order with employers gaining enhanced control and "temporal flexibilities," while workers were faced with increasing pressure to balance responsibilities of paid work and reproductive labour (Shalla 2007, 251). Despite the claims for flexibility, it offered little to employees to either control their hours of work or to construct alternative caregiving strategies. This neoliberal order thereby reinforced long-standing gendered inequalities in the organization of social reproduction by adding to already-existing pressures on women to manage the balance between paid and unpaid work.

Finally, while employment standards legislation applies most directly to non-unionized workers, the employment conditions of unionized workers were also implicated in the reforms process, in particular through the potential "harmonizing down" effects. A union representative captured the significance of the new ESA for unionized workers in the following statement:

> For the unionized sector, [the ESA] forms the floor on which we build our collective agreement. We don't need to argue that wages should be above $5.00 an hour, because they are already $6.85. So you start there. We don't need to argue for two weeks vacation. It's already in the law. What we argue for is three and four. We haven't had to argue for time-and-a-half after 44 hours. It's already in the law. What we want is double time. We want the employer to hire other people, instead of working us overtime. So we put those kinds of provisions into a collective agreement ... That's the floor upon which we build up. When you begin to move the floor downwards, when the main floor becomes the basement, we can expect employers to come along and say "I want to average overtime." They're going to want to negotiate it.[25]

It was not long after the new employment standards legislation was implemented that these tendencies began to appear at the bargaining table. For example, proposals for a sixty-hour work week were tabled by employers during two high-profile strikes undertaken by the Canadian Auto Workers.[26] In the fall of 2001, only months after the ESA 2000 came into effect, ADM Agri-Industries, a food oil processor in Windsor included proposals for a mandatory sixty-hour work week in a package of concessionary demands.[27] ADM workers, members of CAW Local 195, rejected the proposals and undertook a ten-week strike to protect their contract against the concessions. While the sixty-hour work week proposals were eventually dropped by the employer, the final settlement included changes to days off and reduced benefits.[28] The sixty-hour work week was also tabled by Navistar, a Chatham-based truck manufacturer, in 2002 as part of a package of concessionary proposals that the company claimed it required in order to remain competitive.[29] Navistar workers struck for six weeks to prevent concessions to their contract and secured a settlement that did not include either a sixty-hour work week or wage concessions.

While neither ADM nor Navistar were successful in bargaining a sixty-hour work week, the impact on the collective bargaining process was clear. The new hours-of-work provisions provided the means to significantly alter the parameters of collective bargaining. If workers are forced to fight back against concessionary demands that are far below their existing agreements, improving standards in these areas through the collective bargaining process becomes all the more difficult. Thus, the employment standards reforms constituted a central component of broader labour market tendencies towards employer-oriented flexibility, not only for the non-unionized employees most reliant on legislated standards but for those with collective agreements as well.

FLEXIBILITY *AND* FAIRNESS?

In May 2007, the Toronto-area Workers' Action Centre – which provides assistance to people in low-wage and precarious employment with employment-related problems – issued a report on precarious employment in Ontario (WAC 2007). The legacy of the ESA reform process is clearly articulated in the stories collected by the WAC from workers across the Greater Toronto Area. These stories document the continuing problems of unpaid wages and overtime, workers being misclassified as self-employed and therefore exempt from minimum standards, expectations of work hours well in excess of legislated standards, and a general lack of enforcement of the ESA.[30] With many accounts from women and workers from racialized groups, the report is also a testament to the gendered and racialized character of the neoliberal model of labour flexibility, as "[p]overty, racism, the need to establish themselves and their families in a new country and lack of employment choices and protection lead people do whatever employers ask in order to put food on the table" (16).

These problems persisted despite government pledges to make substantial improvements to ESA enforcement practices during the Bill 147 reforms process.[31] In addition to the legislative changes discussed above, the government had increased fines for employment standards violations, introduced a "no-reprisals" provision designed to protect employees who report violations, and pledged to increase educational and awareness activities. Whereas in the 1980s, an employer could be fined up to $10,000 for ESA violations and whereas in the early 1990s, the fines were increased up to a maximum of $50,000, the ESA 2000 increased the maximum fine for a company in violation of employment standards legislation to $500,000.[32] As part of a promotional and educational campaign to inform employers and employees of their respective obligations and rights under the act, employers were required to post notices of employment standards.[33] These steps were meant to ensure that "flexibility" was balanced with "fairness."

A closer examination of these specific changes, along with several broader components of the administrative and enforcement practices – coverage, ministry staffing levels, timelines to file complaints, and the general promotion of "self-reliance" – challenges the assertion that the reforms created fairness for employees. More specifically, previously established patterns of "implicit deregulation" – policy deregulation through a lack of enforcement (Bakker 1996) – were not sufficiently altered to address concerns related to employee vulnerability and insecurity.

As discussed in chapter 3, since the enactment of the ESA, the regulations have been expanded to provide more comprehensive coverage to the various categories of workers in the province, including workers who received very little protection under the original act, such as domestic workers and homeworkers. The employment standards reforms of 2000 remained consistent with this general trajectory. For example, while live-in domestic workers have historically been excluded from many employment standards and while in the labour relations reforms the Progressive Conservative government repealed their right to unionize, employment standards coverage of domestics was not rolled back. The reformed ESA provided coverage for full-time, live-in domestic workers under all of the major standards, including the maximum hours of work provisions (Ontario 2001a). Appendix 3 contains a detailed breakdown of coverage by category of employee and lists exemptions, full and partial, from the key provisions of the ESA 2000.

The policy amendments of 2000 counteracted the effects of extended coverage, however, by increasing the "flexibility" of some of the key general standards such as hours of work, overtime pay, paid public holidays, and vacations with pay. In other words, broader coverage of employment standards protections was countered with policy reforms that, as discussed above, promoted various forms of employer-oriented flexibility. As well, as indicated in appendix 3, the provisions with the most exemptions continued to be those that regulate overtime pay, hours of work, and the minimum wage. Further, the reformed legislation also expanded the definition of the "exceptional circumstances" under which hours of work standards could be avoided, thereby increasing the capacity of employers to temporarily exempt themselves from the maximum-hours and rest-period provisions. Overall, exemptions and exceptions continued to provide a means through which employers could evade the application of legislated standards.

One of the factors inhibiting a more comprehensive enforcement effort is the staffing levels of the Ministry of Labour's Employment Standards Branch. As discussed earlier in this chapter, the broader (neoliberal) regulatory paradigm emphasizes the need to reduce so-called red tape and eliminate inefficiencies, which may include downsizing public sector workforces. In Ontario's public service, adherence to this perspective resulted in general downsizing across the public sector. Ministry downsizing following the election of the Progressive Conservative government in the mid-1990s – which resulted in the termination of approximately one-quarter of the employment standards officers – thus contributed to the implicit deregulation of employment standards (USWA 2000).[34]

A union representative explains the significance of this form of deregulation as follows: "The Ministry of Labour has lost half of its budget since [the Progressive Conservatives] came into power. That's got to come from somewhere ... I remember looking at the Ministry of Labour's budget plans and one-third of their Employment Standards Officers were slated to be laid off ... You lay off one-third of your Employment Standards Officers ... The pretty unmistakable message that's sending to employers is 'we don't care. Enforcement is not a priority for us.'"[35] This limited enforcement capacity led one community worker to simply avoid the ministry and attempt to resolve disputes independently:

> The problem is there is no one to enforce [the ESA]. They cut a lot of officers. When you file a complaint, they don't even have time to really look into the situation ... So instead of going to the Ministry, we have to try to find another way ... If they want us to help, instead of filing a complaint to the Ministry first, then we will try to help. We will write to the employer asking for back wages. Sometimes we get lucky ... I don't go to the Ministry at all. I go to the factory and ask them to pay the workers. I will call them and tell them they have to pay ... Instead of going to directly to the Ministry, this is how I work with my members.[36]

The timeline to file a complaint, which was reduced in Bill 49 from two years to six months, was identified by many community legal workers as insufficient to cover the potential violations a worker may experience in a workplace, particularly in forms of precarious employment. The change to the time limit restriction was particularly significant as violations may occur over a period of years, but workers may not report them until they are able to find another job.[37] The time limit change, combined with the reduced limit on financial claims (a cap of $10,000), creates further barriers to effective enforcement. The racialized dimensions of this are apparent in the impact on immigrant workers without permanent residency status. A representative from a community organization that assists domestic workers with employment concerns explains:

> A change for the worse was when they shortened the time within which you can claim ... If domestic workers already had a disadvantage under the old provision, at least they could actually wait until they got landed and then get encouraged to make a claim for past wrongs. But that stopped working. It's true, really, that there is a qualitative change in terms of how people assert their rights when they don't have any status in the country, and when they do. Certainly if you had a longer time within which to file a claim, then someone who feels she really had a claim to make, but didn't want to do that to jeopardize

her landed immigrant status, once she had that, she could very
well do that. But they took that away.[38]

The significance of this concern is indicated by the fact that the vast
majority of complaints are filed after the employment relationship
has ended (ESWG 1996).

In its 2001–2 business plan, the Ministry of Labour committed
itself to improving compliance in targeted industries by 20 percent
over five years, and the number of targeted inspections in "high
risk" sectors was increased from 1,543 in 2000–1 to 2,560 in 2005–6
(Ontario 2008).[39] The long-standing reliance on individualized
employee complaints remained the primary enforcement mechanism of the ESA, however, with the aim of promoting employer-
employee "self-reliance" a key emphasis in the reforms process
undertaken through Bill 147. As discussed in chapter 3, this individualized, complaints-based process does not take into account
power imbalances that exist in the employer-employee relationship
(Fairey 2007; WAC 2007), imbalances that were exacerbated through
the reforms to the ESA enacted in 2000, which allowed for higher
levels of employer-employee negotiation of the standards regulated
by the act, for example through the flexible procedures that required
employee consent. Further, as discussed in chapter 3, non-compliance
with the act is directly related to power imbalances in the workplace
created through relations of race, class, gender, and immigration
status, which reduce the likelihood that complaints will be filed.

The emphasis on self-reliance as a primary enforcement mechanism
de-emphasizes proactive mechanisms, such as targeted inspections,
that would address power imbalances in the workplace. It indicates
a desire to withdraw from the regulation of workplace disputes and,
given the already existing power imbalances, thereby creates a workplace environment that further tilts power relations in favour of
employers. As discussed above, these tendencies are exacerbated for
workers from racialized groups and newcomers to Canada, who may
be reluctant to complain about employment standards violations
because of fear of job loss, deportation, or general conditions of
economic insecurity (WAC 2007). Other enforcement strategies,
such as the routine-investigations process, which avoids the individualized approach and has been successful in detecting violations, have
been given a priority that is secondary to both the individual complaints process and other strategies that emphasize workplace self-

Table 6
Unpaid Wages and Entitlements, Collected and Uncollected ($ millions), 2001–6

	2001–2	2002–3	2003–4	2004–5	2005–6
Assessed	30.1	28.7	38.2	34.9	37
Collected	10.1	12.2	15.5	14.9	15.7
Total uncollected	20	16.5	22.7	20	21.3,
Percentage uncollected	66	58	59	57	58

Source: WAC (2007); Ontario Ministry of Labour, Employment Practices Branch, *Fiscal Year Reports*, 2001–2 to 2005–6.

reliance, such as educational seminars. Thus, the lack of effective enforcement becomes another specific method of creating a so-called flexible regulatory regime.

In response to the increased monetary value of the fines discussed above, labour and community organizations expressed concern that, regardless of the levels of the fines, they would not act as a deterrent without more effective enforcement practices (ESWG 2000; UNITE 2000). These were not new claims. The Task Force on Hours of Work and Overtime of the 1980s had already determined that the probability of detection, the probability of assessment, and the expected penalty all combined to create a low monetary cost for violators (Ontario 1987a). During interviews, community legal workers questioned the potential effectiveness of the latest enforcement initiatives, citing the low number of actual prosecutions of employers for repeated violations of the act and the low likelihood that assessments for employment standards violations will be collected.[40] As illustrated in table 6, these concerns are born out in enforcement data that demonstrate approximately 60 percent of the value of assessments against employers for unpaid wages and entitlements goes uncollected.

While the government claimed a commitment to fairness for workers, a deeper analysis of the reformed administrative and enforcement practices reveals that the re-regulation of employment standards through new legislation, which provided increased employer control over workplace standards, was accompanied by other forms of flexibility through inadequate enforcement and disputes resolution practices that privatized the complaints process through the promotion of self-reliance. The model of labour flexibility promoted by these "modern" employment standards was premised on norms of insecurity and market regulation. The continuity of worker complaints documented by the Workers' Action Centre several years after the implementation of the Bill 147 ESA reforms confirms that there are many ways in which workers continue to fall through the cracks of minimum employment standards legislation.

EMPLOYMENT STANDARDS ACROSS CANADA

While the Harris government was seen as a leader in neoliberal labour market reform in Canada, comparable patterns of employer-oriented flexibility in the regulation of minimum standards were clearly present in jurisdictions across the country (see appendix 5). For example, many jurisdictions were developing provisions to allow for flexibility in the scheduling of hours of work, primarily through averaging arrangements (HRDC 2001). Averaging agreements that regulate the calculation of overtime rates appeared in British Columbia (up to four weeks) and under the Canada Labour Code (two or more weeks). In the Northwest Territories and Nunavut, a labour standards officer could authorize averaging arrangements for daily and weekly standards (8/40) and for daily and weekly maximums (10/60). In Saskatchewan, averaging arrangements over any period could be used in the calculation of daily and weekly standards (8/40) and overtime hours. In the Yukon, daily and weekly standards (8/40) could be averaged over a period of two or more weeks. Overall, the general tendency was for a model of flexibility that provided the means for employers to assert control over the organization of hours of work, particularly for those in forms of insecure employment.

Two more detailed examples of reforms to provincial standards illustrate this general trend. In the mid-1990s, the Saskatchewan government revised the Labour Standards Act to improve coverage for part-time workers, the majority of whom were women (Broad 2000). The amendments included the pro-rating of benefits, requirements for advanced scheduling of hours, allowance for breaks, length of time between shifts, and pay for work on statutory holidays. While these amendments constituted significant improvements in the employment standards of part-time workers, many part-timers did not benefit, as many were exempted and the legislation was not adequately enforced (Broad 1997, 2000). The amended act also originally included a provision that would have required employers to offer additional hours of work to existing part-time workers, thereby enabling them to secure full-time hours. However, this provision was left out of the final act owing to opposition from the business community. In practice, the revised act did not provide part-time workers with the improved standards they needed.

The extreme neoliberal approach to the regulation of employment standards was also promoted through a comprehensive set of amendments to the Employment Standards Act in British Columbia (BCFL 2002; Fairey 2007; HRDC 2002). Echoing the intentions of the Ontario government, employment standards reform in British Columbia was undertaken in order to "provide greater flexibility, fairness, and efficiency for employers and employees," and to reduce "red tape," and the regulatory burdens for businesses (HRDC 2002, 2). Over several years beginning in 2001, the government introduced a series of changes that reshaped employment standards legislation, regulations, and enforcement practices, with largely negative implications for employee protection in the workplace.

Maximum hours of work were maintained at eight per day and forty per week, with overtime payable after forty hours of work per week. However, averaging agreements that covered periods from one to four weeks were introduced in the determination of overtime, minimum daily hours, and weekly rest period entitlements. The double time rate was eliminated for hours worked in excess of forty-eight and replaced by a rate of time-and-a-half for work during a weekly rest period. To further promote flexible scheduling, the daily threshold for double time was increased from eleven hours to twelve. Requirements to post hours of work notices and to give employees twenty-four hours notice of shift changes were eliminated. As well, minimum daily pay was reduced from four hours to two hours.

The amended act included changes to the enforcement provisions as well. The period of employer liability for the recovery of wages was reduced to six months from twenty-four. Personal liability for directors or officers of bankrupt or insolvent corporations for employee wages was removed. Requirements to post information about employment standards on the work site were eliminated. Going one step further than Ontario, employees covered by a collective agreement were excluded from the ESA even in cases where the standards in the agreement were inferior to those in the ESA. Like the neoliberal reforms in Ontario, the changes to enforcement practices were meant to encourage "self-reliance" between employers and employees by requiring employees to confront employers before filing a complaint and by replacing investigations procedures with a mediation process. These changes were accompanied by staff reductions and office closures in the Employment Standards Branch. As in Ontario, "[e]mployment standards reforms in British Columbia reflect employers' demands for greater flexibility and lower labour market costs, and not employees' needs for more protection and security" (Fairey 2007, 113).

Overall, while employment standards legislation across Canadian jurisdictions is not uniform, there are many similarities in the general regulatory approach to minimum standards. Ontario, followed by British Columbia, has taken the lead in promoting increased employer-oriented flexibility in the scheduling of work hours, overtime, and time off.[41] Even post–Harris-era amendments to Ontario's employment standards legislation, which were implemented by Dalton McGuinty's Liberal government in 2004, have not altered these general tendencies. Bill 63, The Employment Standards Amendment Act (Hours of Work and Other Matters) 2004, purported to eliminate the sixty-hour work week; however, it simply introduced a government approval process for employer/employee agreements for extra hours and overtime averaging arrangements, in no way ending the sixty-hour work week.[42] The legacy of the sixty-hour work week legislation remained largely intact, even after the defeat of the government that brought it into effect.

CONCLUSION

The social organization of employment changed considerably in the final three decades of the twentieth century. Labour market policies were shaped by the principles of neoliberalism, thereby contributing to a shift towards models of labour market regulation that promoted market-based, privatized, and individualized relations between employers and employees. In the context of workplace and labour market restructuring characterized by growth in forms of nonstandard and precarious employment, the Ontario government used ESA policy reforms to further promote employer-oriented forms of flexibility, thereby increasing employee vulnerability at a time of growing insecurity and polarization. The ESA reforms implemented by the Progressive Conservative government through Bill 147 reduced direct government involvement in the regulation of workplace standards, promoted increased employer control over work time, facilitated the normalization of nonstandard employment relation-ships, and increased the vulnerability of workers in non-unionized workplaces. The new ESA was ideologically significant as well, since along with contributing to the restructuring of employment relation-ships, this model of labour market regulation sought to normalize the experiences of so-called flexible employment, to reorganize workers' presumptions about employment, "their attitudes toward work and wages, their expectations about employment continuity and promotion prospects, their economic identities" (Peck 2001, 52). In this way, the restructuring of employment standards became a central component of a much broader process of labour market and workplace reorganization.

5

Working for Better Standards?
Labour Market Regulation
in a Global Economy

Employment standards are regulated primarily through national and sub-national legislation. Yet the development of employment standards and the social·forces that shape their regulation are connected to broader global economic and political processes. Historically, as referenced in chapter 2, the conventions of the International Labour Organization have provided a normative framework for national governments as they develop employment standards legislation. In the case of the contemporary reforms to Ontario's employment standards examined in chapter 4, the neo-liberal provincial government in power claimed it was introducing flexibility into the employment standards regulatory framework in order to respond to competitive pressures created by processes of economic globalization.

Previous chapters have focused on the regulation of employment standards in Canada, primarily using the case of provincial legislation in Ontario. This chapter moves beyond this localized and state-based focus to examine the regulation of labour standards at the supra-national level, through non-state-based forms of regulation.

GLOBALIZATION AND LABOUR STANDARDS

"Economic globalization" signifies a number of processes that have unfolded within the global economy in recent decades, including financial deregulation associated with the breakdown of the Bretton Woods international monetary system; rapid rates of technological change and technology transfer, particularly in communications and transportation technologies; and the spatial expansion of capitalist relations into regions of Eastern Europe, as well as South East Asia. More specific developments related to these general processes include the geographic fragmentation of systems of production; increases in the size, flow, and speed of foreign direct investment; the spread of forms of wage labour across the globe; the predominance of neoliberal approaches to public policy; and the increasing integration of the transnational capitalist class (Harvey 2000; Mittleman 1996; Panitch 1998). Recent globalization scholarship has integrated transnational and international forms of resistance into this frame, in recognition of the ways in which strategies developed by contemporary social movements are often also transnational or global in scope (Munck 2004; Silver 2003).

While capitalism's need for a "spatial fix" has always been present within the system, the contemporary global political economy has intensified "attempts to shift capitalist production to new spaces within the world economy – sites where means of production, labour, and credit can be mobilized in order to produce more profitability" (McNally 1999, 47–8). And while technological developments and free trade agreements are most often associated with the term globalization, it is increasing levels of foreign direct investment (FDI) and the growth in the power of multinational corporations that lie at the heart of contemporary globalization (McNally 2006). Developments like free trade agreements are part of a deeper process of reducing the constraints on the ability of corporate interests to ensure the free movement of capital. "Flexibility" in the context of globalization thus refers to the capacity for capital to alter the geographic organization of production, for example, through increased levels of foreign direct investment. Trade agreements that simultaneously protect the rights of capital and free up its capacity to increase its levels of FDI construct the new rules for this global economy.

This increased geographic flexibility has occurred through the accelerated relocation of manufacturing production from Northern to Southern economies that began during the early years of the long downturn, a shift that was designed primarily to take advantage of lower labour costs in the South (Lipietz 1987). Despite the imagery of globalization, this investment is not randomly scattered around the globe. Production chains have been organized along regional patterns, in particular in three main trading blocs – the European

Union, the North American Free Trade Area (including Mexico), and the Pacific Rim – rather than being randomly spread throughout the global economy (Mitchie and Grieve Smith 1995).

In the late 1990s, for example, over half of all FDI going into the South was located in only five countries: China, Brazil, Mexico, Singapore, and Indonesia (McNally 2006). Nonetheless, the mobility accorded to capital through vertical disintegration strategies is generally considered to be one of the defining characteristics of economic globalization. These transformations to the international division of labour have led to the expansion of export-processing zones, subcontracting relationships, and the prevalence of sweatshop labour within many nations of the South. Employment conditions and labour practices within these production relationships have been associated with largely unregulated, low-wage, labour-intensive production (Ross 2004; Sassen 1998). Further, these production relations intensify existing patterns of gendered inequality, as workers in these production areas are often women (Mitter 1994). Violent resistance to combat workers' efforts to organize unions has been widely documented (ICFTU 1999). Because of these conditions, globalization is associated with downward pressure on labour standards.

These conditions have also facilitated the push towards employer-oriented labour flexibility within Northern labour markets, conditions described in chapters 3 and 4 (Ladipo and Wilkinson 2002). As increased competitive pressures initiated processes of restructuring, the manufacturing downsizing of the 1980s and 1990s contributed to a broader restructuring of employment within North American labour markets by facilitating the introduction of flexible production strategies in manufacturing employment, thereby paving the way for their introduction into other sectors and occupations. Combined with the cross-border relocation of manufacturing production, service sector growth, particularly in the secondary labour market of the service sector, contributed to the emergence of more precarious forms of employment (Broad 2000). As outlined in chapter 4, neoliberal states also play a key role in creating these conditions of labour flexibility by actively re-regulating labour markets as a means to promote competitiveness and create investment climates favourable to corporate interests.

Furthermore, the ideological impact of globalization on employment relations has been as significant as the material process of restructuring. In other words, part of the power of globalization lies in the ways in which a mythic assumption of absolute capital mobility creates the capacity to alter conditions of work (Bradley et al. 2000). But the mobility of manufacturing production is not as absolute as globalization discourses often suggest, in part because of the large capital costs associated with such mobility (Wood 1998). As well, for many service sector industries, where high levels of employment growth were experienced during the final decades of the twentieth century, the possibilities for mobility are either very limited or non-existent (for example, in accommodations, food services, and cleaning services). Nonetheless, the threat of production relocation has provided an impetus for the restructuring of employment relations within the industrialized labour markets (Wells 1998). In the context of increasing levels of capital mobility and international economic competition, employers have pressured unions into concession bargaining, thereby reducing the wages, benefits, and job security of unionized workers and facilitating the introduction of lean production methods (Moody 1988). This has contributed to the pressures that encourage workers to accept flexible employment relationships (Peck 2001).

These processes are associated with a crisis in the governance of labour standards at both national and global/transnational levels, a crisis that is creating pressures for new methods of labour standards regulation. Patterns of global economic competition, intense labour exploitation in the South, and the growth of insecurity in industrialized labour markets have led to concerns that a "race to the bottom" or a "harmonizing down" of labour standards and working conditions will be a key outcome of globalization processes (Wells 2004).

The "race to the bottom" refers to a downward pressure on labour standards resulting from the competitive environment between jurisdictions created by heightened corporate mobility. Competitive pressure leverages a lowering of labour standards as jurisdictions compete to retain or attract investment. Rather than resulting in a generalized process of global convergence towards low standards, these tendencies are concentrated in sectors and occupations that are the most susceptible to global competition, such as the garment industry (Miller 2004; Ross 2004). Yet while each industry has its own specific characteristics and problems, neoliberal ideology generalizes the pressures of globalization. For example, a generalized picture of globalization framed the Ontario government's call to "modernize" the ESA in the late 1990s. The modernization process led to a lowering of Ontario's employment standards, thereby contributing directly to this broader cycle.

The challenge to regulate labour standards takes place in this context. While downward pressures on labour standards have been the result, there have also been various attempts to construct mechanisms capable of improving labour standards in the global economy, indicating that there may be a growing consensus around the need for new forms of global governance and transnational labour market regulation (Adams 2002; Fung et al. 2001). Thus, globalization can be seen not only in global production chains but also in the efforts to develop international labour standards to counter the tendencies of the race to the bottom. These efforts include strategies to develop international and transnational "core" labour standards and to develop alternatives to governmental regulation through privatized initiatives. The remainder of this chapter examines examples of these strategies in order to better understand their potential.

INTERNATIONAL REGULATION: THE ILO

While labour standards are primarily implemented nationally or sub-nationally, the principles underlying their adoption can be traced to international institutions, specifically to the formation of the International Labour Organization (ILO) in 1919. The ILO was created to develop and promote international labour standards to ensure "humane conditions of labour" as a key condition for the establishment of international peace following World War I (ILO 1994, 5). The founding principles of the organization included the following: (a) that "labour is not a commodity," (b) that "freedom of expression and of association are essential to sustained progress," (c) that "poverty anywhere constitutes a danger to prosperity everywhere," and (d) that "the war against want requires to be carried on with unrelenting vigour within each nation" (22). At its first meeting in 1919, the ILO proclaimed its support for the following specific labour standards: the right of association, a "reasonable living wage"; the eight-hour day or forty-eight-hour week; a weekly rest period of at least twenty-four hours, which should include Sunday wherever possible; the abolition of child labour; and the principle of equal pay for work of equal value for male and female workers (*Labour Gazette*, July 1920).

Following World War II, the ILO issued its landmark statement, the Declaration of Philadelphia, which reaffirmed its commitment to its founding principles and also formally identified specific social policy measures that would facilitate the realization of these principles (Haworth and Hughes 1997). The declaration committed the ILO and its members to promoting full employment and rising living standards; employment in occupations that enable workers to enjoy "the satisfaction of giving the fullest measure of their skill and attainments and make their greatest contribution to the common well-being"; a just distribution of wages, hours, and other benefits, including training opportunities; decent working conditions and a minimum living wage for all employed; recognition of the right of collective bargaining and cooperation between management and labour; and safe and healthy work environments (Lowe 2000, 25). The declaration reflected and promoted the normative context of the Keynesian economic framework of the Cold War global order, which in the capitalist West was characterized by political and economic institutions that extended America's New Deal approach to the international stage.[1]

As concerns over declining labour standards resulting from globalization increased during the 1990s, the ILO sought to take a stronger role in promoting core labour standards (ILO 2000). In 1998, it issued its Declaration on Fundamental Principles and Rights at Work, which defined these fundamental rights to be "(a) freedom of association and the effective recognition of the right to collective bargaining; (b) the elimination of all forms of forced or compulsory labour; (c) the effective abolition of child labour; and (d) the elimination of discrimination in respect of employment and occupation" (ILO 2000, 70). Member states, even if they have not ratified the respective ILO conventions that codify these principles, are expected to respect, promote, and realize these fundamental rights.

These core labour standards form the basis of the emerging international human rights consensus that has developed in response to the negative impacts of economic globalization on working conditions. Canada has ratified conventions that reflect these fundamental rights at work, including conventions on the Freedom of Association and Protection of the Right to Organize, the Abolition of Forced Labour, Discrimination in Employment and Occupation, and the Worst Forms of Child Labour. Building on this framework, the ILO has also sought to promote the broader goal of creating "decent work," which involves creating jobs that provide income and employment security, equity, and human dignity (ILO 2002).

While the ILO attempts to establish international standards, it nonetheless does not attempt to replace existing systems of regulation based at national or sub-national levels. Its primary roles are promotional, educational, and normative, since it has no legal capacity to ensure that standards are implemented. The declaration itself is not a binding resolution (Torobin 2000): its role is to encourage member states to implement standards and to assist them in their adoption and promotion.

The inability of the ILO to compel member states to adopt its conventions and its core labour standards continues to hamper its efforts to improve labour standards either at the international level or within member states. While Canada, for example, is an active member of the organization, it has ratified only a small number of ILO standards, 30 out of over 180 ILO conventions. With respect to the core standards, while Canada has ratified the convention on Freedom of Association and Protection of the Right to Organize (Convention 87), it has not ratified the convention on the right to organize and bargain collectively (Convention 98).

Even if states choose to ratify ILO conventions, their implementation is not guaranteed. For example, an analysis of the right to organize and bargain collectively reveals that that despite an official position of support, there are significant gaps between the policies and their practice within Canada (Adams 2002). There are many examples of Canadian governments taking actions that contradict these ILO principles, such as the termination of unionization rights for agricultural workers in Ontario in 1995, the denial of unionization rights to those in the Ontario Workfare program, and the frequent practice of overriding collective bargaining rights through back-to-work legislation or wage controls in non-crisis situations. While the ILO includes the right to bargain and to strike within the concept of freedom of association, the Supreme Court of Canada has historically rejected this inclusion within the Canadian context.[2] Further, rather than promoting bargaining rights for Canadian workers, Canadian governments simply make access to collective bargaining available to specific employee groups.

The ILO has condemned Canadian governments for these actions. For example, the Ontario government's decision to terminate unionization rights for agricultural workers prompted condemnation from the ILO's Freedom of Association Committee, which called on the government to "take the necessary measures to guarantee the excluded groups' access to machinery and procedures that facilitate collective bargaining, to recertify the organizations representing those workers, and to revalidate any collective agreements they entered into" (quoted in Adams 2002, 125). Canadian governments have generally ignored such recommendations, however.

This refusal of governments to respect and practise the principles of ILO standards undermines the legitimacy of the organization (Reed and Yates 2004), and it points to a larger problem with the ILO. Lacking a sanctions-based system to enforce its standards and relying instead on education, training, advice on legislative reform, and moral persuasion to promote labour standards, the ILO thereby assumes that governments will not like negative attention and will take steps to avoid it. Yet this approach is fundamentally flawed.

For example, Canada is not considered to be in compliance with the convention on freedom of association, because of the exclusion of certain occupational groups from collective bargaining legislation in a number of jurisdictions (Torobin 2000). Further, the Canadian Labour Congress has filed many complaints with the ILO over violations of the right to freedom of association, primarily with respect to the limitation of collective bargaining in the public sector through wage controls and restrictions on the right to strike and back-to-work legislation in both the public and private sectors, and over the definition of essential services. Between 1991 and 2001, the CLC filed thirty-five complaints with the ILO, which amounted to more than 80 percent of all complaints received from G7 countries (Panitch and Swartz 2003, 208–9).[3] Yet, even in the face of ILO condemnation, governments continue to act independently of its standards when they see fit, regardless of the ILO's definitions of fundamental rights.

Recent tendencies towards policies that advocate neoliberal variants of labour flexibility further undermine the ILO's mission to promote the decommodification of labour. Specifically, in its 2004–5 *World Employment Report*, the ILO promotes productivity-based strategies as solutions to poverty (ILO 2005). While the goals of employment creation and poverty reduction are presented through its established "decent work" framework, the report prioritizes the need to connect poverty reduction to productivity-enhancing strategies. It asserts that it is unproductive employment, rather than unemployment or substandard remuneration, that is the problem to be addressed, stating that "a substantial share of poor people in the world is already at work: it is not the absence of economic activity that is the source of their poverty, but the less productive nature of that activity" (1). While rejecting traditional notions of flexibility through deregulation, the report calls for constructing a balance between protection for employees and flexibility for employers, both of which, it claims, will promote productivity. If social protection is connected with employer-oriented flexibility, productivity will increase, thereby addressing the problem of low-wage, insecure employment.

The danger in this framing of the issue is twofold. First, it conceals the structural dynamics in the global economy that produces some of the forms of unstable and low-wage employment – the mobility of capital in the search for low-wage, exploitable labour. In other words, low-wage employment may be produced through the power of capital and the exploitation of labour power, regardless of the productivity levels of the workforce. Second, it begs the question as to whether social protection is a worthwhile goal in and of itself if it cannot be made through the business/productivity case. While the ILO nonetheless maintains its primary concern in establishing decent work and core labour standards, emphasising productivity enhancement through "balanced" flexibility downplays the need for stronger mechanisms of social protection.

In summary, the ILO's core labour standards are a clear articulation of important principles that, if implemented, would constitute a cornerstone in the struggle for better working conditions in the global economy. Further, as a prominent international institution, the ILO provides workers and unions with a yardstick against which to measure standards in their respective national boundaries. The ILO, through the Declaration of Philadelphia, played a key, even if symbolic, role in both defining and promoting a postwar global economic system that considered labour rights a key priority. The 1998 Declaration on Fundamental Rights at Work attempts to construct and promote a new global consensus regarding "core labour standards." Yet, in the context of the political economy of globalization, and the pressures of the race to the bottom, its system of deferential governance does not provide the means to effectively foster and implement such a consensus. And the adoption of a softer neoliberalism in recent policy prescriptions further undermines the ILO's principle that labour is not a commodity.

TRANSNATIONAL REGULATION

The North American Agreement on Labour Cooperation

In addition to international standards, mechanisms have been developed to regulate labour standards at the transnational level, within regional trading areas. One method of regionally based regulation operates through the inclusion of labour standards clauses in transnational trade agreements. Within North America, the North American Free Trade Agreement (NAFTA) includes such an arrangement. The North American Agreement on Labour Cooperation (NAALC), a side agreement to NAFTA, was negotiated in response to public pressure stemming from fears that free trade would lead to an erosion of labour standards within North America. The agreement includes a commitment to the promotion of guiding principles in the area of labour standards, subject to each signatory's domestic laws. The principles include freedom of association and the right to organize; the right to bargain collectively; the right to strike; the prohibition of forced labour; labour protections for children and young persons; minimum employment standards, including minimum wages and overtime pay; elimination of employment discrimination on such grounds as race, religion, age, or sex; equal pay for women and men; prevention of occupational injuries and illnesses; compensation in cases of occupational injuries and illnesses; and providing migrant workers in a party's territory with the same legal protection as the party's nationals in respect of working conditions.[4] The NAALC is administered by the North American Commission for Labor Cooperation.

As with the ILO, there are many weaknesses in the regulation of standards through the NAALC. The NAALC does not attempt to establish common labour standards for the NAFTA countries but instead encourages them to comply with their own existing labour laws. The principles themselves are ineffective, as the Commission for Labor Cooperation has very limited power to ensure compliance. The NAALC contains no enforcement mechanisms for most of the principles. Sanctions can be levied only in cases where there is "a consistent pattern of failure [of a signatory] to enforce its own labour laws" (Carr 1999, 54) and only in cases involving child labour, health and safety, or minimum wages.[5] Further, judgments or sanctions cannot be levied against private companies. In Canada, the agreement is limited because it must be ratified by each province. Almost a decade after its ratification by the federal government, only four provinces (Alberta, Manitoba, Quebec, and Prince Edward Island) had done so (Bensusan 2002).

Other weaknesses in the NAALC's regulatory capacity include a lengthy investigation and sanctions process (over a year for investigations) and the lack of periodic monitoring of standards. As well, the investigations are conducted by National Administrative Offices that are established by each national government, thereby maintaining a relationship of questionable independence (Clarkson 2002). Overall assessments of the results of the NAALC complaints process suggest its capacity to effectively regulate labour standards in the NAFTA region is "virtually nil" (Bensusan 2002, 256; see also Bacon 2004; Rockenbach 2001).

A review of twenty-eight NAALC cases filed between 1994 and March 2004 confirms these findings.[6] During this period, eighteen complaints were laid regarding Mexico, nine regarding the United States, and two regarding Canada. Twenty-one complaints included issues related to unionization (freedom of association, the right to organize, the right to bargain collectively, the right to strike). Three were subsequently withdrawn and five were not accepted for review. Fifteen complaints resulted in ministerial consultations, with follow-up activities including seminars, public forums, studies and reports, and government-to-government meetings. In the case of several complaints regarding the conditions of migrant workers, the U.S. and Mexican governments have issued commitments to work to improve the rights of these workers. As these files indicate, however, the application of real sanctions is clearly an option of last resort.

Overall, while the NAALC attempts to promote a model of regulation at the transnational level, like the ILO it nonetheless defers to the existing system of a nationally based regulation of labour standards. Further, while the principle of the NAALC is to ensure that labour standards do not deteriorate within signatory countries as a result of free trade, the model fails to provide mechanisms to improve or even protect existing standards.

The EU Social Chapter

The Social Chapter of the European Union provides a more comprehensive approach to regionally based regulation of labour standards (Rubery and Grimshaw 2003). The regulation of common labour standards for members of the European Union dates back to the Treaty of Rome of 1957, which established the European Economic Community. As in the case of the NAFTA, there was widespread concern that the development of a free trade zone in Europe (established in 1992) would lead to downward pressure on labour standards. Growing social and political pressure led to the development of the Social Chapter, which provided for the development of EU-wide labour standards. Once the European Council of Ministers has passed a labour standard directive, members of the European Union are bound by the directive and must incorporate it into national labour law. This method of regulation obviously differs from that of the ILO, which, as we have seen, promotes, but does not require, member states to adopt and implement its standards. Further, it provides for a process of negotiation of new labour standards through social dialogue between employer and union representatives and thus differs from the NAALC, which provides for no such process.

A number of key labour standards have been developed and implemented through this structure.[7] They include directives on equal treatment of men and women; equal pay for work of equal value; equal treatment irrespective of racial or ethnic origin; protections against discrimination in employment on the basis of religion, disability, age, or sexual orientation; protection of young people; and the establishment of pregnancy, parental, and family emergency leaves. Key standards go much further than the general principles expressed in the NAALC or in the ILO's core labour standards. For example, the Working Time Directive establishes a 48-hour work week and a minimum standard of 4 weeks paid holiday. The European Works Councils directive requires that companies with over 1,000 employees in the EU and at least 150 employees in two member states establish a works council. The EU has also made progress in developing labour standards to ensure protections for workers in nonstandard employment. The part-time workers directive provides for equal treatment between full- and part-time workers and the fixed-term workers directive provides similar protection with respect to contract and permanent workers. Overall, the EU's approach clearly sets a base that is higher than that established through other, more deferential approaches to standards (e.g., those of the ILO and the NAALC) and provides a means not just to establish a level playing field but also to raise the standards of poorer member states (Clarkson 2002).

Despite the EU's regional approach to labour standards, the Social Chapter nonetheless displays a tendency to continue to rely on the regulation of labour standards at the level of individual nation-states (Rubery and Grimshaw 2003). For example, some key areas of labour standards, notably those concerning wages policies (minimum wage), are considered to be outside the scope of the EU, and are to be left to national systems of regulation. Further, there is no intention to harmonize labour standards across the EU. Instead, the EU standards are designed to constitute a minimum base upon which individual states may build. This leaves open the possibility of differential standards within member states, though the common floor clearly delimits the differential. As well, protections against differential treatment (for example, for women, part-timers, contract workers) are to be based on treatment within a respective nation-state, rather than across the EU. While clear steps have been taken towards a *supra*-national model of regulation, like the ILO and the NAALC, the European model still accords a strong role for nationally based labour standards. Nonetheless, of the three models of *supra*-national regulation, the EU model goes much farther than those of the ILO and the NAALC in binding member states to a clear set of standards. Further, its standards on protection against differential treatment for part-timers and contract workers provide an important basis for those engaged in nonstandard employment.

Overall, forms of "deferential governance" practised by both international and transnational regulatory institutions create a fundamental crisis in the governance of workers' rights in the era of globalization. As Northern states have shifted to neoliberal policy models, they have undermined workers' rights. As Southern states have sought export-oriented development strategies – though often pressured by international financial institutions – they have facilitated the creation of export processing zones (EPZs) as a means to attract investment (Wells 2004). The crisis thus stems from the fact that the trans/international institutions that are designed to provide protection defer regulation and enforcement to these same neoliberal actors. Moreover, the deferral to nation states creates a situation whereby labour standards remain vulnerable to the pressures of the "race to the bottom" created through capacities for corporate mobility.

PRIVATIZED REGULATION:
CORPORATE CODES OF CONDUCT

In response growing pressure from NGOs and labour organizations to address the "race to the bottom" in labour standards, a growing number of major transnational corporations have developed their own codes of conduct to regulate sourcing practices in their transnational production chains. Companies such as Nike, Levi, Wal-Mart, and GAP, for example, have been the targets of anti-sweatshop campaigns undertaken to force them to improve the labour practices in their supplier chains (Cavanagh 1997; Miller 2004; Yanz et al. 1999).

Corporate codes of conduct are written statements of principle or policy that establish voluntary guidelines for the behaviour of private enterprises involved in global chains of production and distribution. The codes are designed as an attempt to construct minimum labour standards for their workforces. They are self-regulatory and do not require government intervention; they apply to specific firms or groups of firms, rather than all citizens or workers within a region or state. Since the mid-1990s, many companies with transnational supply chains have sought to develop codes of conduct as part of broader programs of corporate social responsibility that include "ethical sourcing" practices, as well as commitments to improving environmental sustainability.[8]

As a form of privatized regulation, the scope, content, and practices embodied within corporate codes vary considerably. The stronger examples of codes generally build on the core labour rights of the International Labour Organization, commit suppliers to local minimum labour standards legislation, involve some form of independent auditing, and include engagement with stakeholders such as unions and NGOs. For example, ranking in the Top 5 two years in a row in recent surveys of corporate transparency practices conducted by the Ethical Trading Action Group (ETAG 2005, 2006), GAP claims to adhere to the principle that "all individuals who work in garment factories deserve to be treated with dignity and respect, and are entitled to safe and fair working conditions."[9]

To make these principles concrete, the company has developed its Code of Vendor Conduct, which is based on the core labour standards of the ILO regarding discrimination, forced and child labour, safe and healthy working conditions, and freedom of association, and which requires production factories to comply with local labour laws. The company employs vendor compliance officers to inspect supplier factories and ensure they meet the requirements of the code. Companies that violate the code are faced with the prospect of either termination of the business relationship or the adoption of a corrective action plan. Other stakeholders are brought into this process through GAP's involvement in multi-stakeholder organizations such as the Ethical Trading Initiative and Social Accountability International, both of which bring together corporations, human rights organizations, and unions to develop, implement, and monitor labour standards codes for supply chains.

Of Canadian companies, Mountain Equipment Co-operative (MEC) has been highly ranked for its corporate social responsibility efforts by both *Report on Business* magazine and the Ethical Trading Action Group. In describing its commitment to social responsibility, MEC states that it "prides itself on being a leader in ethical sourcing" and that it works "to improve the human condition in factories."[10] In its code of conduct for suppliers, it sets out prohibitions on forced or child labour, harassment or abuse, and discrimination, while aiming to promote healthy and safe working conditions and recognition of freedom of association rights. It worked with NGOs and civil society groups to develop its code and is continuing to do so in developing further workers' rights initiatives. Other steps to improve "social compliance" include plans for public disclosure of its factory locations, further collaboration with other companies in auditing common suppliers, and developing communications strategies to inform MEC customers of its efforts to improve factory conditions.[11]

Other Canadian companies such as the Hudson's Bay Company (HBC) and Roots have developed similar codes. HBC's Vendor Code of Conduct requires suppliers to adhere to local, regional, and national labour laws, in particular concerning wages, hours of work, and benefits. The code also expects suppliers to abide by core ILO standards regarding child labour, forced labour, freedom of association, and discrimination. HBC uses third-party auditors (Intertek Labtest and Independent Global Compliance Services) to ensure compliance with its code. External auditors are chosen in order to lend greater credibility to the auditing process.[12] They conduct factory inspections, review contracts and payroll documents, and conduct interviews with managers and workers. Similarly, Roots requires all suppliers to sign its Workplace Code of Conduct, a document that outlines its requirement that "all suppliers operate with fairness, decency, and responsibility in all aspects of their business."[13] Like HBC's code, the Workplace Code of Conduct stipulates that suppliers operate in accordance with local labour laws and includes the core labour standards of the ILO. And like HBC, Roots employs third-party auditors to monitor is suppliers.

Private codes are supported by the assumption that if a company is involved in developing and implementing a code, they are more likely to follow it. There are several fundamental weaknesses in this approach to the regulation of labour standards, however (Pearson and Seyfang 2001; Ross 2004; Wells 2007). First, because they are voluntary, if companies choose not to develop a supplier code of conduct, there is no regulatory mechanism to compel them to do so. As well, the codes may be self-monitored, without a central or clear enforcement agency. Thus, even if a code is adopted, violations may persist within the supply chain. Companies may establish their own priorities in terms of which violations are to be addressed, and they may design their own strategies for action in dealing with non-compliant venders, strategies ranging from severance of the relationship to forms of remediation and/or education. The lack of regulatory consistency creates great variation in the overall effectiveness of the voluntary approach.

A second weakness is that there is widespread variation in their content, and codes are generally not as specific or as comprehensive as ILO conventions. They may not include provisions for supplier monitoring or define responsibilities vis-à-vis sub-contractors, although some are starting to. They may not guarantee full disclosure of audits of factories or workplaces. They may create enclaves of protected workers, while excluding others, for example, homeworkers. They may or may not involve interaction with other stakeholders (unions, NGOs) or external auditors. Taking into account the ways in which the corporate bottom line influences the negotiation and implementation of corporate codes of conduct, Robert Ross (2004, 314) summarizes the contradictory nature of the voluntary approach to regulating labour standards, stating that "high standards make for narrow participation; wide participation leads to weak standards or toothless enforcement."

Further, as they are corporate-initiated principles, they may avoid key workers' rights, such as freedom of association and the right to collective bargaining. For example, in a survey of 122 U.S. company codes, while most included health and safety measures and regulations involving child labour, only 12 recognized the right to organize and bargain (Pearson and Seyfang 2001). In Canada, efforts to negotiate a base code of conduct for suppliers to Canadian retailers broke down over opposition from the industry representatives to the inclusion of references to the ILO core labour rights regarding unionization, collective bargaining, and protection from employer retaliation during unionization efforts.[14]

Company codes vary, and some companies have gone much further than others in attempting to monitor and regulate labour standards in their production chain. A report by the Ethical Trading Action Group (ETAG 2005) provides a "transparency report card" on corporate practices oriented towards protecting workers' rights in their supply chains. The report surveyed thirty major apparel companies that sell products in the Canadian market, focusing on the content, application, and transparency of codes of conduct. The report also assessed auditing and reporting practices, as well as the extent to which companies engage with external stakeholders (e.g., NGOs, unions) in the regulation of labour standards. Within the companies surveyed, there were significant differences in company practices in labour standards monitoring and reporting. In particular, large companies that had been targeted by anti-sweatshop campaigns or media exposés showed greater levels of transparency in labour standards regulation. Moving beyond simply developing a code of conduct, corporate practices of industry leaders in this area included third-party factory audits, collaboration with unions and NGOs through multi-stakeholder initiatives, training initiatives for local managers, public reporting of audit findings, and public disclosure of supply chain factory locations.[15] Overall, however, none of the companies are "currently providing sufficient, credible and verifiable information to consumers or investors to allow them to make informed ethical choices" (ETAG 2005, 29).

A key mechanism in promoting transparency through private codes lies in the involvement of stakeholders in the development and monitoring of codes. Including unions and NGOs, for example, may promote new forms of information sharing and cooperation between corporate and non-corporate actors and may enhance the amount of publicly available information about working conditions in supply chains.[16] Involvement of such stakeholders may also improve the integrity of the monitoring and enforcement process (ETAG 2005). In its survey of corporate practices, ETAG reported that companies that engaged with stakeholders tended to score higher in other categories of the survey. Yet less than half of the total companies surveyed provided indication of work with stakeholders, and most did not engage with factory workers in their efforts.

Developing stronger and clearer codes of conduct may also create its own form of competitive pressure. In the spring of 2004, GAP issued a highly detailed report on its labour standards in its supply chain that is credited with being much more transparent and thorough than the standards of most other Canadian retailers. The company committed itself to including the ILO standard on freedom of association in its corporate code. In 2005, it conducted inspections of 2,118 of its 4,438 factories and terminated business relationships with 62 for violations of its code. Labour standards activists expressed hope that the transparency of these practices would pressure competitors to act similarly.[17]

Taking the transparency process one step further, in 2005 Nike publicly disclosed through a company website the names and addresses of factories producing in its supply chain. Since then, two other companies – Levi Strauss and Timberland – have followed suit by publicly disclosing the locations of suppliers.[18] While public disclosure of factory locations in no way ensures compliance with labour standards codes, it is an important step in making production conditions in the global economy visible.

Overall, however, since such codes are voluntary, they remain within the purview of individual companies, which may be motivated by market share, rather than a genuine concern for workers' rights. The codes are largely unenforceable and therefore severely compromised in their capacities to adequately protect workers in the global economy. Activists, NGOs, and labour organizers often view them as public relations exercises (Pearson and Seyfang 2001) or "top down" mechanisms that lack accountability.[19] Efforts to develop multilateral monitoring of codes that bring transnational corporations and NGOs together risk being compromised by corporate influence over the monitoring process (Wells 2004). Finally, the inherent philosophy of corporate codes threatens workers' independent capacity to negotiate the terms of their employment, as those codes may replace the principles of freedom of association with a new form of management self-regulation (Reed and Yates 2004).

Thus, despite efforts to expand content and introduce transparency mechanisms, the privatization of labour standards regulation through corporate codes of conduct is not an effective answer to the problem of the race to the bottom in today's global capitalism.

CONCLUSION

Forms of labour standards regulation that take into account the transnational organization of production are necessary in the contemporary global economy. Yet while there may be a growing consensus regarding the need to establish mechanisms to better regulate labour standards globally, a review of existing models of transnational regulation reveals that there remain many challenges to such a project. International institutions such as the ILO or the NAALC clearly establish normative models but lack the means to effectively implement or enforce them. While corporate codes of conduct may present an image of social responsibility, the voluntary and unilateral nature of most codes compromises their ability to offer meaningful protection for workers' rights. What these strategies lack are effective enforcement and accountability mechanisms, practices that would ensure that broader international labour standards norms are implemented in localized workplace-level contexts. In other words – and like the local labour standards studied in previous chapters – transnational strategies designed to confront the race to the bottom need to be combined with a project of labour market re-regulation that works from the bottom up.

Conclusion

Proponents of neoliberal models of labour flexibility often argue that strong employment standards present a threat to competitiveness in the hyper-competitive global marketplace. "Over-regulation" may contribute to inflexibility, through restrictions on hours of work, or to unemployment, through wage floors that do not reflect market principles. As documented throughout this book, neoliberal policies, practices, and ideologies have played a key role in reshaping the regulation of employment standards in recent times, with the effect of enhancing employer power over workers and intensifying conditions of labour market inequality and insecurity.

Yet, "flexibility" need not simply mean employment practices that create worker insecurity and serve only employer's prerogatives (Clement 2001; Fudge 2001). The term "flexibility" itself can be re-defined to refer to workplace relationships that promote greater capacities to negotiate a balance between work and family responsibilities and that provide options for access to educational and skills upgrading programs. Worker-oriented flexibility through stronger minimum standards may produce workplace relations that prevent the unrestrained exercise of market powers, thereby moderating the inherent inequality between employers and workers (ILO 2002). In this regard, alternative visions of employment standards are needed. While neoliberal forms of labour flexibility that prioritize business interests are predominant, worker-oriented flexibility should not be considered utopian.

Returning to the Canadian-based focus of this book, this chapter argues that a new approach to the regulation of minimum standards is necessary to counter the increased insecurity, vulnerability, and polarization currently experienced by many workers in the Canadian labour market. As discussed in chapter 5, in a global economy transnational regulatory strategies are needed to counter the downward pressure on labour standards produced by globalization processes. Yet transnational strategies must be supported with strong localized mechanisms. Thus, this concluding chapter argues that the process of re-regulating labour standards in today's era of globalization must begin with the development of stronger local standards. Re-regulating labour markets from the bottom up is fundamental to raising the floor for the most vulnerable workers.

REFORMING EMPLOYMENT STANDARDS

Reforming employment standards must begin with substantial reforms to existing legislation. Necessary reforms include expanding legislative coverage, improving key standards in the areas of minimum wages and working time, and improving enforcement practices to ensure employers comply with existing standards.

As illustrated through the discussion of exemptions in chapters 3 and 4, some of the most vulnerable groups of workers are not covered by existing minimum standards legislation. Extending that coverage to those groups is thus central to this project of labour market re-regulation. Expanding coverage should include expanding the definition of "employee," since growing numbers of workers are defined as self-employed and are thus exempt from employment standards legislation. But these workers in fact depend on the sale of their labour for income through what could be termed a dependent contractor relationship (WAC 2007). This is an international condition, as the ILO has documented the increasingly widespread phenomenon of a lack of legislative protection for those who are defined as self-employed but who could effectively be considered dependent workers (Saunders 2003). Including these workers within the scope of legislated standards could constitute a significant first step in improving the conditions of their work.

Expanding the scope of employment standards legislation should also include provisions for joint liability in the case of outsourced services, since many workers in the informal economy face the significant problem of a lack of employer accountability for employment standards violations. Currently, because companies that contract out work are not considered to be employers of these workers, they are able to avoid responsibility for any employment standards violations committed by the contractor. This problem is particularly prevalent in the garment industry, where violations by contractors, who often run small, independent, and temporary operations, are frequent.[1] The transitory nature of contracting operations, combined with the lack of responsibility of the source company, means that garment workers, especially homeworkers, are particularly vulnerable to employment standards violations (Ng et al. 1999).[2] A legislative provision for joint responsibility between employers would ensure that companies that have contracted out production and services remain responsible for the working conditions of the workers performing those activities.

Across the provinces, real minimum wages (adjusted for inflation) declined between the late 1970s and 1990 and have since remained constant or only slightly increased (Murray and Mackenzie 2007). As current minimum wage levels are insufficient to provide an income above the poverty line for either single workers or those with dependents in the largest Canadian cities (Saunders 2003), redefining the *minimum* wage as a *living* wage is also key to employment standards reform. A single individual working full-time seeking to generate an income above the poverty line would need to earn *at least* ten dollars per hour (2005 dollars, adjusted for inflation).[3] Yet, close to one in five Canadian workers earns less than this amount. In 2002, of those earning less than ten dollars per hour, one-third were the sole income earners in their families, almost half were over thirty-five, and one-third had a postsecondary degree or diploma.[4] Campaigns to increase the minimum wage to ten dollars per hour and to index future increases to inflation have been launched in light of the growing numbers of working poor.[5]

The relationship between minimum wage increases and employment rates is a key point of dispute in policy discussions regarding the need for a higher minimum wage. Critics of minimum wage increases tend to argue that, as with overall improvements to labour standards, increasing minimum wages will produce job loss (OECD 1998). Yet reviews of the research literature indicate that there is insufficient evidence to demonstrate that minimum wage increases negatively affect employment rates (Saunders 2003). A noted study of minimum wage increases in the United States found that they had no significant impact on employment (Card and Krueger 1995). Similarly, a study in four Canadian provinces found that changes in the minimum wage (positive and negative) produced only minor corresponding shifts in employment levels (negative and positive) (Goldberg and Green 1999). Comparative international research by the OECD (1998) found similar results. Rather than minimum wage increases, employment rates are much more directly affected by large-scale changes in the economy, such as recessions and economic growth (Murray and Mackenzie 2007). And of the positive effects, increasing the minimum wage directly increases the incomes of low-paid workers and thus plays an important role in helping to alleviate both poverty and income polarization.

Working time reduction and increased time sovereignty have been identified as key strategies to address employment insecurity, labour market inequality, and a lack of work-life balance (Beck 2000, 6–7). Working time is a central concern in today's labour market, owing to growing tendencies towards work-life conflict (Duxbury et al. 2003). In recent years, many unions and community groups have argued for reduced work time in order to reduce overwork and promote job creation, particularly in light of employment standards that facilitate further increases to daily and weekly hours of work.[6] In the mid-1990s, the Canadian Labour Congress played an active role in the development of the *Report of the Advisory Group on Working Time and the Distribution of Work,* which called for a standard forty-hour workweek and annual limits on overtime hours. The model of the thirty-five-hour workweek in France and Italy and the generally shorter work time in Western Europe has been presented by some unions as an alternative to the North American model of longer hours of work and a polarization in the distribution in work time (CAW 2000; White 2002).

Creating a more equal distribution of paid and unpaid working time has also been identified as a necessary component of broader gender equality strategies (Mutari and Figart 2000; Rubery et al. 1998). A key focus of proponents of reduced work time is the need to reduce hours in order to increase the ability of workers to balance work and family life, which could, it is hoped, reduce the pressures created through forms of work-life conflict, particularly those that result from caring responsibilities. Approaching working time from the perspective of gender equity requires moving beyond strategies to re-regulate daily or weekly hours of work, however. It also includes, for example, strategies to provide greater access to time off for family care. Existing maternity and paternity leave programs could be further supplemented through extended parental leave, compassionate leave, bereavement leave, and child and elder care leave, as well as supplementary income top-ups for those on maternity leave. In addition, shorter-term forms of family/emergency leave may assist employees with meeting daily and emergency family responsibilities. Given the continued problems of stress, overwork, hours polarization, and gendered inequalities associated with social reproduction, a broad approach to re-regulating work time would provide a much-needed improvement to existing minimum standards.

As demonstrated in chapters 3 and 4, a lack of compliance with existing legislated standards plays a key role in creating and sustaining conditions of labour market vulnerability. Thus, in addition to expanding legislative coverage and improving key standards in the areas of minimum wages and working time, improving compliance with existing standards is essential. There are many recommendations for improving compliance rates. They include increasing fines for violations, increasing proactive inspections and audits of recurring offenders, which itself would require increasing the number of field investigators, and requiring employers to pay the costs of an investigation that detects an employment standards violation (Adams 1987; Fudge 1991; Ng et al. 1999; WAC 2007).[7]

RE-REGULATING THE LABOUR MARKET

The above examples illustrate proposals that could improve existing standards and that could address some of the conditions of labour market vulnerability. Combined, these proposals provide an alternative version of employment standards that is clearly oriented towards addressing key dimensions of labour market insecurity and inequality. Improvements to specific standards will not be sufficient to adequately address the structural transformations that have reshaped labour markets over the past several decades, however, as they remain rooted in a system of labour market regulation built upon the norm of the standard employment relationship. A much more thorough process of labour market re-regulation may be required to reflect the proliferation of nonstandard employment relationships and labour market precariousness. The principles of such a process could include expanding the scope of regulatory strategies by redefining the contract of employment, addressing disparities between those in standard and nonstandard employment, more fully incorporating equity concerns into regulatory strategies, and developing labour laws that improve access to collective representation (Fudge and Vosko 2001b; Vallee 2005).

Employment rights such as statutory employment standards typically apply only to those in traditional employment relationships. However, many types of work that could be conceived of as employment fall outside this legal category. As discussed, the growth in nonstandard forms of employment, particularly in own-account self-employment, leaves a sizeable percentage of the workforce outside the coverage of employment standards laws. Labour market policies and labour laws need to take these workers into account through a new type of employment contract that includes temporary workers, independent contractors, and others who are currently defined as outside the traditional employment contract. In other words, the rise of nonstandard employment creates the need to develop a model of labour market regulation that is not premised on the traditional legal employment contract. Such a model should extend legislative protections to all who depend on the sale of their labour power for income, including those in so-called non-traditional employment relationships.[8]

A second strategy is to legislate standards that apply equally to workers in either standard or nonstandard employment relationships. Currently, there is a great deal of inequality between those who are in SERs and those who are in NSERs in terms of the application of legislative standards and access to non-statutory benefits. Some employment standards come into effect only after the worker has been employed for a minimum period, which means that workers in a series of short-term employment relationships with different employers may lack access to the full range of statutory minimum standards. For example, they often do not have full access to non-statutory benefits plans. A study by Saunders (2003) revealed that only 17 percent of part-time workers and 14 percent of temporary workers were covered by extended medical, dental, life, and disability insurance plans, as compared to 58 percent of full-time workers and 57 percent of permanent workers. A strategy for addressing such disparities could include statutory requirements that provide nonstandard workers with full access to the benefits accorded to full-time workers, as well as mechanisms to allow workers on short-term contracts to carry benefits with them through different contracts.

A more thorough process of labour market regulation would need to more directly incorporate equity into new regulatory strategies. Indeed, addressing equity is at the heart of the process of re-regulation outlined in this chapter. The above proposals are designed to address many of the gendered and racialized inequities that are currently created through forms of precarious employment, for example by reducing working time to promote an increased work-life balance and by eliminating disparities between the treatment of those in nonstandard forms of employment and those in full-time, full-year employment. As discussed, to fully address these concerns it is necessary to construct a new regulatory model, not based on the norms of the standard employment relationship, but on a basis that will capture the multiplicity of employment experiences of the contemporary labour market. Further, to truly address gender equity, this project must also incorporate social reproduction into its regulatory framework, for example, by promoting greater access to time away from work, as well as more equitable distributions of paid working time. Re-regulating employment standards is far from all that is required. It is, however, an important first step in that process.

Finally, as discussed in chapter 3, legislated standards are often not enforceable without strong union representation: employment standards provide

> a form of regulation that actually doesn't work unless there is a union there. The problem with regulations is that, suppose there are regulations about breaks, management doesn't follow them. The point is what is a worker going to do about it? They complain and they will get fired. So the balance of forces at the local level are such that there is no enforcement mechanism … The point about this kind of enforcement mechanism is that it actually depends on an enforcement mechanism locally. Given the balance of class forces, it doesn't exist unless there is a union.[9]

The goal of securing strong and effective legislated standards is thus directly connected to efforts to expand unionization into areas of precarious employment. Current labour laws are biased against workers in small workplaces and in nonstandard employment. In order to facilitate the unionization of many workers currently reliant on employment standards legislation, such as those in small workplaces and part-time and temporary workers, changes to existing labour relations legislation are required. Labour law reforms that allow for broader-based bargaining structures – the extension of the benefits of a collective agreement to all workers within a sector, sub-sector, geographic region, or chain of production – could overcome some of the obstacles to union representation experienced by many workers who are most reliant on legislated standards and who are most vulnerable to employer violations (Shields and Russell 1994; Yanz et al. 1999).[10] Currently, such bargaining arrangements are possible, but only subject to employer agreement.[11] The rise of nonstandard employment relationships creates the need for a new system of labour law that facilitates unionization amongst a wider range of employment categories.

While it is non-unionized workers who are most reliant on employment standards, it is also in the interest of the labour movement to secure strong legislation. As employment standards set the floor upon which collective agreements are negotiated, organized labour must challenge legislative initiatives that lower that floor. The impact on collective agreements may not be immediate; however, over the long term, declining employment standards threaten standards within collective agreements. Minimum standards should be regarded not as a secondary form of protection but as a central component in a broad project of labour market re-regulation that is in the interests of both unionized and non-unionized workers.

ORGANIZING FOR BETTER STANDARDS

The momentum to create such a project of labour market re-regulation will not materialize on its own, but, as with early minimum standards legislation, will emerge through the efforts of labour and social movements to challenge the exploitative working conditions of contemporary capitalism. Constructing alternatives to the conditions of insecurity and the race to the bottom has become a key concern for contemporary labour and social movements. Campaigns to pressure for stronger labour standards have taken a range of forms and include union organizing in sectors of the labour market with low union density, community coalitions using diverse and innovative campaign strategies, and the formation of cross-border solidarity networks to combat the effects of globalization. While the first half of this chapter focused on the need for labour market regulatory reforms, this final section looks at examples of these labour and social movement strategies, focusing on both local and transnational efforts.

The conditions of work specific to the private service sector – where the largest proportion of non-unionized workers in the Canadian labour market, and consequently those who are most reliant on employment standards legislation, may be found – pose specific obstacles for organizing campaigns. It is difficult to organize workers in service workplaces, owing to their small size. Once organized, these sites do not provide a dues base comparable to large manufacturing plants, as the jobs are generally low-wage and part-time, thereby placing a strain on union resources. These jobs are often nonstandard, presenting further challenges for organizing in the service sector, as union contracts have traditionally been based on the gendered norms of the standard employment relationship (Zeitinoglu and Muteshi 2000). The fear of job loss associated with precarious employment makes organizing all the more difficult. Moreover, the lack of attachment to a single workplace that is common amongst contract workers reduces or eliminates possibilities for worksite-based organizing. In this employment context, the labour movement needs "new and creative approaches to organizing and bargaining," in order to provide effective representation for nonstandard workers (duRivage et al. 1998, 265; see also Cobble and Vosko 2000).

As the majority of workers in nonstandard and precarious forms of work are women, members of racialized groups, and recent immigrants, workers who have not generally had high rates of union representation in the Canadian labour market, unions also face the need to address equity concerns, both within the workplace and within the labour movement itself (CLC 1997a, 1997b). Organizing a racialized, feminized working class is paramount not only to combating the race to the bottom by organizing workers in non-unionized, precarious forms of employment but also to revitalizing labour movements in the North, movements that have historically been primarily institutions of white, male workers.

Models of "community unionism" provide an example of such potential. These models rely on strategies of community-based organizing, which involves unions organizing in coalition with community organizations directly in workers' communities (Leah 1999). These strategies include campaigns to organize workers previously considered unorganizable, most often workers engaged in forms of precarious employment (Needleman 1998). This form of organizing has brought unions into community-based campaigns designed to organize women workers and recent immigrants, who may be employed in sweatshop or under-regulated conditions. The community-based model has been particularly important where workplace organizing is difficult or impossible or where workers may not be eligible for traditional union representation. Community-based organizing often involves the use of drop-in community centres, which provide services to workers, as well as a collective space for education, organizing, and socializing (Ness 1998).

Canadian organizations such as the Homeworkers' Association of UNITE and INTERCEDE provide examples of the model of community unionism. These organizations have formed to provide collective associations for new immigrant workers engaged in forms of employment where unionization is prohibited by provincial labour laws. Both organizations assist their members with employment standards complaints, and both have been involved in political campaigns to improve legislated standards for low-wage immigrant workers.

The Homeworkers Association (HWA), which formed in 1992 and consists of immigrant women who sew garments from their own homes, represents approximately five thousand homeworkers in the Toronto area. It was formed out of the efforts of the International Ladies Garment Workers Union to organize homeworkers in the early 1990s (Leah 1999). The organization is connected to UNITE through its Associate Membership Program. The objectives are to provide education about workers' rights to homeworkers, to provide homeworkers with assistance in enforcing those rights, including legal assistance and social services, and generally to "be a vehicle through which homeworkers come together to develop their own capacity to respond to issues, share strategies and to find collective solutions."[12] INTERCEDE for the Rights of Domestic Workers, Caregivers, and Newcomers, which formed in 1979, represents migrant and immigrant women who work as domestic workers and caregivers across Canada (Arat-Koç 2001).

Neither the HWA nor INTERCEDE is a union, and therefore neither is directly involved in negotiating wages and working conditions for its members. As members must rely on legislated standards, both organizations provide assistance in the event of employment standards violations. Owing to the difficulties experienced by workers with the complaints process, the HWA has opted to deal directly with employers to address employment standards complaints. Association staff contact employers directly to pressure for settlements before filing complaints with the MOL. Because UNITE is a well-recognized union, the affiliation with UNITE has sometimes assisted HWA staff in securing payments from employers without an intervention from the MOL.[13]

As collective organizations, both the HWA and INTERCEDE reduce the individualistic tendencies of the employment standards complaints process and are able to provide some assistance to the worker as the complaints process is carried out (Yalnizyan 1993). As the HWA's members are recent immigrants, the association also provides social activities to reduce the isolation of homework, as well as ESL classes. Similarly, as the women in the Live-In Caregiver Program are not Canadian citizens, INTERCEDE assists them with settlement services. Both organizations are also involved in broader political campaigns. INTERCEDE successfully pressured the Ontario government to include domestic workers under ESA minimum wage and overtime provisions,[14] while the HWA works on anti-sweatshop campaigns through UNITE. Following the principles of community unionism, both use organizing strategies that are designed to reach recent immigrant women workers in their own communities and that are based on coalition work with other community organizations.

Coalition-based strategies between labour and social movements have also been adopted to push for better international labour standards as concerns over their erosion have become a key issue for movements in both the North and the South. The coalition-based strategy is perhaps most evident in the anti-sweatshop campaigns that began in the 1990s and that have attempted to challenge labour and human rights abuses in transnational production chains by using public awareness tactics in the North to support labour organizing in the South (Featherstone 2002; Ross 1997; Ross 2006). Using a combination of strategies targeting Northern consumers and governments, including legislative tactics and consumer boycotts, these campaigns have sought to support Southern workers' efforts to organize and engage in collective bargaining and to thereby transform sweatshop labour conditions. Based on the assumption that because production is transnational, labour organizing must be as well, these initiatives bring together Northern and Southern labour and social justice organizations.

In Canada, labour organizations such as UNITE, the United Steelworkers, and the Canadian Labour Congress have participated in coalition-based efforts through the Maquila Solidarity Network and the Ethical Trading Action Group (ETAG) in order to raise awareness about sweatshop labour, to promote codes of conduct for Canadian businesses, and to support unionization and collective bargaining efforts of workers in the South who are facing employer repression.[15] Specific strategies include organizing conferences and panel discussions involving activists from Mexico and Central America, developing education/action materials, conducting "no sweat" fashion shows, pressuring governments lobbying to improve local labour standards, and supporting campaigns designed to pressure Canadian universities to adopt codes of conduct for retail and purchasing practices.[16]

These illustrate of some of the creative ways in which, in the context of globalization, transnational connections can be established between nationally and locally based movements. Transnational linkages between workers, unions, and human rights organizations are forged through efforts to improve labour standards and working conditions at local and international levels. By supporting and promoting labour rights activism at local levels, in Toronto, Canada, and in workplaces in Mexico, El Salvador, and Bangladesh, and by simultaneously highlighting the connections between these struggles and transnational production processes, these campaigns bridge the distance between the local and the global in the contemporary global economy and may create the social pressure needed to build momentum towards stronger employment standards and alternatives to the neoliberal model of labour flexibility.

RE-REGULATING FROM THE BOTTOM UP

The challenge to construct a viable alternative is multidimensional. In the era of globalization, transnational models of regulation are needed to combat the competitive pressure that corporations can exert between nation-states. While recognizing that localized conditions of employment such as wage rates and hours of work will vary, ensuring a level playing field across national borders – at least in terms of procedural rights such as freedom of association and substantive rights such as a living wage – will reduce the potential for downward pressure on labour standards. International and supra-national institutions may also provide the process of re-regulation both with direction – through regulations for equal treatment for part-time workers in the EU – and with normative support, as is the case with the ILO. A key challenge for models of international regulation rests with developing mechanisms to ensure that policy principles are effectively implemented and enforced at localized levels.

While transnational regulatory mechanisms are needed, so too are meaningful national and sub-national models of regulation, such as those based on principles outlined in the first half of this chapter. Effective localized implementation and enforcement of strong employment standards are keys to constructing the base for a broader regulatory regime that provides meaningful protection for workers. This process – that of re-regulating the labour market from the bottom up – defines a process of raising the floor for the most vulnerable workers. It is a project of labour market reform that attempts to begin to address some of the harshest inequalities engendered through the organization of employment in today's global economy. And it is a process that hinges on the formation of independent workers' organizations to develop, promote, and enforce labour and employment standards, as legislative and policy reforms cannot be viewed as a substitute for labour organizing. As this book has emphasized, workers have long been engaged in struggles with employers and governments to improve employment standards. In light of continued and growing concerns over labour market vulnerability and insecurity, efforts to secure better employment standards constitute a cornerstone in the continuing struggles over the organization of work.

APPENDICES

Research Methodology

Archival records were obtained from the Archives of Ontario's Ontario Ministry of Labour Record Groups. These records included materials produced by government departments and officials, women's and labour organizations, and employer associations. Labour movement materials consisted primarily, but not exclusively, of records of the Ontario Federation of Labour (OFL). Records of some individual unions and other labour organizations were used where possible. Records from women's organizations included the Business and Professional Women's Club and the Ontario Committee on the Status of Women. Employer records included those of the Canadian Manufacturers' Association (CMA) and the Ontario Chamber of Commerce.

These various records were used to construct an analysis of the development of employment standards legislation in Ontario and to examine the influence of organizations external to the state on the policy development process. While the archival records extended back to the 1930s, the files that began in the 1960s, and particularly those that covered the period following the enactment of the ESA, were much more complete than the pre-1960 records. Articles from the *Labour Gazette*, a publication of the federal government, were used to construct a more complete analysis of early minimum standards legislation. The *Gazette* provided regular reports on developments in federal and provincial labour legislation, the activities of business and labour organizations, and general reports on working conditions. Articles covering the period from 1901 to 1970 were used to supplement the archival records.

Contemporary government documents provided the basis for an analysis of employment standards policies in the contemporary context. Government of Ontario documents included the reports of the *Task Force on Hours of*

Work and Overtime (Ontario 1987), as well as discussion papers, fact sheets, and business plans from the Progressive Conservative government that took office in 1995. These documents outlined employment standards policies and policy changes. Annual reports of the Employment Practices Branch of the Ontario Ministry of Labour from the early 1980s to 2006 provided statistical details of the branch's administrative and enforcement activities, as well as data on employment standards violations. Quantitative labour market data compiled by Statistics Canada were used to develop a statistical profile of the contemporary Canadian labour market. These data were used in conjunction with secondary sources to outline patterns of labour market change over the past three decades and to provide the basis for an analysis of the relationship between changes to the employment standards and the structure of the labour market.

Because the documents discussed above were either produced or collected by state agencies and/or officials, two other sources of data were used to gain a perspective on employment standards from outside the state. First, documents obtained directly from labour, women's, business, and community organizations illustrated the views of these various actors on contemporary employment standards policies. Of particular importance were submissions to the Ontario Ministry of Labour during the consultations process prior to the contemporary employment standards reforms in the late 1990s.[1] These submissions formed the basis of an analysis of the positions of labour, community, women's, and business organizations.

Finally, the document-based analysis was supplemented with key informant interviews, which were conducted between August 2001 and May 2004, and during June and July 2007. Interviews were conducted with representatives from labour organizations (provincial, national, and international); representatives from community organizations engaged in employment standards reform; community legal workers who provide assistance to, and work with, non-unionized workers who experience employment standards violations; officials from the Ontario Ministry of Labour; representatives from non-governmental organizations involved in promoting international labour standards; and representatives from corporations engaged in corporate social responsibility programs.[2]

NOTES

1 Selected organizations included the African Canadian Legal Clinic,
   the Canadian Auto Workers, the Canadian Federation of
   Independent Business, the Canadian Union of Public Employees,

the Employment Standards Work Group, INTERCEDE, the National Action Committee on the Status of Women, the Ontario Chamber of Commerce, the Ontario Federation of Labour, the Retail Council of Canada, UNITE, and the United Steelworkers of America.

2 Interviews are referenced in endnotes where appropriate. Interviews are coded as follows: ER – representatives from non-unionized employee organizations; CL – community legal workers; U – union representatives; G – representatives from the Ontario Ministry of Labour; NGO – representatives from NGOs engaged in international labour standards work; CSR – corporate representatives.

Developments in Ontario Minimum Standards Legislation

1884 Factories Act. Hours of work and safety standards for women and children; sixty-hour work week introduced.

1920 Minimum Wage Act. Board established to determine minimum wages, hours, and working conditions for women and youth.

1935 Industrial Standards Act. Process established to determine minimum wages and standards within industries.

1936 Government Contracts Hours and Wages Act. Regulation of wages and hours of work for employees in public works.

1944 Hours of Work and Vacations with Pay Act. Eight-hour day, forty-eight-hour week maximums; coverage extended to men; vacations with pay (replaces Factories, Shops and Office Buildings Act).

1951 Fair Remuneration to Female Employees Act. Wage discrimination on bases of sex prohibited (equal pay for equal work).

1963 Minimum wage amendments. Common minimum wage for male and female workers phased in.

1968 Employment Standards Act. Consolidated legislation on hours of work, minimum wages, and vacations; provides overtime pay.

1975 ESA. Overtime threshold reduced from forty-eight to forty-four hours.

1981 Coverage extended to domestic workers under the ESA.

1987 ESA amended to include severance and termination standards.

1991 Employee Wage Protection Program introduced.

1995 Employee Wage Protection Program phased out; minimum wage frozen at $6.85.

1996 Bill 49. Privatization of ESA collections; reduced time to file complaints.

2000 Bill 147 amendments; see table 5 chapter 4.

Sources: Brennan (2000); Klee (2000); Quintal (2000); Ursel (1992).

Developments in Federal Minimum Standards Legislation

1900 Department of Labour established; House of Commons Policy on Fair Wages.

1906 Lord's Day Act.

1919 International Labour Organization established; ILO Convention 1: eight-hour day and forty-eight-hour week supported by Canada, (ratified in 1935).

1930 Fair Wages and Eight-Hour Day Act. For workers in the federal jurisdiction.

1935 Fair Wages and Hours of Labour Act. Eight-hour day and forty-four-hour week.

1956 Female Employees Equal Pay Act. Equal pay for equal work for employees under federal jurisdiction.

1958 Vacations with Pay Act. For workers under federal jurisdiction.

1965 Canada Labour (Standards) Code. Minimum standards for hours of work (8/40), wages, annual vacations with pay, and statutory holidays with pay for workers in the federal jurisdiction; applied to men and women.

1966 Canada Labour (Safety) Code. Codified laws and regulations regarding safety standards for workers in the federal jurisdiction.

1967 Canada Labour Code. Consolidated minimum standards and safety legislation.

1994 North American Agreement on Labour Cooperation. Side agreement to North American Free Trade Agreement.

Sources: Brennan (2000); HRDC (2000); Ursel (1992).

APPENDIX FOUR

Table A1
ESA Coverage and Exemptions, 2001

Occupational Category	Minimum Wage	Hours of Work	Overtime Pay	Paid Public Holidays	Vacation with Pay	Pregnancy, Parental, Emergency Leave	Termination Notice
Ambulance drivers, helpers, and attendants	C	C	N	C	C	C	C
Construction employees (on-site)	C	N	S	S	C	C	N
Continuous operation employees (e.g., oil refineries, steel works, breweries)	C	C	C	S	C	C	C
Crown employees	N	N	N	N	N	C	C
Domestic workers employed by a householder	S	C	C	C	C	C	C
Drivers of highway transport trucks	C	C	S	C	C	C	C
Embalmers and funeral directors	C	N	C	C	C	C	C
Farm employees (directly employed in primary production of eggs, milk, grain, seeds, fruit, vegetables, etc.)	N	N	N	N	N	C	C
"Near farming" (workers directly employed in growing mushrooms, flowers, trees, or shrubs for sale, etc.)	C	N	N	N	C	C	C
Firefighters	C	N	N	N	C	C	C
Fishers (commercial)	N	N	N	N	N	C	C
Harvesters of fruit, vegetables, tobacco	S	C	C	S	S	C	C
Homemakers (employed by third party)	S	N	N	C	C	C	C
Homeworkers	S	C	C	C	C	C	C

Table A1 (continued)

Occupational Category	Minimum Wage	Hours of Work	Overtime Pay	Paid Public Holidays	Vacation with Pay	Pregnancy, Parental, Emergency Leave	Termination Notice
Hospital employees	C	C	C	S	C	C	C
Hotel, motel, tourist resort, restaurant, or tavern employees (not seasonal)	C	C	C	S	C	C	C
Information technology professionals	C	N	N	C	C	C	C
Landscape gardeners	C	N	N	N	C	C	C
Liquor servers	S	C	S	S	C	C	C
Managerial and supervisory employees	C	N	N	C	C	C	C
Registered real estate salespersons	N	N	N	N	N	C	C
Residential care workers	S	N	N	C	C	C	C
Salespersons – commission	N	N	N	N	N	C	C
Students under 18	S	C	C	C	C	C	C
Superintendents, janitors, and caretakers who reside in building	N	N	N	N	C	C	C
Taxicab drivers	C	C	C	C	C	C	C

Source: Ontario (2001a).

Note: C = full coverage; N = not covered; S = special regulations. This table does not provide complete list of exemptions. For the complete list of full and partial exemptions, see *Regulations Made under the Employment Standards Act, 2000*, Exemptions, Special Rules and Establishment of Minimum Wage – O.Reg. 285/01 – O.Reg. 285/01, www.gov. on.ca/LAB/esa/esa_e/reg_e_4.htm.

APPENDIX FIVE

Table A2
Employment Standards in Canada, 2006

Jurisdiction	Maximum Hours	Minimum Wage ($)[1] & Effective Date	Annual Paid Vacation (Weeks)	Paid Holidays (Days)	Maternity/Parental Leave[2] (Weeks)
Federal (Canada Labour Code)[3]	48/week	–	2; 3 after 6 years	9	17/37
Alberta	12/day	7.00; 1/09/2005	2; 3 after 5 years	9	15/37
British Columbia	NA[4]	8.00; 1/11/2001	2; 3 after 5 years	9	17/37
Manitoba	NA	8.00; 1/04/2007	2; 3 after 5 years	7	17/37
New Brunswick	NA	7.25; 1/07/2007	2; 3 after 8 years	6	17/37
Newfoundland and Labrador	14/day	7.00; 1/01/2007	2; 3 after 15 years	5	17/35
North West Territories and Nunavut	10/day; 60/week	7.00; 1/04/2001	2; 3 after 6 years	10	17/37
Nova Scotia	NA	7.60; 1/05/2007	2; 3 after 8 years	5	17/52
Ontario	8/day; 48/week[5]	8.00; 1/02/2007	2	8	17/37
Prince Edward Island	NA	7.50; 1/04/2007	2	5	17/35
Quebec	NA	8.00; 1/05/2007	2; 3 after 5 years	8	18/52
Saskatchewan	44/week	7.95; 1/03/2007	3; 4 after 10 years	9	18/37
Yukon	NA	8.37; 1/04/2007	2	9	17/37

Source: Human Resources and Social Development Canada, http://www.hrsdc.gc.ca/en/lp/spila/clli/eslc/01Employment_Standards_Legislation_in_Canada.shtml. Accessed June 2007.

[1] Rates provided are for adult workers. Some provinces and territories have different rates for young workers and for specific occupations.

[2] All jurisdictions also allow for adoption leave of equivalent duration to parental leave. The exceptions are Newfoundland, Prince Edward Island, and Saskatchewan, which allow for 52 weeks of adoption leave.

[3] The minimum wage rate for workers under federal jurisdiction is the adult minimum rate of the province or territory within which work is performed.

[4] No maximum. However, an employer must ensure that employees working split shifts complete their shift within 12 hours of starting work. Also, an employer "must not require or allow an employee to work excessive hours or hours detrimental to the employee's health and safety.

[5] Employers and employees may negotiate agreements whereby the work week may be extended to 60 hours.

Notes

INTRODUCTION

1 For a general discussion of concerns related to job quality, see Lowe (2007). Lowe's survey of job quality finds that recent economic growth in Canada has not translated into improvements in workers' experiences with job quality. Of particular concern is growth in the numbers of people having either short or long weekly work hours and growing inequalities in earned family income. A survey by Duxbury and Higgins (2001) on work-life balance documents increased problems owing to increasing role overload, work-family conflicts, and job stress.

2 For recent reports of income inequality and economic insecurity see Campaign 2000 (2008), CLC (2002), Chaykowski (2005), and Yalnizyan (2007).

3 For example, see CLC (2005), ESWG (1996), Fudge et al. (2002), Saunders (2003), Vallee (2005), and WAC (2007).

CHAPTER ONE

1 Further, assessments of the U.S. model in comparison with Western European labour markets indicate that some highly regulated labour markets (for example, Denmark) outperformed the United States in the late 1990s (Jackson et al. 2000; Stanford 2000).

2 See Murray et al. (2000) for a discussion of the concept of re-regulation.

3 This analysis was influential in shaping the assumptions of regulation theory, which posited that the Keynesian welfare state was a central

component in the Fordist system of accumulation during the
post–World War II period in the advanced capitalist economies.
See Lipietz (1987), Jessop (1992), and Peck (1996) for a discussion
of this framework.

4 The commodification of labour power is a condition specific to
capitalist societies, whereby workers are required to sell their labour
power within a labour market in order to secure the means of survival.
The commodification of labour power creates a situation of competition between workers, a lack of social power vis-à-vis the market, a lack
of control over the conditions of employment, and little capacity to
act collectively. See Esping-Andersen (1990), chapters 1 and 2. But
while labour power is commodified, it is unique as a commodity form:
"[workers] must survive and reproduce themselves and the society
they live in" (37). Thus, some form of de-commodification is
necessary in order to maintain social reproduction.

5 "De-commodification," according to Esping-Andersen (1990), does
not denote the complete elimination of the commodity status of
labour power. Rather, it "refers to the degree to which individuals, or
families, can uphold a socially acceptable standard of living
independently of market participation" (37).

6 Burawoy also argues that workers engage in "games" – "informal rules
and practices aimed at creating space and time, controlling earnings,
and making work more interesting" – on the shopfloor, thus achieving some freedom within the larger structural constraints of management control (Thompson 1989:160). The significance of the games
is that they represent a shift from coercive to consensual shopfloor
relations in that "participation in games has the effect of concealing
relations of production while coordinating the interests of workers
and management" (Burawoy 1985, 38). Insofar as these games do
not challenge the larger constraints of the capitalist relations, but
make the labour process more "bearable," they reproduce workers'
consent. The widespread practice of such games is also a part of
Burawoy's concept of "hegemonic regime."

7 The Anti-Inflation Program applied to federal and Crown
corporation employees, some provincial public sector workers, workers in large private sector firms, and professionals. The "six-and-five"
program limited the wage increases of federal government employees
to 6 percent in 1982 and 5 percent in 1983. The 1991 federal
budget implemented further pay restraints on federal employees.
See McBride and Shields (1997).

8 The Ontario Social Contract froze the wages of public sector workers in Ontario from 1993 to 1996. See Panitch and Schwartz (2003) and Russell (1997).

9 The changing orientation in public policy also initiated a shift in the employment practices of the state. Following the private sector, public sector workplaces have been restructured along the lines of flexible models and lean methods, producing work intensification and employment insecurity for public sector workers (Armstrong and Armstrong 1996; Shields and Evans 1998). In the context of neoliberal restructuring, the state has contributed to trends of gendered labour market polarization as public sector restructuring has eroded the primary source of stable employment for women (Sears 1999).

10 This comment builds upon Hyman's (1975) critique of institutionalist approaches to the study of industrial relations and Fudge and Vosko's (2003) critique of institutionalist approaches to political economy.

11 See Peck (1996,46–82) for a detailed overview of the development of segmentation theories.

12 First-generation segmentation theorists argued that primary sector production relies on high levels of both technological investment and technological change. This, in turn, requires high levels of skill and thus high levels of employment stability in order to retain skilled workers. The need to retain skilled workers contributes to the development of internal labour markets, which further promote security. In contrast, the secondary labour market is considered to be "technologically backward," and much more subject to competitive pressures. A second generation of segmentation theory is typified in the work of Edwards (1979), who argues that capitalist labour markets are characterized by different forms of control within primary and secondary sectors. Further, segmentation itself became incorporated into the system of capitalist control, as workers were divided and sub-divided according to their structural location within the labour market. Thus, "labour segmentation provided a means by which capital could overcome the contradictions inherent in deskilling" by constructing divisions within the working class through internal and labour market hierarchies (Peck 1996,53). Further, these divisions are based not only on skill, but also on race and gender, as women and racialized minority group members tend to be over-represented in the secondary labour market.

13 In 1998, the ten most common jobs for women were retail salespersons, secretaries, cashiers, registered nurses, accounting clerks, elementary teachers, food servers, general office clerks, baby-sitters, and receptionists (Statistics Canada 1998). For a detailed analysis of the feminization of the labour market and of the gendering of jobs see Armstrong and Armstrong (1994).

14 This definition of "nonstandard" that will be used throughout this book.

15 Barker and Christensen define contingent work as jobs that are temporary, self-employed, or involuntary part-time. In this usage of the term, contingent work is equivalent to nonstandard employment.

16 See also, Luxton (1980), Maroney and Luxton (1997), and Peck (1996, 36–8).

17 For example, in addition to labour relations legislation that primarily benefited male workers, the Unemployment Insurance system that was central to Canada's welfare state promoted women's dependence on a male breadwinner through eligibility restrictions that discriminated against women workers (Pulkingham 1998).

18 These practices are often referred to as "family friendly." As they clearly have positive implications for workers regardless of their family status, the term "family friendly" is not used in this chapter.

19 Similarly, Rosenfeld's (2001) study of such policies in the United States found that those most likely to benefit from them are single men in professional or highly skilled occupations.

20 Katherine Harding, "Success Redefined," *Globe and Mail,* 7 May 2003, C1, C8; and "Balance Tops List of Job Desires," *Globe and Mail,* 7 May 2003, C1, C6. See also Duxbury et al. (2003).

21 Duxbury and Higgins (2001) estimate that absenteeism resulting from work-life conflict costs Canadian businesses close to $3 billion a year.

22 This potential is raised by O'Conner et al. (1999), who suggest that a key question to be addressed in the evaluation of welfare state policies is the extent to which they promote personal autonomy and access to paid employment for all household members. See also McKeen and Porter (2003).

CHAPTER TWO

1 AO RG 7-1, File 7-1-0-1178, box 37, Labour Standards and Poverty in Ontario, Ontario Department of Labour, 22 November 1965.

2 An abbreviated version of this chapter has been published as Thomas (2004).

3 AO RG 7-1, File 7-1-0-1407.2, box 47, Notes for an Address by the Hon. Dalton Bales, Q.C., Minister of Labour for Ontario, During 2nd reading of: The Employment Standards Act, 1968, 31 May 1968.

4 While this periodization of labour law has been used to analyze the regulation of labour relations – legislation regulating union certification, collective bargaining, and strikes – the framework also provides a useful lens through which to view the development of minimum standards legislation. It indicates the general framework through which the state attempted to regulate the labour market and indicates the ways in which labour legislation developed in relation to patterns of labour market segmentation, and subsequently reinforced them.

5 Prior to the 1880s, the Lord's Day Act was the only legislation governing what are today considered to be employment standards. The act, which was initially constituted as part of the law of Upper Canada through the Constitutional Act of 1791, provided that "[n]o tradesman, artificer, workman, labourer, or other person whatsoever, shall do or exercise any worldly labour, business, or work of their ordinary calling upon the Lord's Day, or any part thereof" (*Labour Gazette*, January 1902,415). The act remained in force until 1845, when it was first repealed, but then was re-enacted with the explicit exclusion of those who delivered mail and those who sold drugs or medicines.

6 The push for shorter hours was an attempt to provide relief from overwork and work intensification and was also considered necessary to provide time for moral, social, and intellectual improvement. The need to secure greater leisure time in order to promote these broader goals of social development within the working class was a central proposition not only within the Canadian Nine-Hour Leagues but within shorter-hours movements in the United States and Western Europe as well (Ross 1991). For further discussion of the movement, see also Heron (1996, 14–17) and Palmer (1992, 106–8).

7 The movement also represented a turning point in the formation of the Canadian labour movement and was instrumental in the formation of the first nationally based, cross-occupational workers' political organization, the Canadian Labour Union (CLU), the predecessor to the Trades and Labour Congress (TLC) (Battye 1976; Heron 1996).

8 See Heron (1996, 20–6) and Palmer (1992, 121–7) for a discussion of the Knights of Labour.

9 See Kealey (1973). A similar strategy was explored following the labour revolt of 1919. The federal government brought together representatives from government, labour, and business in order to explore the possibilities of reforms that would regulate and contain class struggle without significant incursion into the capitalist labour market. The Royal Commission on Industrial Relations (RCIR) held hearings across the country beginning in mid-April 1919 and reported its recommendations in June 1919. The commission's recommendations included minimum wages for women, girls, and unskilled labourers, an eight-hour day, and unemployment and health insurance (Fudge and Tucker 2001). A National Industrial Conference (NIC) followed the report of the commission in September 1919. While employers remained opposed to most of the recommendations of the RCIR's majority report, they accepted a recommendation calling for the establishment of minimum wage boards for women (McCallum 1986).

10 The history and role of the ILO is examined in chapter 5.

11 The primary piece of labour relations legislation prior to World War II was the Industrial Disputes Investigation Act (IDIA) of 1907, which was designed to prevent labour disputes over union recognition by enacting a process of conciliation. The process established by the act was voluntary, however, as the state was unwilling to force employers to accept compulsory union recognition. It was simply an attempt to reduce the frequency of union recognition strikes and establish a "conciliatory" approach to labour relations (McBride 1995). In 1925, the scope of the IDIA was reduced to cover only those areas of economic activity under federal jurisdiction, such as transportation and mining.

12 AO RG 7-1, File 7-1-0-69, box 2, The *Fair Wages and Eight-Hour Day Act*, 1934, 2d Draft.

13 AO RG 7-1, File 7-1-0-154, box 5, Report of a Conference between Members of the Canadian Manufacturers' Association and Hon. A.W. Roebuck, K.C., Minister of Labour for the Province of Ontario, 30 January 1935.

14 AO RG 7-1, File 7-1-0-130, box 4, Memorandum, Re: Minimum Wage, 26 February 1937.

15 AO RG 7-1, File 7-1-0-130, box 4, Memorandum, Re: Minimum Wage, 26 February 1937. Municipal councils that passed resolutions in

support of a male minimum wage included those of Brampton, Port
Colborne, Orillia, Iroquois Falls, St Thomas, and Ottawa. See also
Labour Gazette (February 1935b,150).

16 AO RG 7-1, File 7-1-0-130, box 4, Letter, Toronto District Labor
Council, No Date (approximately March, 1937).

17 AO RG 7-1, File 7-1-0-130, box 4. Memorandum, Re: Minimum Wage,
26 February 1937; AO RG 7-1, File 7-1-0-130, box 4, Letter, From The
Board of Trade of the City of Toronto, 17 March 1937; AO RG 7-14,
File 7-14-0-130, box 3, Letter, From Canadian Manufacturers'
Association, To J.F. Marsh, Deputy Minister of Labour, 13 March
1937; AO RG 7-14, File 7-14-0-130, box 3, Letter, From Canadian
Manufacturers' Association, To J.F. Marsh, Deputy Minister of Labour,
13 March 1937. See also *Labour Gazette* (June 1937).

18 AO RG 7-1, File 7-1-0-154, box 5, Report of the Executive Committee
of the Toronto Branch of the Canadian Manufacturers' Association
to the Annual Meeting of the Branch, Toronto, 28 April 1938.

19 AO RG 7-1, File 7-1-0-130, box 4, Memorandum, Re: Minimum Wage,
26 February 1937.

20 AO RG 7-1, File 7-1-0-130, box 4, Letter, To Toronto District Labour
Council, From David Croll, Minister of Labour, 22 March 1937.

21 There was also very little standardization across provinces. Movement
towards a harmonized approach to minimum standards across the
provinces was considered in the report of the Royal Commission on
Dominion-Provincial Relations in the late 1930s, but no consensus
emerged as to a desire for the federal government to exert greater
control over the establishment of minimum standards. The mandate
of the commission was to "re-examine the economic and financial
basis of Confederation and the distribution of legislative powers in
the light of the economic and social developments of the last
70 years" (*Labour Gazette,* June 1940, 545). The commission made
wide-ranging recommendations in the areas of unemployment insurance, employment services, provincial welfare, old age pensions,
health insurance, worker's compensation, and labour legislation.
In its recommendations on labour legislation, the commission made
several recommendations in the area of minimum employment
standards, specifically in the areas of minimum age of employment,
hours of work, minimum wages, and weekly days of rest. It also recommended that the federal government be given jurisdiction to set
standards for minimum wages, maximum hours, and minimum age
of employment.

22 The "liberal" welfare state that developed in Canada during the postwar period was premised on a general policy commitment to provide social security for Canadian citizens within the context of an economic system of private enterprise. For a typology of welfare state models that developed during the postwar period see Esping-Andersen (1990).

23 The policies of the postwar welfare state were much less ambitious than the recommendations contained in Leonard Marsh's *Report on Social Security in Canada*, which was presented to the federal government in 1943. For a discussion of the Marsh report and the development of the welfare state in Canada see McBride and Shields (1997), chapter 2, "The Post-War Canadian State."

24 The other key element of the postwar labour relations system, the mandatory dues check-off, was established by Supreme Court Justice Ivan Rand in attempt to resolve a 1945 strike at the Ford plant in Windsor involving ten thousand auto workers. Rand ruled that since all workers in a unionized shop benefit from the union contract, all must pay dues through mandatory paycheque deductions. Through the Rand Formula, unions were guaranteed a financial base upon which to provide organizational representation to their members, so long as they acted within the bounds of the conciliatory processes established under PC 1003. For a discussion of the wartime struggles that led up to the establishment of PC 1003 and the Rand Formula, see Palmer (1992), 278–84.

25 See Fudge and Tucker, "Pluralism or Fragmentation," 275–9, for a discussion of legislative developments in the area of labour relations during this period.

26 The labour rights established by the system were not absolute, however. The postwar system was designed to establish a framework to ensure stability in labour relations. While it provided for processes of free collective bargaining, the legislation also imposed a number of restrictions on those rights, such as limiting the scope of collective bargaining and the right to strike (Wells 1995).

27 AO RG 7-14, File 7-14-0-90, box 3, Ontario Legislative Assembly, 14 February 1951, 3. In the early 1940s, approximately 40 percent of male employees and 50 percent of female employees in Ontario worked forty-eight hours per week or less. A one-week annual vacation with pay was a generally accepted standard. AO RG 7-14, File 7-14-0-93, box 3, An Act Respecting Hours of Work and Vacations with Pay in Industrial Undertakings, August 1944.

As women were more likely to be employed in part-time work, many worked far fewer hours than forty-eight per week.

28 AO RG 7-1, File 7-1-0-854, The Hours of Work and Vacations with Pay Act, 1964.

29 Even though large industrialists were primarily intent on preventing organized labour from securing increased power through new labour relations legislation, they also pressured the state to exercise caution with improvements to minimum standards legislation. For example, in response to the Hours of Work and Vacations with Pay Act, the Hamilton-Brantford branch of the CMA called on the government to delay the changes until the end of the war out of fear that reduced hours of work would exacerbate labour shortages (CMA 1944).

30 AO RG 7-14, File 7-14-0-93, box 3, Regulations under the Hours of Work and Vacations with Pay Act, 1944, 6 July 1944.

31 AO RG 7-14, File 7-14-0-93, box 3, Regulations under the Hours of Work and Vacations with Pay Act, 1944, 6 July 1944.

32 AO RG 7-14, File 7-14-0-93, box 3, The Effect of the Hours of Work and Vacations with Pay Act 1944 on Business and Industry in Ontario, 1944; AO RG 7-14, File 7-14-0-93, box 3, An Act Respecting Hours of Work and Vacations with Pay in Industrial Undertakings, August 1944.

33 AO RG 7-1, File 7-1-0-447, box 10, Memorandum to all Members of Cabinet Committee, T.M. Eberlee, 1961.

34 AO RG 7-14, File 7-14-0-90, box 3, Ontario Legislative Assembly, 14 February 1951.

35 AO RG 7-14, File 7-14-0-90, box 3, Ontario Legislative Assembly, 14 February 1951, 4.

36 AO RG 7-14, File 7-14-0-130, box 3. The Minimum Wage Act, Order No. 2 made by the Industry and Labour Board under the Act, 1947. Zone One included the largest municipalities: Toronto, Hamilton, Windsor, Ottawa, London, and surrounding municipalities. In Zone Two were municipalities with populations of 3,000 and over, while Zone Three consisted of municipalities with populations under 3,000.

37 Along with pressuring for legislation, unions also attempted to secure equal pay through collective bargaining, although at the time equal pay provisions were "not frequent" (*Labour Gazette*, September 1959).

38 AO RG 7-1, File 7-1-0-447, box 10. Memorandum to all Members of Cabinet Committee, T.M. Eberlee, 1961. The other piece of anti-discrimination legislation passed in Ontario at that time was the 1951

Fair Employment Practices Act, which prohibited employers from "refusing to employ, from firing or from discriminating against any person because of race, creed, colour, nationality, ancestry or place of origin" (*Labour Gazette*, April 1951, 443). The act was the first of its kind in Canada; however, critics raised the concern that it did not include discrimination on the basis of sex (*Labour Gazette*, June 1951). As well, the act excluded workplaces with fewer than five workers, as well as domestic workers, and non-profit, religious, philanthropic, educational, fraternal, and social organizations.

39 See *Labour Gazette* (February 1961) for a discussion of the various provisions of these acts.

40 The act was immediately criticized, as it applied only to the "same work," and therefore did not take into account "work of equal value." As well, it contained an individualized complaints process that placed the onus on the worker to report a violation. A report produced by the federal government at the end of the decade found that the practice of paying women less than men for the same work remained "widespread" (*Labour Gazette,* September 1959).

41 "Labour Delegates Clash on Official Coddling," *Globe and Mail,* 13 January 1951. In AO RG 7-14, File 7-14-0-90, box 3, Ontario Legislative Assembly, 14 February 1951.

42 The CCL formed in 1940 through a merger of the ACCL and the CIO industrial unions expelled from the TLC.

43 "Labour Delegates Clash on Official Coddling," *Globe and Mail,* 13 January 1951. In AO RG 7-14, File 7-14-0-90, box 3, Ontario Legislative Assembly, 14 February 1951, 3.

44 AO RG 7-14, File 7-14-0-130, box 3, Comments on Minimum Wages and Codes, No Date (1940s).

45 AO RG 7-14, File 7-14-0-90, box 3, Ontario Legislative Assembly, 14 February 1951, 3–4.

46 AO RG 7-1, File 7-1-0-730, box 19, Legislative Proposals, 1963, To the Prime Minister and Other Members of the Government of Ontario, Submitted by Ontario Federation of Labour CLC, 22 February 1963.

47 For an overview of labour militancy in the 1960s, see Heron (1996,92–8) and Palmer (1992,320-5). For a discussion of the "war on poverty" see Palmer (1992,276, 337). See Fudge and Tucker (2000,283–9), for general developments in labour and employment law in the context of this heightened militancy.

48 AO RG 7-1, File 7-1-0-1178, box 37, Labour Standards and Poverty in Ontario, Ontario Department of Labour, 22 November 1965, 5.

49 AO RG 7-1, File 7-1-0-1182, box 37, Memorandum, to H.L. Rowntree, Minister of Labour, Re: Proposed Provincial Labour Code, 17 October 1966.

50 Memorandum Re: Meetings of Cabinet Committee Appointed to Consider a Minimum Wage for Men, 1961.

51 AO RG 7-1, File 7-1-0-1178, box 37, Labour Standards and Poverty in Ontario, Ontario Department of Labour, 22 November 1965, 5.

52 AO RG 7-1, File 7-1-0-1178, box 37, Labour Standards and Poverty in Ontario, Ontario Department of Labour, 22 November 1965.

53 AO RG 7-1, File 7-1-0-731, box 19, Statement by the Honourable H.L. Rowntree, Minister of Labour, on the Government's Minimum Wage Policy, ND, 1963, 1–2.

54 AO RG 7-1, File 7-1-0-475, box 11, Memorandum, Minimum Wage for Men, Industry and Labour Board, 1961.

55 AO RG 7-1, File 7-1-0-447, box 10, Memorandum Re: Meetings of Cabinet Committee Appointed to Consider a Minimum Wage for Men, 1961, 1. The possibility of a general minimum wage for all male and female workers was also considered. Two concerns stemmed from this possibility, however. First, while the committee felt the economy could support a $1.00 per hour minimum for male workers, it claimed it did not have enough information to assess the impact of such a minimum for all workers (male and female). This raised the possibility of a differential minimum for male and female workers, which would conflict with the principles of equal pay for equal work established by the Female Employees Fair Remuneration Act (see below).

56 By the early 1960s the OFL was calling for a general minimum wage of $1.25 per hour for male and female workers. AO RG 7-1, File 7-1-0-730, box 19, Legislative Proposals, 1963, To the Prime Minister and Other Members of the Government of Ontario, Submitted by Ontario Federation of Labour C.L.C., 22 February 1963; AO RG 7-1, File 7-1-0-731, box 19, Statement by the Honourable H.L. Rowntree, Minister of Labour, on the Government's Minimum Wage Policy, 1–2.

57 AO RG 7-1, File 7-1-0-447, box 10, Memorandum to all Members of Cabinet Committee, T.M. Eberlee, 1961, 2

58 AO RG 7-1, File 7-1-0-1189, box 37, Circular no. 24, The Minimum Wage Act, Labour Standards Branch, Department of Labour, 1 March 1966. The only industry-based differentiation was for construction workers, whose hourly minimum wage was set at $1.25. Lower rates were set for persons under the age of eighteen and for some workers,

such as apprentices. Some salesmen, some professionals, domestic workers, and farm workers, were exempted from the new rates (*Labour* Gazette, August 1963, July 1964; Whittington 1970).

59 AO RG 7-1, File 7-1-0-653, box 16, Report of the Ontario Division Executive Committee to the 44th Annual Meeting of the Ontario Division, the Canadian Manufacturers' Association, 2 May 1963.

60 AO RG 7-1, File 7-1-0-447, box 10, Memorandum to all Members of Cabinet Committee, T.M. Eberlee, 1961.

61 AO RG 7-1, File 7-1-0-447, box 10, Memorandum to all Members of Cabinet Committee, T.M. Eberlee, 1961, 3.

62 AO RG 7-1, File 7-1-0-854, box 23, The Hours of Work and Vacations with Pay Amendment Act, 1964: Reasons for Maintaining the forty-hour week, 1964.

63 AO RG 7-1, File 7-1-0-992, box 30, Notes for Statement by Hon. Allan J. MacEachen, Minister of Labour on resumption of debate in the House of Commons on Bill C-126, The Canada Labour (Standards) Code, 16 February 1965. Overtime averaging, with overtime rates calculated after an average of forty hours per week, was permitted up to a period of thirteen weeks.

64 AO RG 7-1, File 7-1-0-992, box 30, Notes for Statement by Hon. Allan J. MacEachen, Minister of Labour on resumption of debate in the House of Commons on Bill C-126, The Canada Labour (Standards) Code, 16 February 1965.

65 AO RG 7-1, File 7-1-0-992, box 30. Bill C-126 – Canada Labour Standards Code (produced by Ontario Department of Labour), 11 February 1965, 2.

66 AO RG 7-1, File 7-1-0-992, box 30, Letter, To W.M. McIntyre, Deputy Minister, Department of the Prime Minister, From H.L. Rowntree, Minister of Labour, 28 April 1965.

67 AO RG 7-1, File 7-1-0-1181, box 37, Legislative Proposal Respecting "The Hours of Work and Vacations with Pay Act"; AO RG 7-1, File 7-1-0-1407.3, box 47, The Labour Standards Act, Background Memorandum, 25 January 1968, 2; AO RG 7-1, File 7-1-0-731, box 19, Statement by the Honourable H.L. Rowntree, Minister of Labour, on the Government's Minimum Wage Policy, 1–2.

68 AO RG 7-1, File 7-1-0-1322, box 43, Ontario Federation of Labour Legislative Proposals to the Prime Minister and Other Members of the Government of Ontario, 1967.

69 AO RG 7-1, File 7-1-0-1322, box 43, Submission of the Ontario Federation of Labour to Hon. Dalton Bales, Minister of Labour, January 1967.

70 AO RG 7-1, File 7-1-0-1322, box 43, Ontario Federation of Labour Legislative Proposals to the Prime Minister and Other Members of the Government of Ontario, 1967.

71 AO RG 7-1, File 7-1-0-1435, box 49, Brief on Women's Minimum Wage Rates, Submitted by the Congress of Canadian Women, 28 February 1968.

72 AO RG 7-1, File 7-1-0-1181, box 37, Report on Proposed Amendments to the Ontario Human Rights Code.

73 AO RG 7-1, File 7-1-0-1532.3, box 54, Summary of Representations Made by Associations in regard to the Employment Standards Act, 1968, 1969.

74 AO RG 7-1, File 7-1-0-872, box 24, Letter, From Building Products Ltd, To Hon. H.L. Rowntree, Minister of Labour, 9 March 1964.

75 AO RG 7-1, File 7-1-0-1178, box 37, Labour Standards and Poverty in Ontario, Ontario Department of Labour, 22 November 1965, 5.

76 AO RG 7-1, File 7-1-0-1407.1, box 47. Minimum Wage Regulations, 1968.

77 AO RG 7-1, File 7-1-0-1407.3, box 47, Labour Standards Act, 1968, Background Memorandum, 25 January 1968.

78 AO RG 7-1, File 7-1-0-447, box 10, Memorandum to all Members of Cabinet Committee, T.M. Eberlee, 1961.

79 AO RG 7-1, File 7-1-0-1178, box 37, Labour Standards and Poverty in Ontario, Ontario Department of Labour, 22 November 1965.

80 AO RG 7-1, File 7-1-0-1407.3, box 47, The Labour Standards Act, Background Memorandum, 25 January 1968.

81 AO RG 7-1, File 7-1-0-1385.1, box 46, Memorandum to: W.M. McIntyre, Esq., Secretary of the Cabinet, Parliament Buildings, From Dalton Bales, Minister of Labour, 25 March 1968.

82 AO RG 7-1, File 7-1-0-1021, box 31, "Longer Hours Unlikely for Lumber Dealers," *Globe and Mail*, 27 March 1965; AO RG 7-1, File 7-1-0-1021, box 31, Memorandum, From E.G. Gibb, Re: *Globe and Mail* Article, 29 March 1965.

83 AO RG 7-1, File 7-1-0-1407.2, box 47, Memorandum Re: Employment Standards Act.

84 AO RG 7-1, File 1407.3, box 47, The Labour Standards Code, 1968, No Date (1968).

85 AO RG 7-1, File 7-1-0-1117.2, box 34, Comments of the Department of Labour on the Brief of the Ontario Federation of Labour, Presented to Cabinet, 30 March 1966.

86 AO RG 7-1, File 7-1-0-1407.1, box 47, Minimum Wage Regulations, 1968.

87 Minimum Wage Regulations, 1968; also AO RG 7-1, File 7-1-0-1407.1, box 47, Interim Paper on a $1.25 Minimum Wage.

88 AO RG 7-1, File 7-1-0-1407.1, box 47, Employment Standards Act, 1968, 1969. The act received Cabinet approval on 13 May 1968. It was given First Reading on 27 May and received Royal Assent on 13 June.

89 AO RG 7-1, File 7-1-0-1532.1, box 54, Notice to Employers and Employees, 1969.

90 AO RG 7-1, File 7-1-0-1407.2, box 47, Bales' New Labour Code Includes 1 ½ overtime pay, Ontario Department of Labour Information Release, 27 May 1968.

91 The construction rate was increased to $1.55.

92 While the Business and Professional Women's Clubs of Ontario supported the transfer of authority for the equal pay laws, it continued to voice its dissatisfaction with the government's resistance to incorporating the terms of work of comparable character into the legislation. AO RG 7-1, File 7-1-0-1408.2, box 47, Letter, To Hon. D. Bales, 25 September 1968.

93 AO RG 7-1, File 7-1-0-1533.1, box 54, Memorandum, From R.M. Warren, Executive Director, Manpower Services, 3 February 1969.

94 For example, managerial and supervisory employees were exempted from the hours of work and overtime provisions. While exemptions were made for seasonal employees in fruit and vegetable processing, there was reluctance to grant exemptions to all seasonal employees, as "it is often those employees who have little or no other choice but to work in these seasonal industries who must need the protection of our legislation." AO RG 7-1, File 7-1-0-1532.3, box 54, Memorandum, Re: Representation from the Ontario Ski Area Operators Association, 28 April 1969.

95 AO RG 7-1, File 1505.1, box 53, Legislative Proposals to the Government of Ontario, 1969, Submitted by – Ontario Federation of Labour.

96 AO RG 7-1, File 7-1-0-1532.2, box 54, "The Minimum Wage Must Be a Living Wage," *Toronto Daily Star*, 10 July 1969; AO RG 7-1, File 7-1-0-1533.1, box 54, "Employment Standards Act Comes under Fire as Well," *Oshawa Times*, 18 October 1968.

97 AO RG 7-1, File 7-1-0-1532.3, box 54, Summary of Representations Made by Associations in regard to the Employment Standards Act, 1968, 1969.

98 AO RG 7-1, File 7-1-0-1407.1, box 47, Letter to Honourable Dalton Bales, Minister of Labour, 23 August 1968.

99 AO RG 7-1, File 7-1-0-1407.1, box 47, Letter to M.E. Howard,
Director, Labour Standards Branch, 31 July 1968.

100 AO RG 7-1, File 7-1-0-1408.2, Letter to Hon. D.A. Bales,
13 September 1968.

101 Ibid.

102 AO RG 7-1, File 7-1-0-1407.1, box 47, Notes on Minimum Wage and
Employment Standards Policy; AO RG 7-1, File 7-1-0-1505.1, box 53,
Memorandum to Hon. J.P. Robarts, From Dalton Bales, Minister of
Labour, 18 March 1969. To indicate the significance of the increase
to $1.30, the government argued that at the time there were
150,000 workers who received a raise with the implementation
of the ESA.

103 AO RG 7-1, File 7-1-0-1581, Memorandum to the Minister Re:
OFL Brief, 19 March 1969.

CHAPTER THREE

1 AO RG 7-130. Research Studies – Policy and Legislation. The Nature
and Level of Employment Standards Services and Techniques for
Achieving Compliance. Paper presented to the Canadian Association
of Administrators of Labour Legislation. June 1974, 1.

2 AO 7-1. File 7-1-0-1532.2, box 54. Letter, From Dalton Bales, Minister,
8 August 1969.

3 A detailed analysis of the causes of the "long downturn" was
produced by Brenner (1998); he attributed declining rates of profitability to an accumulation of fixed capital controlled by U.S. industry
that began to face competitive pressures from German and Japanese
capital. An intensified competition cycle generated overproduction
and declining profits. In response, McNally (1999) argues, currency
devaluations and revaluations were central to the internationalisation
of the economic crisis. See also Foster (1999). For Brenner's
response to McNally and Foster, see Brenner (1999).

4 AO RG 7-78. Initial Submission , Management by Results and
Estimates, 1979/80. 12 July 1978, 2; AO RG 7-78. Explanatory
Material for 1982/83 Estimates. Descriptive Summaries by Program
and Activity as of 31 March 1982.

5 See Bakker (1996) for a discussion of this concept.

6 The four types of self-employment are incorporated, without paid
help (own account); incorporated, with paid help; unincorporated,
without paid help; unincorporated, with paid help.

7 Cranford et al. (2003) developed a multi-dimensional measure of "precariousness employment" to indicate a continuum of employment experiences based on job security, control over the labour process and working conditions, degree of regulatory protection, and income level. This continuum of precariousness proceeds from full-time permanent employment to full-time temporary, to part-time permanent, to part-time temporary. The measure is a more accurate reflection of the variety of labour market conditions that shape labour market vulnerability than the dualistic standard/ nonstandard distinction.

8 Between 1967 and 1997, men's unionization rate decreased to 32.4 percent, while women's increased to 29.6 percent. In 2000, 29.6 percent of women and 31.1 percent of men were unionized. The dramatic increase in women's unionization rates can be explained to a large degree by women's high rates of employment in the highly unionized public sector (Akyeampong 1997, 2000; Krahn et al. 2006).

9 AO RG 7-78, Memorandum, Manpower Adjustment Service, February 1972; AO RG 7-78, Discussion Paper on Advance Notice of Termination, No Date (prior to 1979); AO RG 7-78, Pregnancy Leave in Ontario, A Policy Discussion, Women's Bureau, March 1977; AO RG 7-78, Legislated Hours of Work and Premium Pay Provisions. Research Branch, March 1977; AO RG 7-78, Equal Pay in Ontario, Women's Bureau, March 1977; AO RG 7-78, Ontario Labour Legislation of Interest to Working Women, Women's Bureau, Ontario Ministry of Labour; AO RG 7-78. Pregnancy Leave in Ontario, A Policy Discussion, Women's Bureau, March 1977; AO RG 7-186, News Release, Year-End Review of Ministry, 30 December 1975; AO RG 7-78, News Release, 20 February 1978. The differential rate was introduced under pressure from the hospitality industry owing to "the substantial tip income received by such workers." AO RG 7-186, News Release, Minimum Wages for Students and Tipped Workers, 10 March, 1976; AO RG 7-78, Letter, To Ontario Hotel and Motel Association, 3 November 1975; AO RG 7-78, Adoption Leave – A Background Paper, March 1977; AO RG 7-78, Protection from Arbitrary Dismissal: No Dismissal without a Just Cause – A New Employment Standard? September 1976; AO RG 7-78, Cabinet Submission, Priorities of Wage Claims in Insolvencies and Bankruptcies, 3 April 1974. AO RG 7-78, Termination of Employment – Current Issue Report, 2 June 1976.

10 AO RG 7-78, Employment Standards Review, Current
Recommendations, By Employment Standards Review Committee,
26 November 1981; RG 7-78, ESR Committee Files, Consecutive Days
of Work, 1982. AO RG 7-78, Briefing Notes on Proposed Revisions to
the Employment Standards Act, March, 1982; AO RG 7-168,
Committee of Resources Deputies, Meeting Minutes, 29 April 1982.

11 AO RG 7-78, Revision of the Employment Standards Act, 1982, 1.

12 AO RG 7-168, Memorandum, To S.J. Wychowanec, Deputy Provincial
Secretary for Justice, From T.E. Armstrong, Deputy Minister of
Labour, 22 April 1985; AO RG 7-168, Termination Pay (Pay in Lieu of
Notice), 1985; AO RG 7-168, Wage Protection in Business Failure,
13 May 1984.

13 AO RG 7-168, Policy Subject Files, Interim Report of the Inquiry into
Wage Protection, 15 December 1983.

14 AO RG 7-168, Policy Subject Files, Protection of Wages in Bankruptcy
and Insolvency, February 1980.

15 AO RG 7-168, Policy Subject Files, Letter, R.H. Ramsay, to Laurell
Ritchie, Canadian Textile and Chemical Union, 2 July 1984.

16 AO RG 7-78, Wage Recovery, Bankruptcies and Insolvencies – Current
Issue Report, 20 May 1976.

17 AO RG 7-78, Memorandum, Protections of Workers' Wages, 2 June
1977; AO RG 7-78, Cabinet Submission, Priorities of Wage Claims in
Insolvencies and Bankruptcies, 3 April 1974.

18 AO RG 7-130, Research Studies – Policy and Legislation, The Nature
and Level of Employment Standards Services and Techniques for
Achieving Compliance, Paper Presented to the Canadian Association
of Administrators of Labour Legislation, June 1974.

19 AO RG 7-168, Policy Subject Files, Wage Protection in Business
Failure, 13 May 1984.

20 AO RG 7-186, Policy and Program Development, News Releases,
Minister of Labour Issues Commission Report on Wage Protection,
25 November 1985.

21 AO RG 7-186, News Release, Ontario Labour Minister Elgie Presents
Ministry Year-End Review, 11 January 1982. See Bill 68 (c.55, SO
1983) and Bill 62 (c.31, SO 1984).

22 AO RG 7-78, Comparison of Ontario Employment Standards Act and
Canada Labour Code Proposed Revisions, Minutes of the Executive
Committee Meeting, 17 May 1982; AO RG 7-78, Program, Statistics,
and Current Legislation, 1982. "Mass termination" was defined as
involving "a group of 50 or greater who are terminated over

6 months in a complete or partial closure of an establishment."
AO RG 7-168, Notes on Severance Pay Provision, No Date (1984).

23 See Bill 128, (c.51, SO 1986); Bill 85, (c.30, SO 1987), and Ontario (1987c).

24 Matt Maychak, "New Law Would Entitle 1.5 Million to Layoff Pay," *Toronto Star*, Tuesday, 16 June 1987, A1.

25 AO RG 7-78, Submission to the Resources Development Policy Field: Equal Pay for Equal Work (No Date, 1973–1977); AO RG 7-78, Equal Pay in Ontario, Women's Bureau, March 1977; AO RG 7-78, Equal Pay for Equal Work – Current Issue Report, 1 June 1976; AO RG 7-186, Policy and Program Development, News Releases, Equal Pay for Work of Equal Value Discussion Paper Released, 18 October 1976; AO RG 7-168, Cabinet Meeting, Agenda Item – Report of the Cabinet Committee on Resources Development, 19 December 1979.

26 AO RG 7-168, Legislative Assembly of Ontario, Statement by Ms. Bryden (NDP), 5 June 1984.

27 AO RG 7-168, Equal Pay-Composite, 9 March 1983.

28 AO RG 7-168, Amendments to the Equal Pay Provisions of the Employment Standards Act, 15 November 1982.

29 AO RG 7-168, Proposed Administrative Procedures for a Composite Approach to Equal Pay, 25 October 1983.

30 Despite this broader conceptualization of equal pay, however, numerous shortcomings were identified within the Pay Equity Act, including that its coverage was not as wide as that of the ESA, that it did not apply to private sector workplaces with fewer than ten employees, and that it was difficult to enforce for workers without union representation.

31 AO RG 7-78, Program, Statistics, and Current Legislation, 1982; AO RG 7-168, Draft Outline for Study on Hours of Work and Job Creation, 26 November 1982.

32 In particular, there was pressure from locals within the CAW and USWA. Interview, U3, November 2001.

33 Task Force on Hours of Work and Overtime, Letter to William Wrye, Minister of Labour, May 1987. See Ontario (1987).

34 The report concluded that reductions in work time would not necessarily lead to increases in employment levels at all, owing to potential increases in moonlighting, alternative compensation arrangements, lack of fit between labour demand and labour supply, noncompliance with legislative standards, and higher labour costs.

35 AO RG 7-78, Minister of Labour Announces Changes to Minimum Wage, 27 June 1991.

36 AO RG 7-186, News Release, Ontario's General Minimum Wage to Increase to $5.40 an Hour, 25 June 1990.

37 AO RG 7-186, News Release, Questions and Answers for the 1993 Minimum Wage Announcement, 1993.

38 Other ESA initiatives included a proposal to add eighteen weeks of unpaid parental leave for parents of both newborn and adopted children, expanding the coverage provided to homeworkers under the ESA, amendments to the appeals process, and proposals to increase the protections for workers who chose not to work on Sundays. AO RG 7-186, News Release, Parental Leave Package Proposed by Minister of Labour, 22 November 1990; AO RG 7-186, News Release, Sunday Shopping Committee Tables Recommendations, 4 March 1993.

39 AO RG 7-186, Policy and Program Development, News Releases. Consultations on Wage Protection Fund, 24 January 1991. At the time of its inception, the Wage Protection Program was expected to benefit between 40,000 and 67,000 workers. AO RG 7-78, Field Operations, Wage Protection Fund, Discussion Paper, December 1990.

40 AO RG 7-186, News Release, Labour Minister Announces Government Plan to Assist Laid-off Workers, 24 January 1991; AO RG 7-186, News Release, Consultations on Wage Protection Fund, 24 January 1991.

41 AO RG 7-186, News Release, Labour Minister Announces the Creation of the Employee Wage Protection Program, 11 April 1991; AO RG 7-186, News Release, Employee Wage Protection Program Gets Royal Assent, Minister Tells Workers "Cheques are Ready to Roll," 16 October 1991. The program was introduced in Bill 70, An Act to Amend the Employment Standards Act to Provide for an Employee Wage Protection Program and to Make Certain Other Amendments, which received Royal Assent on 16 October 1991. See Bill 70, c.16, so 1991.

42 Interview, ER1, September 2001.

43 AO RG 7-78. Initial Submission, Management By Results and Estimates, 1979/80. 12 July 1978, 6.

44 AO RG 7-78, Letter, John R. Scott, Director, Re: The Employment Standards Act, 1974 & The Automatic Car Wash Industry, 4 April 1975; AO RG 7-78, Letter, John P. MacBeth, Minister of Labour, 24 June 1975.

45 AO RG 7-78, Memorandum, Re: Ontario Federation of Labour, 6 April 1976.

46 While unions, women's organizations, and community groups
   pressured the state to expand ESA coverage, employer associations
   sought to restrict its application by requesting exemptions for specific
   categories of work. Their requests generally sought to emphasize the
   uniqueness of the specific occupation in question, particularly in
   cases of seasonal employment or businesses with nonstandard
   (e.g., continuous) scheduling, and the ways in which application of
   the ESA might impact on the financial viability of that specific
   business. OFL Briefs to the Ministry of Labour. In AO RG 7-78,
   Employment Standards – Overtime/Excess Hour Permits, Labour
   Services Division, Staff Branch, 6 April 1976. AO RG 7-78,
   Memorandum, Ontario Swimming Pool Association, 20 June 1975;
   AO RG 7-78, Letter, From Ready Mixed Concrete Association of
   Ontario, 22 October 1974; AO RG 7-78, Memorandum, Re: Ontario
   Milk Distributors Association, 8 January 1969; AO RG 7-78, Further
   Presentation of the Ontario Hotel and Motel Association to the
   Industry and Labour Board for Ontario, 16 May 1967.
47 AO RG 7-168, Policy Subject Files, Memorandum, Employment
   Standards Branch, 17 May 1985, 6.
48 AO RG 7-78, Overview of Domestic Workers in Ontario, Women's
   Bureau, Ontario Ministry of Labour, November, 1976, 25.
49 AO RG 7-78, Program, Statistics, and Current Legislation, 1982;
   AO RG 7-186, Policy and Program Development, News Releases,
   New Provisions Relating to Terms and Conditions of Employment
   Applicable to Domestic Workers in Ontario, 20 December 1980.
50 AO RG 7-186, Policy and Program Development, News Releases, New
   Time-Off Rules for Live-In Domestics and Nannies Take Effect on
   Saturday, 24 February 1984; AO RG 7-186, Policy and Program
   Development, News Releases, Ministers Announce Increased
   Minimum Wage for Domestic Workers, 30 November 1984.
51 AO RG 7-168, Memorandum (Untitled), To John R. Scott, Director,
   Employment Standards Branch, 12 April 1985; AO RG 7-168,
   Memorandum (Untitled), 17 May 1985.
52 AO RG 7-186, Policy and Program Development, News Releases,
   Overtime Pay and Other Benefits Set for Household Domestics,
   9 June 1987.
53 AO RG 7-78, Current Issue, From W.B. Cook, Administrator,
   Industrial Standards, Re: Homeworkers – Garment Industry,
   17 September 1982.

54 AO RG 7-78, Current Issue, From W.B. Cook, Administrator,
   Industrial Standards, Re: Homeworkers – Garment Industry,
   17 September 1982.

55 AO RG 7-186, Policy and Program Development, News Releases,
   Homeworkers to Get Improved Working Conditions, 16 December
   1993.

56 Between 1947 and 1948, 4,527 male Polish war veterans were
   admitted to Canada and were required to sign contracts that obli-
   gated them to work for a designated farmer for two years at pay rates
   set by the Department of Labour. Between 1947 and 1954, over
   7,000 displaced persons were required to sign a one-year
   employment contract.

57 In a review of the disputes resolution processes of the Seasonal
   Agricultural Workers Program, Brem (2006) points to the contradictory role of the liaison officers responsible for ensuring that workers
   are not subjected to employer abuse. While officially maintaining a
   role as the workers' advocate, the officers are also responsible for
   ensuring the continuity of the program and for maintaining amicable
   relationships with Canadian employers. This contradictory role limits
   the effectiveness of the liaison officers in ensuring worker concerns
   are addressed.

58 This discrepancy is reported as creating confusion in determining
   eligibility for vacation pay and public holidays, as workers sometimes
   move between harvesting work and farm work. See Verma
   (2003, 66).

59 AO RG 7-78, Program, Statistics, and Current Legislation, 1982, 16.

60 AO RG 7-78, Legislated Hours of Work and Premium Pay Provisions,
   Research Branch, March 1977.

61 Ibid.

62 Ibid., 4.

63 Jonathan Eaton, "Employment Standards Rules Require Better
   Enforcement," *Toronto Star*, Monday, 6 May 1996, B3.

64 Annual Reports – Employment Practices Branch, 1990–91 to
   2000–1.

65 Similarly, a study of precarious employment in the city of Toronto
   found that workers in low-wage forms of nonstandard employment
   were particularly vulnerable to employment standards violations
   (de Wolff 2000).

66 Interview, CL1, September 2001.

67 Interview, CL2, September 2001.

68 AO RG 7-78, Letter, Gary C. Yee, Metro Toronto Chinese & Southeast Asian Legal Clinic, to Penny Dutton, Director, Employment Standards Branch.

69 AO RG 7-78, Report of the Chinese Restaurant Workers Advisory Committee, June 1987.

70 AO RG 7-78, Letter, Chinese Canadian National Council, Toronto Chapter, to Gregory Sorbara, Minister of Labour, 3 May 1988.

71 Being exempt from key standards of the ESA, the conditions for workers in the Seasonal Agricultural Workers Program are largely governed through the employment contracts between the participating governments. Dispute resolution procedures take place through liaison offices of the respective governments, with liaison officers designated to resolve complaints from workers regarding working conditions. Without an independent advocate for workers, these disputes resolution processes have been largely ineffective in addressing workers' concerns, leaving them vulnerable to employer abuse. See Verma (2003) for a detailed discussion.

72 Interview, ER1, September 2001.

73 AO RG 7-78, Management by Results, 1977-78, 4th Quarter; AO RG 7-78, Management by Results (No Date, 76–78).

74 AO RG 7-78, No. 1 MBR Commitment, No Date (1976–78), 1.

75 AO RG 7-130, Research Studies – Policy and Legislation, The Nature and Level of Employment Standards Services and Techniques for Achieving Compliance, Paper Presented to the Canadian Association of Administrators of Labour Legislation, June 1974.

76 AO RG 7-78, Employment Standards Branch – Future Outlook, 1982–83, 7.

77 AO RG 7-78, Employment Standards Branch – Future Outlook, 1982–83.

78 AO RG 7-78, Field Operations, Overview – Field Operational Status, 9 December 1991.

79 AO RG 7-78, Employment Standards – Comments on Program Indicators, 1982; AO RG 7-78, Employment Standards Branch – Future Outlook, 1982–83.

80 AO RG 7-78, Management by Results (General Program Description), No Date (1976–78); AO RG 7-78, Explanatory Material for 1982/83 Estimates, Descriptive Summaries by Program and Activity as of 31 March 1982; Ministry of Labour, Business Plan, 2000–1.

81 Approximately 70 percent of complaints are verified as violations of the ESA Employment Practices Branch, Fiscal Year Reports, 1990–91 to 2000–1.

82 AO RG 7-78, Choosing a Tribunal to Adjudicate Unjust Dismissal Cases, No Date (1976–77).

83 Interview, CL2, September 2001; Interview, U2, August 2001. As the ESWG (1996,4) stated in their report on working conditions in low-wage workplaces in the province, "[w]orkers who speak out are vulnerable."

84 Interview, U1, August 2001.

85 AO RG 7-130, Research Studies – Policy and Legislation, The Nature and Level of Employment Standards Services and Techniques for Achieving Compliance, Paper Presented to the Canadian Association of Administrators of Labour Legislation, June 1974.

86 AO RG 7-78, Letter, Chinese Canadian National Council, Toronto Chapter, to Gregory Sorbara, Minister of Labour, 3 May 1988.

87 Interview, CL1, September 2001.

88 Ministry of Labour, Annual Reports, 1981–82 to 1988–89.

89 AO RG 7-78, Field Operations, Overview – Field Operational Status, 9 December 1991.

90 AO RG 7-78, Letter, from Centre for Spanish Speaking Peoples, to Gregory Sorbara, Minister of Labour, 26 July 1988.

91 Employment Practices Branch, Fiscal Year Reports, 1997–98 to 2000–1.

92 AO RG 7-78, Field Operations, Wage Protection Fund, Discussion Paper, December 1990.

CHAPTER FOUR

1 See Winson and Leach (2002, 13–44) for a discussion of the need to study how macro-level, or global, social processes are "brought down to earth" in localized contexts.

2 For an overview of the origins of neoliberalism, see Clarke and Barlow (1997).

3 Interview, U2, August 2001.

4 For a detailed discussion of the neoliberal policy changes implemented by the Mulroney and Chrétien governments, see McBride and Shields (1997), chapters 3 and 4. See also Brodie (1996b) and Sears (1999).

5 AO RG 7-130, A Review of Ontario's Fair Wage Programme, Research
   Branch, January 1971.
6 See Bill 49 (c.23, SO 1996).
7 Jonathan Eaton, "Province Shifts Employment Standards
   Responsibility: Changes Put Onus on Unions to Ensure Rules Are
   Applied," *Toronto Star*, Monday, 2 December 1996, C3; David Ivey,
   "Changes to Basic Employment Rights Affect All Ontarians," *Hamilton
   Spectator*, Saturday, 7 December 1996, B2.
8 Jonathan Eaton, "Province Shifts Employment Standards
   Responsibility."
9 Interview, CL1, September 2001. When first introduced, the bill also
   included a provision that would allow employers and unions to contract out of the ESA or negotiate standards below those written in the
   act for hours of work, holidays, and overtime, vacation, and severance
   pay. The only restriction to this proposed clause was that any negotiated settlement must, as a whole package, provide total benefits
   greater than those contained in the ESA. Following widespread criticism from organized labour owing to concerns that this proposal
   would contribute to the erosion of the minimum standards contained
   in the act, this specific proposal was withdrawn from the bill.
   Although withdrawn, the proposal signalled another way in which the
   government intended to explore methods of promoting the privatization of minimum standards through the language of "self-reliance."
   Jonathan Eaton, "New Law Will Gut Workplace Standards"; Canadian
   Press, "Delay Study of Job Rules, Tories Urged: Hearings Called a
   'Sham' After Major Change is Withdrawn," *Toronto Star*, Tuesday,
   20 August 1996, B3.
10 See, for example, OCC (2000).
11 Toronto Board of Trade, Letter to Chris Stockwell, Minister of
   Labour, Re: Bill 147, The Employment Standards Act, 2000,
   7 December 2000.
12 See ACLC (2000), CAW (2000), CUPE (2000), ESWG (2000),
   INTERCEDE (2000), NAC (2000), OFL (2000), UNITE (2000), USWA
   (2000).
13 Interview, CL2, September 2001.
14 Interview, CL2, September 2001.
15 Interview, CL1, September 2001.
16 Bill 147, the amended ESA, received third reading on 20 December
   2000.

17 This change was associated with an amendment to the Employment Insurance Act that increased parental benefits from ten to thirty-five weeks, as of 31 December 2000. In order to facilitate employee eligibility for this extension, parental leaves in all provinces and in the Canada Labour Code were adjusted to reflect the new EI benefits. While there are variations across the provinces, maternity leave of a minimum of fifteen weeks is present in all jurisdictions, as is parental/adoption leave of a minimum of thirty-five weeks. Further, in December 2000 the parental leave provisions of the Canada Labour Code were extended to same-sex partners adopting a child. In Ontario, the ESA was amended in March 2000 to prohibit employers from differentiating between employees or their beneficiaries, survivors, or dependents on the grounds of age, sex, or marital status, including same-sex partnership status, when "establishing or providing a fund, plan, arrangement or benefit" (HRDC 2000b,13).

18 Interview, CL2, September 2001.

19 Interview, CL2, September 2001.

20 Interview, ER2, November 2001.

21 Interview, CL2, September 2001.

22 Under considerable pressure from labour and anti-poverty organizations, Dalton McGuinty's Liberal government introduced a series of increases to Ontario's minimum wage with the aim to raise it to $10.25 by 31 March 2010.

23 See "Understanding the Racialization of Poverty in Ontario" (www. colourofpoverty.ca), Campaign 2000 et al. (2008), and WAC (2007) for an overview of these patterns.

24 Interview, ER1, September 2001.

25 Interview, U2, August 2001.

26 In an effort to prevent the Big Three companies from attempting to use legislative reforms as a rationale for seeking contract concessions, the Canadian Auto Workers had the pre-2000 employment standards legislation incorporated into each of its master auto agreements when it became apparent that the provincial government was intent on reforming the ESA. Interview, CAW representative, summer 2003.

27 Colin Perkel, "Strikers Outraged by 60-Hour Work Weeks," *Hamilton Spectator*, 11 January 2002, c8.

28 Canadian Press, "Windsor Workers End 10-Week Strike," 20 February 2002.

29 John Saunders, "Navistar Still Awaits Word on Money to Keep Plant," *Globe and Mail,* 12 May 2003, B1, B6; Tony Van Alphen, "Navistar Workers Okay Concessions to Save Plant," *Toronto Star,* 14 May 2003.

30 The report was compiled from complaints received through the centre's telephone hotline and through in-depth interviews conducted by centre staff and volunteers (WAC 2007,11).

31 Interview, G1, 24 July 2002.

32 Employment Standards Act, 2000 (S.O. 2000, c. 41).

33 Interview, G1, 24 July 2002.

34 Interview, CL1, September 2001.

35 Interview, U1, August 2001.

36 Interview, ER2, November 2001.

37 Canadian Press, "Labour Activists Compile 'Bad Boss' Inventory," *Hamilton Spectator,* 10 September 1996, A2.).

38 Interview, ER1, September 2001.

39 Business Plan – Ministry of Labour, 2001–2.

40 Interview, CL1, September 2001; Interview, CL2, September 2001.

41 Interview, U2, August 2001.

42 Cavalluzzo, Hayes, Shilton, McIntyre and Cornish (2004), *Update: Ending the 60 Hour Work Week?* December 2004. Accessed on 19 April 2005, at http://www.cavalluzzo.com/.

CHAPTER FIVE

1 See Arrighi and Silver (1999, 202–11) for a discussion of this context.

2 See Panitch and Swartz (2003), chapter 4, for a discussion of the Supreme Court rulings on the right to freedom of association.

3 Reports of the Committee of Freedom of Association may be accessed at http://www.ilo.org/public/english/standards/norm/enforced/foa/cfa.htm.

4 North American Agreement on Labour Cooperation (NAALC) between the Government of Canada, the Government of the United Mexican States and the Government of the United States Of America 1993. Final Draft, 13 September 1993.

5 From the NAALC website: "If a matter related to occupational safety and health or other technical labor standards (NAALC's Labor Principles 4–11) has not been resolved after ministerial consultations, any country may request the establishment of an independent Evaluation Committee of Experts (ECE). The ECE shall analyze, in

the light of the objectives of the Agreement and in a non-adversarial manner, patterns of practice by each country in the enforcement of these labor standards. The ECE will present a final report to the Council. ECEs may not be convened to examine matters that are deemed not trade-related, not covered by mutually recognized labor laws, or related to the NAALC's Labor Principles 1 to 3. If after consideration of a final ECE report a country believes that there is still a persistent pattern of failure by another country to effectively enforce its occupational safety and health, child labor, or minimum wage technical labor standards, it may request further consultation, and eventually, the establishment of an independent Arbitral Panel. Arbitral Panels consist of five members who examine effective enforcement of laws related to Labor Principles 5, 6, and 9. Based on the panel's final report and its recommendations, the disputing parties may agree on a mutually satisfactory action plan. Failure to implement the plan could result in fines or trade sanctions." http://www.naalc.org/english/ece.shtml, accessed on 3 March 2005.

6 NAALC, Summary of Public Communications (as of March 2004), http://www.naalc.org/english/public.shtml, accessed on 3 March 2005.

7 See Rubery and Grimshaw (2003), 252–3, for a comprehensive list of EU labour standards directives.

8 Interview, NGO1, July 2007.

9 Accessed at http://www.gapinc.com/public/SocialResponsibility/sr_factories.shtml. Accessed June 2007.

10 Accessed at http://www.mec.ca/Main/content_text. jsp?FOLDER%3C%3Efolder_id=1408474396038947&FOLDER%3C%3 EbrowsePath=1408474396038947&bmUID=1181593804784. Accessed June 2007.

11 Interview, CSR2, July 2007.

12 Interview CSR1, June 2007.

13 Accessed at http://www.roots.com/index.php?/canada/content/view/18/58/lang,en/. Accessed June 2007.

14 ETAG Press Release, "Retailers to Adopt Sweatshop Standards," 3 May 2000; Naomi Klein, "No Sweat: Canada's Retailers Come Up Short on Delivering a Fair International Labour Code," *Globe and Mail*, 3 May 2000. The RCC claimed it would develop and implement a code on its own.

15 The "Top 5" companies in the report (in order) are Levi Strauss, Nike, Gap, Liz Claiborne, and Mountain Equipment Cooperative

(2005). In an updated version of the report issued in 2006, the "Top 5" had changed to Reebok, MEC, Adidas, Gap, and Levi Strauss (ETAG 2006).

16 Interview NGO1, July 2007.

17 Shawn McCarthy, "Gap Pressures Other Retailers with First Report on Sweat Shops," *Globe and Mail*, 13 May 2004, B1, B10.

18 Factory lists can be found at http://www.levistrauss.com/Citizenship/ProductSourcing.aspx; http://www.nike.com/nikebiz/nikeresponsibility/; http://www.timberland.com/include/csr_reports.

19 Interview, NGO2, July 2007.

CONCLUSION

1 Interviews, U1, August 2001; ER2, November 2001.

2 A court case between a Toronto-area garment worker and several clothing retailers illustrates the inadequacy of existing legislation in this regard. The worker claimed to be owed wages, overtime pay, and vacation pay for work performed over a two-month period. The worker further claimed that the ESA violation was the responsibility of the retailers who had contracted the work. The retailers, however, claimed that they exercised no control over the manufacturers with which they contracted the work or over any other parties subcontracted in the production chain. The Ontario Superior Court of Justice ruled in favour of the defendants, stating that "there is no evidence of a vertically integrated business relationship between any of the defendants" and the subcontracted manufacturer. The decision confirmed that while the retailers are able to benefit from the efficiencies and reduced labour costs achieved through subcontracted relationships, they are not legally responsible for the wages and working conditions of the workers who produce the products they sell. Nonetheless, while the court case did not secure compensation for the worker, the union that supported the worker considered the case successful in raising the profile of the abuses in the garment industry and in highlighting the need for legislative reform. A standard of joint liability is crucial in order to address the abuses faced by workers in subcontracted employment relationships. Ontario Superior Court of Justice, Between Fan Jin Lian (Plaintiff), and J. Crew Group Inc., Venator Group Canada Inc., Clothing for Modern Times Ltd., E. Knitted Garment Inc., and Eliz World Inc.

(Defendants), February 2001. Interviews, ER2, November 2001; U4, August 2002.

3 This figure is based on the 2005 before-tax low-income cut-off of $20,778 (Murray and Mackenzie 2007).

4 Judith Maxwell, "No Way Up the Pay Scale." *Globe and Mail,* Tuesday, 8 October 2002, A21.

5 Interviews, CL2, September 2002; ER3, September 2002; WAC (2007). As a result of this movement, and a growing awareness of the social problems associated with low-wage and precarious employment, in the spring of 2007 the Ontario provincial government announced a new schedule of minimum wage increases to take the minimum wage to $10.25 by 31 March 2010. Yet, even with this increase, minimum wage workers will continue to earn sub-poverty wages, as the increase will be outpaced by inflation (WAC 2007). A real minimum wage of $10 per hour (2005) would be $11.10 in 2010 (Murray and Mackenzie 2007).

6 For an overview of union strategies to re-regulate working time, see Thomas (2006).

7 In response to public concerns over the lack of enforcement, the Ontario Ministry of Labour claims to have adopted a more determined stance to enforce Ontario's employment standards legislation, which includes increased fines for ESA violations and targeted inspections of problem industries. The ministry has also indicated that it plans to increase the number of ESA officers for ESA complaints and to undertake a promotional and educational campaign to inform employers and employees of their respective obligations and rights under the act. Given the poor enforcement record to date, community legal workers have expressed scepticism as to the likely effectiveness of the ministry's new compliance strategy. Interviews, G1, July 2002; CL3, July 2002; CL4 August 2002.

8 For a detailed discussion of labour law reforms in this context, see Fudge et al. (2002).

9 Interview, U3, November 2001. Similar sentiments were reflected in other interviews: CL2, September 2002; U1, U2, August 2001;U4, August 2002.

10 Such proposals were advanced by the Ontario Labour Law Reform Committee in the early 1990s. See Shields and Russell (1994,342).

11 The notable legislative alternative is the decree system in Quebec, which allows for the extension of collective agreement provisions

across sectors and which includes non-unionized workers in coverage (Yanz et al. 1999). Another alternative is sectoral certification, which would allow workers in a given sector to opt in to an existing master agreement in the sector.

12 See "Homeworkers Association," <www.unite-svti.org>.

13 Interview, ER2, November 2001.

14 Interview, ER1, September 2001.

15 ETAG Press Release, "Retailers to Adopt Sweatshop Standards", 3 May 2000; Naomi Klein, "No Sweat: Canada's Retailers Come Up Short on Delivering a Fair International Labour Code," *Globe and Mail*, 3 May 2000.

16 "Sweatshops, Free Trade and the Americas – Highlighting Women behind the Labels," Conference Agenda, 2 November 1999. "Students against Sweatshops Networking Conference," Conference Agenda, 4–5 March 2000; "A Forum on Issues and Practices Affecting Licensing Policies for Use of University Insignia," Agenda, 31 January 2000. ETAG Update, 5 October 2000; Network Update, "Lobbying Mexico's New President on Worker Rights," 25 August 2000; MSN Update, "Wal-Mart Campaign and Call for Action," 19 July 2000; Memo for MSN members and friends, "The Harris Grinch is Trying to Steal Your Time Off and Money from Your Pocket."

Bibliography

ARCHIVAL SOURCES

Archives of Ontario Record Group 7-1, Ministry of Labour, Minister, Correspondence.
– Record Group 7-14, Ministry of Labour, Legislation and Regulation Files.
– Record Group 7-78, Ministry of Labour, Employment Standards Branch, Director's Correspondence.
– Record Group 7-130, Ministry of Labour, Research Studies, Policy and Legislation.
– Record Group 7-168, Ministry of Labour, Policy Subject Files.
– Record Group 7-186, Ministry of Labour, Policy and Program Development.

PRINTED SOURCES

Acker, Joan. 2006. *Class Questions, Feminist Answers*. Toronto: Rowman and Littlefield Publishers.
Adams, Roy J. 1987. "Employment Standards in Ontario: An Industrial Relations Systems Analysis." *Relations Industrielles/Industrial Relations* 42, no. 1: 46–64.
– 2002. "Implications of the International Human Rights Consensus for Canadian Labour and Management." *Canadian Labour and Employment Law Journal* 9, no. 1: 119–39.
Adib, Amel, and Yvonne Guerrier. 2003. "The Interlocking of Gender with Nationality, Race, Ethnicity and Class: The Narratives of Women in Hotel Work." *Gender, Work & Organization* 10, no. 4: 413–32.

African Canadian Legal Clinic (ACLC). 2000. *Deputation to the Ministry of Labour, Employment Standards Act Project Team.* Toronto: ACLC.

Akyeampong, Ernest B. 1997. "A Statistical Portrait of the Trade Union Movement." *Perspectives on Labour and Income* 9, no. 4: 45–54.

– 2000. "Unionization – An Update." *Perspectives on Labour and Income.* Ottawa: Statistics Canada.

Albo, Greg, and Chris Roberts. 1998. "European Industrial Relations: Impasse or Model?" In *Rising from the Ashes? Labour in the Age of "Global" Capitalism,* eds. E. Meiksins Wood, P. Meiksins, and Michael Yates, 164–79. New York: Monthly Review Press.

Arat-Koç, Sedef. 2001. *Caregivers Break the Silence.* Toronto: INTERCEDE.

– 2006. "Whose Social Reproduction? Transnational Motherhood and Challenges to Feminist Political Economy." In *Social Reproduction: Feminist Political Economy Challenges Neo-liberalism,* eds. K. Bezanson and M. Luxton, 75–92. Montreal and Kingston: McGill-Queen's University Press.

Armstrong, Pat. 1996. "The Feminization of the Labour Force: Harmonizing Down in a Global Economy." In *Rethinking Restructuring: Gender and Change in Canada,* ed. I. Bakker, 29–54. Toronto: University of Toronto Press.

Armstrong, Pat, and Hugh Armstrong. 1994. *The Double Ghetto: Canadian Women and Their Segregated Work.* 3d ed. Toronto: McClelland & Stewart.

– 1996. *Wasting Away: The Undermining of Canadian Health Care.* Toronto: Oxford University Press.

Armstrong, Pat, Mary Cornish, and Elizabeth Millar. 2003. "Pay Equity: Complexity and Contradiction in Legal Rights and Social Processes." In *Changing Canada: Political Economy as Transformation,* ed. W. Clement and L. Vosko, 161–82. Montreal and Kingston: McGill-Queen's University Press.

Arrighi, Giovanni, and Beverly J. Silver. 1999. *Chaos and Governance in the Modern World System.* Minneapolis: University of Minnesota Press.

Bacon, David. 2004. *The Children of NAFTA: Labor Wars on the U.S./Mexico Border.* Berkeley: University of California Press.

Baines, Donna, and Nandita Sharma. 2002. "Migrant Workers as Non-Citizens: The Case against Citizenship as a Social Policy Concept." *Studies in Political Economy* 69: 75–107.

Bakker, Isabella. 1996. "The Gendered Foundations of Restructuring in Canada." In *Rethinking Restructuring: Gender and Change in Canada,* ed. I. Bakker, 2–25. Toronto: University of Toronto Press.

Bannerji, Himani. 1995. *Thinking Through: Essays on Feminism, Marxism, and Anti-Racism.* Toronto: Women's Press.

Barker, Kathleen, and Kathleen Christensen. 1998. *Contingent Work: American Employment Relations in Transition.* Cornell University.

Basok, Tanya. 2002. *Tortillas and Tomatoes: Transmigrant Mexican Harvesters in Canada.* Montreal and Kingston: McGill-Queen's University Press.

Battye, John. 1979. "The Nine Hour Pioneers: The Genesis of the Canadian Labour Movement." *Labour/Le Travail* 4: 25–56.

Beck, Ulrich. 2000. *The Brave New World of Work.* Translated by P. Camiller. Cambridge: Polity.

Bensusan, Graciela. 2002. "NAFTA and Labor: Impacts and Outlooks." In *NAFTA in the New Millennium*, eds. E.J. Chambers and P.H. Smith, 243–64. La Jolla, CA: Centre for U.S.-Mexican Studies.

Bezanson, Kate, and Meg Luxton. 2006. *Social Reproduction: Feminist Political Economy Challenges Neoliberalism.* Montreal: McGill-Queen's University Press.

Black, Errol, and Jim Silver. 2001. *Building a Better World: An Introduction to Trade Unionism in Canada.* Halifax: Fernwood.

Block, Richard N., and Karen Roberts. 2000. "A Comparison of Labour Standards in the United States and Canada." *Relations Industrielles/ Industrial Relations* 55, no. 2: 273–307.

Boyer, Robert, ed. 1988. *The Search for Labour Market Flexibility: The European Countries in Transition.* Oxford: Clarendon Press.

Bradley, Harriet, Mark Erickson, Carol Stephenson, and Steve Williams. 2000. *Myths at Work.* Cambridge: Polity.

Brand, Dionne. 1991. *No Burden to Carry: Narratives of Black Working Women in Ontario, 1920s to 1950s.* Toronto: Women's Press.

– 1999. "Black Women and Work: The Impact of Racially Constructed Gender Roles on the Sexual Division of Labour." In *Scratching the Surface: Canadian Anti-Racist Feminist Thought*, eds. E. Dua and A. Robertson, 83–96. Toronto: Women's Press.

Brem, Maxwell. 2006. *Migrant Workers in Canada: A Review of the Seasonal Agricultural Workers Program.* Ottawa: North-South Institute.

Brennan, Geoffrey. 2000. "Minimum Wages and Working Time during the Last Century." *Workplace Gazette – Centennial Issue* 3, no. 4: 61–73.

Brenner, Robert. 1998. "The Economics of Global Turbulence." *New Left Review* 229.

– 1999. "Competition and Class: A Reply to Foster and McNally." *Monthly Review* 51, no. 7: 24–44.

British Columbia Federation of Labour (BCFL). 2002. *Summary of Employment Standards Changes.* Victoria: BCFL.

Broad, Dave. 1997. "The Casualization of the Labour Force." In *Good Jobs, Bad Jobs, No Jobs: The Transformation of Work in the 21st Century*, eds. A. Duffy, D. Glenday, and N. Pupo, 53–73. Toronto: Harcourt Canada.

– 2000. *Hollow Work, Hollow Society? Globalization and the Casual Labour Problem in Canada.* Halifax: Fernwood.

Brodie, Janine. 1996a. "Canadian Women, Changing State Forms, and Public Policy." In *Women and Canadian Public Policy*, ed. J. Brodie, 1–28. Toronto: Harcourt Brace Canada.

– 1996b. "Restructuring and the New Citizenship." In *Rethinking Restructuring: Gender and Change in Canada*, ed. I. Bakker, 126–40. Toronto: University of Toronto Press.

Burawoy, Michael. 1985. *The Politics of Production: Factory Regimes under Capitalism and Socialism.* London & New York: Verso.

Burchell, Brendan, David Ladipo, and Frank Wilkinson, eds. 2002. *Job Insecurity and Work Intensification.* London and New York: Routledge.

Burman, Patrick. 1997. "Changes in the Patterns of Unemployment: The New Realities of Joblessness." In *Good Jobs, Bad Jobs, No Jobs: The Transformation of Work in the 20th Century*, ed. A. Duffy, D. Glenday, and N. Pupo, 190–216. Toronto: Harcourt Canada.

Calliste, Agnes. 2000."Nurses and Porters: Racism, Sexism and Resistance in Segmented Labour Markets." In *Anti-Racist Feminism: Critical Race and Gender Studies*, eds. A. Calliste and G. Sefa Dei, 143–64. Halifax: Fernwood Publishing.

Campaign 2000 (2008) *Work Isn't Working for Ontario Families: The Role of Good Jobs in Ontario's Poverty Reduction Strategy.* Toronto: Campaign 2000.

Canada. Human Resources and Development (HRD). 1996. Unpublished Departmental Files. Ottawa: Human Resources Development.

Canadian Auto Workers (CAW). 1996. *Working Conditions Study: Benchmarking Auto Assembly Plants.* Toronto: CAW.

– 2000. *New Rights for a New Century: Modern Rights for Ontario Workers.* Toronto: CAW.

Canadian Federation of Independent Business (CFIB). 2000. *CFIB Submission to the Ontario Government on Its July 2000 Consultation Paper, Time for Change: Ontario's Employment Standards Legislation.* Toronto: CFIB.

Canadian Labour Congress (CLC). 1997a. *Women's Work: A Report.* Ottawa: CLC.

- 1997b. *Challenging Racism: Going Beyond Recommendations.* Ottawa: CLC.
- 2002. *Is Work Working For You? Report Card 2002.* Ottawa: CLC.
- 2005. *Labour Standards for the 21st Century: Canadian Labour Congress Issues Paper on Part III of the Canada Labour Code.* Ottawa: CLC.
Canadian Manufacturers' Association (CMA). 1944. "Annual Meetings of Divisions and Provincial and City Branches." *Industrial Canada* 45, no. 2. Toronto: CMA.
Canadian Union of Public Employees (CUPE). 2000. *Ontario Division Submission to Ministry of Labour on Time for Change: Ontario's Employment Standards Legislation.* Toronto: CUPE.
Card, David, and Alan Krueger. 1995. *Myth and Measurement: The New Economics of the Minimum Wage.* Princeton: Princeton University Press.
Carr, Barry. 1999. "Globalization from Below: Labour Internationalism under NAFTA." *International Social Science Journal* 159: 49–59.
Cavanagh, John. 1997. "The Global Resistance to Sweatshops." In *No Sweat: Fashion, Free Trade, and the Rights of Garment Workers,* ed. A. Ross, 39–50. London and New York: Verso.
Cecil, R.G., and G.E. Banks. 1992. "The Caribbean Migrant Farm Worker Programme in Ontario: Seasonal Expansion of West Indian Economic Spaces." *International Migration* 30: 19–36.
Chaykowski, Richard. 2005. *Non-standard Work and Economic Vulnerability.* Ottawa: Canadian Policy Research Networks.
Cheung, Leslie. 2005. *Racial Status and Employment Outcomes.* Ottawa: Canadian Labour Congress.
Clarke, Tony, and Maude Barlow. 1997. *MAI: The Multilateral Agreement on Investment and the Threat to Canadian Sovereignty.* Toronto: Stoddard.
Clarkson, Stephen. 2002. *Uncle Sam and Us: Globalization, Neoconservatism, and the Canadian State.* Toronto: University of Toronto Press.
Clement, Wallace. 2001. "Who Works: Comparing Labour Market Practices." In *Reconfigurations of Class and Gender,* eds. J. Baxter and M. Western, 55–80. Stanford, CA: Stanford University Press.
- 2007. Methodological Considerations: Thinking about Researching Work." In *Work in Tumultuous Times: Critical Perspectives,* eds. V. Shalla and W. Clement, 30–51. Kingston & Montreal: McGill-Queen's University Press.
- ed. 1997. *Understanding Canada: Building on the New Canadian Political Economy.* Montreal & Kingston: McGill-Queen's University Press.
Clement, Wallace, and John Myles. 1994. *Relations of Ruling: Class and Gender in Postindustrial Societies.* Montreal and Kingston: McGill-Queen's University Press.

Cobble, Dorothy Sue, and Leah F. Vosko. 2000. "Historical Perspectives on Representing Nonstandard Workers." In *Nonstandard Work: The Nature and Challenges of Changing Employment Arrangements*, eds. F. Carré, M.A. Ferber, L. Golden, and S.A. Herzenberg, 291–312. Champaign, IL: Industrial Relations Research Association.

Commission for Labor Cooperation. 2002. *Protection of Migrant Agricultural Workers in Canada, Mexico and the United States*. Washington: Commission for Labor Cooperation.

Cook, Joanne, and Jennifer Roberts. 2000. "Towards a Gendered Political Economy." In *Towards a Gendered Political Economy*, eds. J. Cook, J. Roberts, and G. Waylen, 3–13. London: MacMillan.

Cranford, Cynthia J., Leah F. Vosko, and Nancy Zukewich. 2003. "Precarious Employment in the Canadian Labour Market: A Statistical Portrait." *Just Labour* 3: 6–22.

Creese, Gillian. 1999. *Contracting Masculinity: Gender, Class, and Race in a White-Collar Union, 1944–1994*. Toronto: Oxford.

– 2006. "Exclusion or Solidarity? Vancouver Workers Confront the 'Oriental Problem.'" In *Canadian Working Class History: Selected Readings*. 3d ed., eds. L. Sefton McDowell and Ian Radforth, 199–216. Toronto: Canadian Scholars Press.

Dagg, Alexandra. 1997. "Worker Representation and Protection in the 'New Economy.'" In *Collective Reflection on the Changing Workplace: Report of the Advisory Committee on the Changing Workplace*, 75–118. Canada: Human Resources Development Canada.

Department of Labour. 1902a. "Sunday Shopping in Canada – some of its Legal Aspects." *Labour Gazette* 2 (January): 415–18.

– 1902b. "Labour Congress Interview with Dominion Government." *Labour Gazette* 2 (April): 590–5.

– 1904. "The Trades and Labour Congress of Canada, Nineteenth Annual Convention." *Labour Gazette* 4 (October): 320–9.

– 1908. "Legislation with Regard to Child and Female Labour in Canada." *Labour Gazette* 8 (March): 1100–20.

– 1909. "Night Work for Women in Ontario: Representations to Government on Behalf of Labour." *Labour Gazette* 9 (April): 1119–20.

– 1912. "Twenty-Seventh Annual Convention of the Trades and Labour Congress of Canada." *Labour Gazette* 12 (October): 338–49.

– 1920. "Canada and the International Labour Office." *Labour Gazette* 20 (July): 844–65.

– 1921. "Jubilee Convention of Canadian Manufacturers' Association." *Labour Gazette* 21 (June): 802–5.

– 1922a. "Notes on Current Matters of Industrial Interest: Labour Legislation Proposals for Ontario." *Labour Gazette* 22 (February): 115.
– 1922b. "Canadian Manufacturers' Association Annual Convention." *Labour Gazette* 22 (August): 844–7.
– 1924. "Recent Labour Legislation in Ontario and New Brunswick." *Labour Gazette* 24 (June): 479–82.
– 1925a. "Judgement of the Supreme Court of Canada Regarding the Eight Hour Day Convention of the International Labour Conference." *Labour Gazette* 25 (July): 671–2.
– 1925b. "Trades and Labour Congress of Canada: Summary of the Proceedings of the 41st Annual Convention." *Labour Gazette* 25 (August): 891–900.
– 1925c. "Canadian Manufacturers' Association: Fifty-Fourth Annual General Meeting." *Labour Gazette* 25 (August): 783–5.
– 1926a. "Notes on Current Matters of Industrial Interest: Benefit of Uniform Labour Laws." *Labour Gazette* 26 (April): 305.
– 1926b. "Labour Subjects at Recent Session of Dominion Parliament." *Labour Gazette* 26 (July): 651–5.
– 1926c. "Trades and Labour Congress of Canada: Summary of the Proceedings of the 42nd Annual Convention." *Labour Gazette* 26 (October): 964–77.
– 1929. "Minimum Wage Rates for Women in Ontario in 1928." *Labour Gazette* 29 (August): 885–6.
– 1931. "Canadian Manufacturers' Association: Sixtieth Annual Convention." *Labour Gazette* 31 (June): 668–72.
– 1933. "Canadian Manufacturers' Association: Proceedings at Sixty-Second Annual Convention." *Labour Gazette* 33 (June): 616–21.
– 1935a. "Ontario Executive of Trades and Labour Congress Presents Legislative Program to Provincial Government." *Labour Gazette* 35 (February): 160–1.
– 1935b. Untitled. *Labour Gazette* 35 (February): 150.
– 1936. "Annual Convention of the Canadian Manufacturers' Association." *Labour Gazette* 36 (June): 503–5.
– 1937a. "Notes on Current Matters of Industrial Interest: Ontario Bill Provides Minimum Wages for Men." *Labour Gazette* 37 (March): 264.
– 1937b. "Annual Report of Industrial Relations Committee, Canadian Manufacturers' Association." *Labour Gazette* 37 (June): 642–3.
– 1940. "Royal Commission on Dominion-Provincial Relations: Recommendations Concerning Unemployment Insurance, Labour

Legislation, etc.: Demarcation of Jurisdiction in Social Services."
Labour Gazette 40 (June): 545–54.

– 1944a. "Labour Legislation in Ontario and Saskatchewan in 1944."
Labour Gazette 44 (July).

– 1944b. "Recent Regulations under Dominion and Provincial
Legislation." *Labour Gazette* 44 (September): 1177–81.

– 1947. "Conventions of Labour Organizations." *Labour Gazette* 47
(November): 1568–89.

– 1951a. "Notes of Current Interest: Fair Employment Practices and
Equal Pay Bills in Ontario." *Labour Gazette* 51 (April): 443–4.

– 1951b. "Labour Legislation in Ontario in 1951." *Labour Gazette* 51
(June): 846–52.

– 1952. "The 12th Annual Convention of the Canadian Congress of
Labour." *Labour Gazette* 52 (October): 1312–28.

– 1956. "First Constitutional Convention of the Canadian Labour
Congress." *Labour Gazette* 56 (June): 634–58.

– 1957a. "Labour's Briefs to the Cabinet." *Labour Gazette* 57 (February):
147–58.

– 1957b. "Canadian Labour Congress Submits Annual Memorandum to
Cabinet." *Labour Gazette* 57 (November): 1289–95.

– 1958. "Equal Pay Legislation in Canada." *Labour Gazette* 58
(November): 1227–9.

– 1959. "Equal Pay for Equal Work." *Labour Gazette* 59 (September): 903–5.

– 1961. "Labour Legislation of the Past Decade – III." *Labour Gazette* 61
(February): 140–4.

– 1962a. "Progress toward Shorter Work Week." *Labour Gazette* 62
(March): 289–91.

– 1962b. "Six Provincial Labour Federations Held Annual Conventions
This Fall." *Labour Gazette* 62 (December): 1355–66.

– 1963. "Recent Regulations under Provincial Legislation." *Labour
Gazette* 63 (August): 713–26.

– 1964a. "Federal-Provincial Labour Conference." *Labour Gazette* 64
(April): 264–8.

– 1964b. "Recent Regulations, Federal and Provincial." *Labour Gazette* 64
(July): 592–7.

– 1964c. "Canada Labour (Standards) Code." *Labour Gazette* 64
(December): 1058–63.

– 1967. "Minimum Standards Legislation and Economic Policy." *Labour
Gazette* 67 (September): 567.

- 1968. "Annual Conventions of the Ontario and Quebec Federation of Labour." *Labour Gazette* 68 (February): 76–9.
- 1969a. "News Briefs: Ontario Ups Minimum Wage, Passes New Standards Act." *Labour Gazette* 69 (January): 27.
- 1969b. "Labour Standards Legislation in 1967–68." *Labour Gazette* 69 (January): 19–24.
Dewees, Donald N. 1987. *Special Treatment under Ontario Hours of Work and Overtime Legislation: General Issues.* A Report Prepared for the Ontario Task Force on Hours of Work and Overtime. Toronto: Ontario Task Force on Hours of Work and Overtime.
de Wolff, Alice. 2000. *Breaking the Myth of Flexible Work: Contingent Work in Toronto.* Toronto: Contingent Workers Project.
Doeringer, Peter B., and Michael J. Piore. 1971. *Internal Labor Markets and Manpower Analysis.* Lexington, MA: Heath.
Drache, Daniel. 1992. *Getting on Track: Social Democratic Strategies for Ontario.* Montreal and Kingston: McGill-Queen's University Press.
Duchesne, Doreen. 1997. "Working Overtime in Today's Labour Market." *Perspectives on Labour and Income* 9, no. 4: 9–24.
Duffy, Ann. 1997. "The Part-Time Solution: Toward Entrapment or Empowerment?" In *Good Jobs, Bad Jobs, No Jobs: The Transformation of Work in the 21st Century*, eds. A. Duffy, D. Glenday and N. Pupo, 166–88. Toronto: Harcourt Brace and Company Canada.
duRivage, Virginia L., Françoise J. Carré, and Chris Tilly. 1998. "Making Labor Law Work for Part-time and Contingent Workers." In *Contingent Work: American Employment Relations in Transition*, eds. K. Barker and K. Christensen, 263–80. Ithaca, NY: Cornell University Press.
Duxbury, Linda, and Chris Higgins. 2001. *Work-Life Balance in the New Millennium: Where Are We? Where Do We Need to Go?* Ottawa: Canadian Policy Research Networks.
Duxbury, Linda, Chris Higgins, and Donna Coghill. 2003. *Voices of Canadians: Seeking Work-Life Balance.* Ottawa: Human Resources Development Canada.
Edwards, P.K. 1994. "A Comparison of National Regimes of Labor Regulation and the Problem of the Workplace." In *Workplace Industrial Relations and the Global Challenge*, eds. P. Edwards, J. Belanger, and Larry Haiven, 23–42. Ithaca, NY: ILR Press.
Edwards, Richard. 1979. *Contested Terrain: The Transformation of the Workplace in the Twentieth Century.* New York: Basic Books.

Elliott, Kimberly Ann, and Richard B. Freeman. 2003. *Can Labor Standards Improve under Globalization?* Washington: Institute for International Economics.

Employment Standards Work Group (ESWG). 1996. *Bad Boss Stories: Workers Whose Bosses Break the Law.* Toronto: ESWG.

– 2000. *Time for Change: Tories Turn Back the Clock but Working People Want to Move Forward. A Response to Time for Change.* Toronto: ESWG.

Esping-Andersen, Gosta. 1990. *The Three Worlds of Welfare Capitalism.* Princeton: Princeton University Press.

Ethical Trading Action Group (ETAG). 2005. *Coming Clean on the Clothes We Wear.* Toronto: ETAG.

– 2006. *Revealing Clothing.* Toronto: ETAG.

Fairey, David. 2007. "New 'Flexible' Employment Standards Regulation in British Columbia." *Journal of Law and Social Policy* 21: 91–113.

Featherstone, Liza. 2002. *Students against Sweatshops.* London and New York: Verso.

Felstead, Alan, and Nick Jewson, eds. 1999. *Global Trends in Flexible Labour.* London: Macmillan.

Frager, Ruth A. 1992. *Sweatshop Strife: Class, Ethnicity, and Gender in the Jewish Labour Movement of Toronto, 1900–1939.* Toronto: University of Toronto Press.

Frances, Raelene, Linda Kealey, and Joan Sangster. 1996. "Women and Wage Labour in Australia and Canada, 1880–1980." *Labour/Le Travail* 38: 54–89.

Fudge, Judy. 1991. *Labour Law's Little Sister: The Employment Standards Act and the Feminization of Labour.* Ottawa: Canadian Centre for Policy Alternatives.

– 1996. "Fragmentation and Feminization: The Challenge of Equity for Labour-Relations Policy." In *Women and Canadian Public Policy*, ed. J. Brodie, 57–87. Toronto: Harcourt Brace Canada.

– 2001. "Flexibility and Feminization: The New Ontario Employment Standards Act." *Journal of Law and Social Policy* 16:1–22.

Fudge, Judy, and Eric Tucker 2000. "Pluralism or Fragmentation? The Twentieth-Century Employment Law Regime in Canada." *Labour/ Le Travail* 46:251–306.

– 2001. *Labour before the Law: The Regulation of Workers' Collective Action in Canada, 1900–1948.* Don Mills, ON: Oxford University Press.

Fudge, Judy, and Leah F. Vosko. 2001a. "Gender, Segmentation and the Standard Employment Relationship in Canadian Labour Law, Legislation and Policy." *Economic and Industrial Democracy* 22, no. 2: 271–310.

– 2001b. "By Whose Standards? Reregulating the Canadian Labour Market." *Economic and Industrial Democracy* 22, no. 3: 327–56.

– 2003. "Gender Paradoxes and the Rise of Contingent Work: Towards a Transformative Political Economy of the Labour Market." In *Changing Canada: Political Economy as Transformation*, eds. W. Clement and L.F. Vosko, 183–209. Montreal and Kingston: McGill-Queen's University Press.

Fudge, Judy, Eric Tucker, and Leah Vosko. 2002. *The Legal Concept of Employment: Marginalizing Workers.* Report for the Law Commission of Canada.

Fung, Archon, Dara O'Rourke, and Charles Sabel. 2001. *Can We Put an End to Sweatshops?* Boston: Beacon Press.

Gabriel, Christina. 1999. "Restructuring at the Margins: Women of Colour and the Changing Economy." In *Scratching the Surface: Canadian Anti-Racist Feminist Thought*, eds. E. Dua and A. Robertson, 127–64. Toronto: Women's Press.

Galabuzi, Grace-Edward. 2001. *Canada's Creeping Economic Apartheid: The Economic Segregation and Social Marginalization of Racialised Groups.* Toronto: Centre for Social Justice.

– 2006. *Canada's Economic Apartheid: The Social Exclusion of Racialized Groups in the New Century.* Toronto: Canadian Scholars Press.

Gibb, Heather. 2006. *Farmworkers from Afar: Results from an International Study of Seasonal Farmworkers from Mexico and the Caribbean Working on Ontario Farms.* Ottawa: North-South Institute.

Gindin, Sam. 1995. *The Canadian Auto Workers.* Toronto: Lorimer.

Glenn, Evelyn Nakano. 2001. "Gender, Race, and the Organization of Reproductive Labor." In *The Critical Study of Work: Labor, Technology, and Global Production*, eds. R. Baldoz, C. Kroeber, and P. Kraft, 71–82. Philadelphia: Temple University Press.

Goldberg, Michael, and David Green. 1999. *Raising the Floor: The Social and Economic Benefits of Minimum Wages in Canada.* Ottawa: Canadian Centre for Policy Alternatives.

Goutor, David. 2007. "Standing by Our Principles: The Trades and Labor Congress of Canada and Immigration, 1933–1939." *Just Labour: A Canadian Journal of Work and Society* 11: 55–65.

Haiven, Larry. 1995. "PC 1003 and the (Non)Right to Strike." In *Labour Gains, Labour Pains: 50 Years of PC 1003*, eds. C. Gonick, P. Phillips, and J. Vorst, 215–36. Halifax: Fernwood.

Hall, Karen. 1999. "Hours Polarization at the End of the 1990s." *Perspectives on Labour and Income* 11, no. 2: 28–37.

Harrison, Bennett. 1994. *Lean and Mean: The Changing Landscape of Corporate Power in the Age of Flexibility.* New York: BasicBooks.

Harvey, David. 1990. *The Condition of Postmodernity: An Enquiry into the Origins of Cultural Change.* Oxford: Blackwell.

– 2000. *Spaces of Hope.* Toronto: Oxford University Press.

Haworth, Nigel, and Stephen Hughes. 1997. "Trade and International Labour Standards: Issues and Debates over a Social Clause." *Journal of Industrial Relations* 39, no. 2: 179–95.

Haythorne, George V. 1960. *Labour in Canadian Agriculture.* Cambridge: Harvard University Press.

Heron, Craig. 1996. *The Canadian Labour Movement: A Short History.* Toronto: Lorimer.

Hudson, Maria. 2002. "Disappearing Pathways and the Struggle for a Fair Day's Pay." In *Job Insecurity and Work Intensification*, eds. B. Burchell, D. Ladipo, and F. Wilkinson, 77–91. London and New York: Routledge.

Human Resources Development Canada (HRDC). 2000a. *Workplace Gazette: Centennial Issue* 3, no. 4. Ottawa: Public Works and Government Services Canada.

– 2000b. *Highlights of Major Developments in Labour Legislation, August 1, 1999 to July 31, 2000.* Ottawa: HRDC.

– 2001. *Hours of Work and Overtime.* Ottawa: HRDC.

– 2002. *Minimum Employment Standards in Canada: Legislative Changes from September 1, 2001 to August 14, 2002.* Ottawa: HRDC.

Hurl, Lorna F. 1988. "Restricting Child Factory Labour in Late Nineteenth Century Ontario." *Labour/Le Travail* 21: 87–121.

Hyman, Richard. 1975. *Industrial Relations: A Marxist Introduction.* London: Macmillan.

– 1994. "Economic Restructuring, Market Liberalism and the Future of National Industrial Relations Systems." In *New Frontiers in European Industrial Relations*, eds. R. Hyman and A. Ferner, 1–14. Oxford: Blackwell.

Iacovetta, Franca, Michael Quinlan, and Ian Radforth. 1996. "Immigration and Labour: Australia and Canada Compared." *Labour/Le Travail* 38: 90–115.

INTERCEDE. 1993. *Meeting the Needs of Vulnerable Workers: Proposals for Improved Employment Legislation and Access to Collective Bargaining for Domestic Workers and Industrial Homeworkers.* Toronto: INTERCEDE.

International Confederation of Free Trade Unions (ICFTU). 1999. *Building Workers' Human Rights into the Global Trading System.* Brussels: ICFTU.

International Labour Organization (ILO). 1994. *Visions of the Future of Social Justice: Essays on the Occasion of the ILO's 75th Anniversary.* Geneva: International Labour Office.

– 2000. *Your Voice at Work.* Geneva: International Labour Office.

– 2002. "Towards a Policy Framework for Decent Work." *International Labour Review* 141, nos. 1–2: 161–74.

– 2005. *World Employment Report, 2004–5: Employment, Productivity and Poverty Reduction.* Geneva: International Labour Office.

Jackson, Andrew. 2003. "Regulating Precarious Employment: What Can We Learn from New European Models?" Unpublished paper.

– 2005. *Work and Labour in Canada: Critical Issues.* Toronto: Canadian Scholars Press.

Jackson, Andrew, David Robinson, Bob Baldwin, and Cindy Wiggins. 2000. *Falling Behind: The State of Working Canada 2000.* Ottawa: Canadian Centre for Policy Alternatives.

Jenson, Jane, Rianne Mahon, and Susan D. Phillips. 2003. "No Minor Matter: The Political Economy of Childcare in Canada." In *Changing Canada: Political Economy as Transformation,* eds. W. Clement and L. Vosko, 135–60. Montreal and Kingston: McGill-Queen's University Press.

Jessop, Bob. 1992. "Fordism and Post-Fordism: A Critical Reformulation." In *Pathways to Industrialization and Regional Development,* eds. M. Storper and A.J. Scott, 46–69. London and New York: Routledge.

– 1993. "Towards a Schumpeterian Workfare State? Preliminary Remarks on Post-Fordist Political Economy." *Studies in Political Economy* 40: 7–39.

Johnson, Andrew F., Stephen McBride, and Patrick J. Smith. 1994. *Continuities and Discontinuities: The Political Economy of Social Welfare and Labour Market Policy in Canada.* Toronto: University of Toronto Press.

Kalleberg, Arne L. 2001a. "Organizing Flexibility: The Flexible Firm in a New Century." *British Journal of Industrial Relations* 39, no. 4: 479–504.

– 2001b. "The Advent of the Flexible Workplace: Implications for Theory and Research." In *Working in Restructured Workplaces: Challenges and New Directions for the Sociology of Work,* eds. D. Cornfield, K. Campbell, and H. McCammon, 437–54. Thousand Oaks, CA: Sage.

Kealey, Gregory S. 1973. *Canada Investigates Industrialism: The Royal Commission on the Relations of Labor and Capital, 1889.* (Abridged). Toronto: University of Toronto Press.

– 1980. *Toronto Workers Respond to Industrial Capitalism, 1867–1892.* Toronto: University of Toronto Press.

Kinley, John. 1987. *Evolution of Legislated Standards on Hours of Work in Ontario*. A Report Prepared for the Ontario Task Force on Hours of Work and Overtime. Toronto: Ontario Task Force on Hours of Work and Overtime.

Klee, Marcus. 2000. "Fighting the Sweatshop in Depression Ontario: Capital, Labour and the Industrial Standards Act." *Labour/Le Travail* 45:13–51.

Krahn, Harvey. 1995. "Non-standard Work on the Rise." *Perspectives on Labour and Income* 7, no. 4: 35–42.

Krahn, Harvey, Graham S. Lowe, and Karen D. Hughes. 2006. *Work, Industry, and Canadian Society*. 5td ed. Toronto: Thomson Nelson.

Ladipo, David, and Frank Wilkinson. 2002. "More Pressure, Less Protection." In *Job Insecurity and Work Intensification*, eds. B. Burchell, D. Ladipo, and F. Wilkinson, 8–38. London and New York: Routledge.

Leah, Ronnie Joy. 1999. "Do You Call Me 'Sister'? Women of Colour and the Canadian Labour Movement." In *Scratching the Surface: Canadian Anti-Racist Feminist Thought*, eds. E. Dua and A. Robertson, 97–125. Toronto: Women's Press.

Little, Margaret. 1998. *"No Car, No Radio, No Liquor Permit": The Moral Regulation of Single Mothers in Ontario, 1920–1997*. Toronto: Oxford University Press.

Lipietz, Alain. 1987. *Mirages and Miracles: The Crisis in Global Fordism*. Trans. David Macey. London: Verso.

Lowe, Graham. 2000. *The Quality of Work: A People-Centred Agenda*. Toronto: Oxford University Press.

– 2007. *21st Century Job Quality: Achieving What Canadians Want*. Ottawa: Canadian Policy Research Networks.

Luxton, Meg. 1980. *More Than a Labour of Love: Three Generations of Women's Work in the Home*. Toronto: Women's Press.

Luxton, Meg, and June Corman. 2001. *Getting By in Hard Times: Gendered Labour at Home and on the Job*. Toronto: University of Toronto Press.

Macklin, Audrey. 1994. "On the Inside Looking In: Foreign Domestic Workers in Canada." In *Maid in the Market: Women's Paid Domestic Labour*, eds. W. Giles and S. Arat-Koç, 13–39. Halifax: Fernwood.

Mann, Michael. 1997. "Has Globalization Ended the Rise and Rise of the Nation-State?" *Review of International Political Economy* 4, no. 3: 472–96.

Maroney, Heather Jon, and Meg Luxton. 1997. "Gender at Work: Canadian Feminist Political Economy since 1988." In *Understanding Canada: Building on the New Canadian Political Economy*, ed. W. Clement, 85–117. Montreal and Kingston: McGill-Queen's University Press.

McBride, Stephen. 1995. "Coercion and Consent: The Recurring Corporatist Temptation in Canadian Labour Relations." In *Labour Gains, Labour Pains: 50 Years of PC 1003*, eds. C. Gonick, P. Phillips, and J. Vorst, 79–96. Halifax: Fernwood.

McBride, Stephen, and John Shields. 1997. *Dismantling a Nation: The Transition to Corporate Rule in Canada.* Halifax: Fernwood.

McCallum, Margaret E. 1986. "Keeping Women in Their Place: The Minimum Wage in Canada, 1910–25." *Labour/Le Travail* 17:29–56.

McInnis, Peter S. 2002. *Harnessing Labour Confrontation: Shaping the Postwar Settlement in Canada, 1943–1950.* Toronto: University of Toronto Press.

McIntosh, Robert. 1993. "Sweated Labour: Female Needleworkers in Industrializing Canada." *Labour/Le Travail* 32:105–38.

McKeen, Wendy, and Ann Porter. 2003. "Politics and Transformation: Welfare State Restructuring in Canada." In *Changing Canada: Political Economy as Transformation*, eds. W. Clement and L. Vosko, 109–34. Montreal and Kingston: McGill-Queen's University Press.

McNally, David. 1999. "Turbulence in the World Economy." *Monthly Review* 51, no. 2: 38–52.

– 2006. *Another World is Possible: Globalization and Anti-Capitalism.* 2d ed. Winnipeg: Arbeiter Ring Publishing.

Miller, Doug. 2004. "Preparing for the Long Haul: Negotiating International Framework Agreements in the Global Textile, Garment and Footwear Sector." *Global Social Policy* 4, no. 2: 215–39.

Mitchie, Jonathan, and John Grieve Smith, eds. 1995. *Managing the Global Economy.* Oxford: Oxford University Press.

Mitchell, Elizabeth. 2003. "The Employment Standards Act 2000: Ontario Opts for Efficiency over Rights." *Canadian Labour and Employment Law Journal* 10, no. 2: 269–86.

Mitter, Swasti. 1994. "On Organizing Women in Casualized Work: A Global Overview." In *Dignity and Daily Bread: New Forms of Economic Organizing among Poor Women in the Third World and the First*, eds. S. Mitter and S. Rowbotham, 14–52. London and New York: Routledge.

Mittleman, James H. 1996. "The Dynamics of Globalization." In ed. J.H. Mittleman. *Globalization: Critical Reflections*, London: Lynne Rienner, 1–19.

Moody, Kim. 1988. *An Injury to All: The Decline of American Unionism.* London and New York: Verso.

– 1997. *Workers in a Lean World: Unions in the International Economy.* London and New York: Verso.

Munck, Ronaldo, ed. 2004. *Labour and Globalisation: Results and Prospects.* Liverpool: Liverpool University Press.

Munro, Marcella. 1997. "Ontario's Days of Action and Strategic Choices for the Left in Canada." *Studies in Political Economy* 53: 125–40.

Murray, Gregor, Christian Levesque, and Guylaine Vallee. 2000. "The Re-Regulation of Labour in a Global Context: Conceptual Vignettes from Canada." *Journal of Industrial Relations* 42, no. 2: 234–57.

Murray, Stuart, and Hugh Mackenzie. 2007. *Bringing Minimum Wages above the Poverty Line.* Ottawa: Canadian Centre for Policy Alternatives.

Mutari, E., and D.M. Figart. 2000. "The Social Implications of European Work Time Policies: Promoting Gender Equity?" In *Working Time: International Trends, Theory and Policy Perspectives,* eds. L. Golden and D. Figart, 232–50. London and New York: Routledge.

Mysyk, Avis Darlene. 1994. *Class, Race, and Ethnic Relations in Manitoba Commercial Market Gardening, 1945–1993.* University of Manitoba. Unpublished thesis.

National Action Committee on the Status of Women (NAC). 2000. *Submission by the NAC on the Consultation Paper Time for Change: Ontario's Employment Standards Legislation.* Toronto: NAC.

Needleman, Ruth. 1998. "Building Relationships for the Long Haul: Unions and Community-Based Groups Working Together to Organize Low-Wage Workers." In *Organizing to Win: New Research on Union Strategies,* eds. K. Bronfenbrenner, S. Friedman, R. Hurd, R. Oswald, and R. Seeber, 71–86. Ithaca: Cornell University Press.

Ness, I. 1998. "Organizing Immigrant Communities: UNITE'S Workers Centre Strategy." In *Organizing to Win: New Research on Union Strategies,* eds. K. Bronfenbrenner, S. Friedman, R.W. Hurd, R. A. Oswald, and R.L. Seeber, 87–101. Ithaca: Cornell University Press.

Newton, Janice. 1995. *The Feminist Challenge to the Canadian Left, 1900–1918.* Kingston and Montreal: McGill-Queen's University Press.

Ng, Roxana, Renita Yuk-Lin Wong, and Angela Choi. 1999. *Homeworking: Home Office or Home Sweatshop?* Toronto: UNITE.

O'Conner, Julia, Ann Orloff, and Sheila Shaver. 1999. *States, Markets, Families.* Cambridge, UK: Cambridge University Press.

Ontario. 1985. *Final Report of the Commission of Inquiry into Wage Protection in Insolvency Situations.* Toronto: Ministry of Labour.

– 1987a. *Working Times: The Report of the Ontario Task Force on Hours of Work and Overtime.* Toronto: Ministry of Labour.

– 1987b. *Working Times: Phase II, The Report of the Ontario Task Force on Hours of Work and Overtime.* Toronto: Ministry of Labour.

– 1987c. *Bill 85 Amendments to the Employment Standards Act.* Employment Standards Bulletin. Toronto: Ministry of Labour.
– 1991. *Employee Wage Protection Program.* Background no. 91–05. Toronto: Ministry of Labour.
– 1998a. *Employer's Guide to the Employment Standards Act.* Toronto: Minister of Labour.
– 1998b. *The Future of Work in Ontario.* Toronto: Ministry of Labour.
– 2000a. "Ontario Government Releases Employment Standards Consultation Paper." Backgrounder. Toronto: Ministry of Labour.
– 2000b. *Time for Change: Ontario's Employment Standards Legislation. A Consultation Paper.* Toronto: Ministry of Labour.
– 2001a. *Who Is Covered by the ESA.* Toronto: Ministry of Labour.
– 2001b. *Your Guide to the Employment Standards Act.* Toronto: Ministry of Labour.
– 2007. *Agricultural Workers: Employment Standards Fact Sheet.* Toronto: Ministry of Labour.
– 2008. *Report Card: Employment Standards.* Toronto: Ministry of Labour.
– Various years. *Annual Report, Ministry of Labour.* Toronto: Ministry of Labour.
– Various years. *Business Plan, Ministry of Labour.* Toronto: Ministry of Labour.
– Various years. *Fiscal Year Report, Ministry of Labour Employment Practices Branch.* Toronto: Ministry of Labour.
Ontario Chamber of Commerce (OCC). 2000. *Response to the Ministry of Labour's Employment Standards Act Consultation Paper.* Toronto: OCC.
Ontario Federation of Labour (OFL). 1999. *The Future of Work in Ontario: Discussion Paper.* Submission by the OFL. Toronto: OFL.
– 2000. *Submission by the Ontario Federation of Labour on the Consultation Paper "Time For Change: Ontario's Employment Standards Legislation."* Toronto: OFL.
Organization for Economic Cooperation and Development. 1998. *Employment Outlook 1998.* OECD: Paris.
Palmer, Bryan D. 1987. *Solidarity: The Rise and Fall of an Opposition in British Columbia.* Vancouver: New Star Books.
– 1992. *Working Class Experience: Rethinking the History of Canadian Labour, 1800–1991.* 2d ed. Toronto: McClelland and Stewart.
Panitch, Leo. 1996. "Rethinking the Role of the State in an Era of Globalization." In *Globalization: Critical Reflections,* ed. J. Mittleman, 83–113. London: Lynne Rienner Publishers.

– 1998. "The State in a Changing World: Social-Democratizing Global Capitalism?" *Monthly Review* 50, no. 5: 11–22.

Panitch, Leo, and Donald Swartz. 2003. *From Consent to Coercion: The Assault on Trade Union Freedoms.* 3d ed. Toronto: Garamond.

Pearson, Ruth, and Gill Seyfang. 2001. "New Hope or False Dawn? Voluntary Codes of Conduct, Labour Regulation and Social Policy in a Globalizing World." *Global Social Policy* 1, no. 1: 49–78.

Peck, Jamie. 1996. *Work-Place: The Social Regulation of Labor Markets.* New York and London: The Guilford Press.

– 2001. *Workfare States.* New York and London: The Guilford Press.

Phillips, Paul. 1997. "Labour in the New Canadian Political Economy." In *Understanding Canada: Building on the New Canadian Political Economy,* ed. W. Clement, 64–84. Montreal and Kingston: McGill-Queen's University Press.

Porter, Ann. 2003. *Gendered States: Women, Unemployment Insurance, and the Political Economy of the Welfare State in Canada, 1945–1997.* Toronto: University of Toronto Press.

Preibisch, Kerry, and Leigh Binford. 2007. "Interrogating Racialized Global Labour Supply: An Exploration of the Racial/National Replacement of Foreign Agricultural Workers in Canada." *Canadian Review of Sociology and Anthropology* 44, no. 1, 5–36.

Progressive Conservative Party of Ontario (PCPO). 1995. *The Common Sense Revolution.* 7th Printing. Toronto: PCPO.

Pulkingham, Jane. 1998. "Remaking the Social Divisions of Welfare: Gender, 'Dependency,' and UI Reform." *Studies in Political Economy* 56:7–48.

Pupo, Norene. 1997. "Always Working, Never Done: The Expansion of the Double Day." In *Good Jobs, Bad Jobs, No Jobs: The Transformation of Work in the 21st Century,* eds. A. Duffy, D. Glenday, and N. Pupo, 144–65. Toronto: Harcourt.

Red Tape Review Commission (RTRC). 1997. *Cutting the Red Tape Barriers to Jobs and Better Government: Final Report of the Red Tape Review Commission.* Toronto: Red Tape Review Secretariat.

Reed, Augusta, and Charlotte Yates. 2004. "The Limitations to Global Labour Standards: The ILO Declaration on Fundamental Principles and Rights at Work." In *The Auto Pact: Investment, Labour, and the WTO,* ed. M. Irish, 243–56. London: Kluwer Law International.

Retail Council of Canada (RCC). 1996. *Presentation to the Standing Committee on Resources Development.* Toronto: RCC.

Rinehart, James. 2006. *The Tyranny of Work: Alienation and the Labour Process.* 5th ed. Toronto: Harcourt Canada.

Rockenbach, Leslie. 2001. *The Mexican-American Border: NAFTA and Global Linkages.* London and New York: Routledge.

Rosenberg, Samuel, ed. 1989. *The State and the Labour Market.* New York: Plenum Press.

Rosenfeld, Rachael A. 2001. "Employment Flexibility in the United States: Changing and Maintaining Gender, Class, and Ethnic Work Relationships." In *Reconfigurations of Class and Gender,* eds. J. Baxter and M. Western, 105–30. Stanford, CA: Stanford University Press.

Ross, Andrew. 1997. *No Sweat: Fashion, Free Trade, and the Rights of Garment Workers.* London and New York: Verso.

Ross, Robert. 2004. *Slaves to Fashion: Poverty and Abuse in the New Sweatshops.* Ann Arbor: University of Michigan Press.

– 2006. "A Tale of Two Factories: Successful Resistance to Sweatshops and the Limits of Firefighting." *Labor Studies Journal* 30, no. 4: 65–85.

Ross, Steven J. 1991. "Living for the Weekend: The Shorter Hours Movement in International Perspective." *Labour/Le Travail* 27: 267–82.

Rubery, Jill. 1992. "Productive Systems, International Integration and the Single European Market." In *International Integration and Labour Market Organization,* eds. A. Castro, P. Méhaut, and J. Rubery, 244–61. London: Academic Press.

Rubery, Jill, and Damian Grimshaw. 2003. *The Organization of Employment: An International Perspective.* Houndsmills, Basingstoke, Hampshire: Palgrave MacMillan.

Rubery, Jill, Mark Smith, and Colette Fagan. 1998. "National Working-Time Regimes and Equal Opportunities." *Feminist Economics* 4, no. 1: 71–101.

Rubery, Jill, and Frank Wilkinson, eds. 1994. *Employer Strategy and the Labour Market.* Oxford: Oxford University Press.

Russell, Bob. 1990. *Back to Work: Labour, State and Industrial Relations in Canada.* Scarborough: Nelson.

– 1991. "A Fair or a Minimum Wage? Women Workers, the State and the Origins in Wage Regulation in Western Canada." *Labour/Le Travail* 28: 59–88.

– 1997. "Reinventing a Labour Movement?" In *Organizing Dissent: Contemporary Social Movements in Theory and Practice.* 2d ed., ed. W.K. Carroll, 117–33. Toronto: Garamond Press.

Salais, Robert. 1992. "Labor Conventions, Economic Fluctuations, and Flexibility." In *Pathways to Industrialization and Regional Development*, ed. M. Storper and A.J. Scott, 276–99. London and New York: Routledge.

Sangster, Joan. 1995. "Women Workers, Employment Policy and the State: The Establishment of the Ontario Women's Bureau, 1963–1970." *Labour/Le Travail* 36: 119–45.

Sassen, Saskia. 1998. *Globalization and Its Discontents: Essays on the New Mobility of People and Money.* New York: The New Press.

– 2000. "Territory and Territoriality in the Global Economy." *International Sociology* 15, no. 2: 372–93.

Saunders, Ron. 2003. *Defining Vulnerability in the Labour Market.* Ottawa: Canadian Policy Research Networks.

Satzewich, Vic. 1990. "Rethinking Post-1945 Migration to Canada: Towards a Political Economy of Labour Migration." *International Migration* 28, no. 3, 327–45.

– 1991. *Racism and the Incorporation of Foreign Labour: Farm Labour Migration to Canada since 1945.* London and New York: Routledge.

Schenk, Chris. 1995. "Fifty Years after PC 1003: The Need For New Directions." In *Labour Gains, Labour Pains: 50 Years after PC 1003*, eds. C. Gonick, P. Phillips, and J. Vorst, 193–214. Halifax: Fernwood.

Sears, Alan. 1999. "The 'Lean' State and Capitalist Restructuring: Towards a Theoretical Account." *Studies in Political Economy* 59: 91–114.

Sengenberger, Werner, and Frank Wilkinson. 1995. "Globalization and Labour Standards." In *Managing the Global Economy*, eds. J. Mitchie and J. Grieve Smith, 111–34. Oxford: Oxford University Press.

Shalla, Vivian. 2007. "Shifting Temporalities: Economic Restructuring and the Politics of Working Time". In *Work in Tumultuous Times: Critical Perspectives*, eds. V. Shalla and W. Clement, 227–61. Montreal and Kingston: McGill-Queen's University Press.

Sharma, Nandita. 2001. "On Being *Not* Canadian: The Social Organization of 'Migrant Workers' in Canada." *Canadian Review of Sociology and Anthropology* 38, 415–39.

– 2006. *Home Economics: Nationalism and the Making of 'Migrant Workers' in Canada.* Toronto: University of Toronto Press.

Shields, John, and B. Mitchell Evans. 1998. *Shrinking the State: Globalization and Public Administration "Reform."* Halifax: Fernwood.

Shields, John, and Bob Russell. 1994. "Part-time Workers, the Welfare State, and Labour Market Relations." In *Continuities and Discontinuities:*

The Political Economy of Social Welfare and Labour Market Policy in Canada, eds. A.F. Johnson, S. McBride, and P.J. Smith, 268–90. Toronto: University of Toronto Press.

Shields, M. 2000. "Long Working Hours and Health." *Perspectives on Labour and Income* 12, no. 1: 49–56.

Silver, Beverly. 2003. *Forces of Labor: Workers' Movements and Globalization since 1870.* Cambridge: Cambridge University Press.

Smith, Vicki. 1997. "New Forms of Work Organization." *Annual Review of Sociology* 23: 315–39.

Standing, Guy. 1992. "Alternative Routes to Labor Flexibility." In *Pathways to Industrialization and Regional Development,* eds. M. Storper and A.J. Scott, 255–75. London and New York: Routledge.

– 1999. *Global Labour Flexibility: Seeking Distributive Justice.* London: Macmillan.

Stanford, Jim. 2000. "Canadian Labour Market Developments in International Context: Flexibility, Regulation, and Demand." *Canadian Public Policy* 26: 27–58.

Stanford, Jim, and Leah F. Vosko, eds. 2004. *Challenging the Market: The Struggle to Regulate Work and Income.* Montreal: McGill-Queen's University Press.

Stasiulis, Daiva. 1997. "The Political Economy of Race, Ethnicity, and Migration." In *Understanding Canada: Building on the New Canadian Political Economy,* ed. W. Clement, 141–71. Montreal and Kingston: McGill-Queen's University Press.

Stasiulis, Daiva, and Abigail B. Bakan. 2005. *Negotiating Citizenship: Migrant Women in Canada and the Global System.* Toronto: University of Toronto Press.

Statistics Canada. 1997–2001. "Key Labour and Income Facts." *Perspectives on Labour and Income.* Ottawa: Statistics Canada.

Steedman, Mercedes. 1997. *Angels of the Workplace: Women and the Construction of Gender Relations in the Canadian Clothing Industry, 1890–1940.* Toronto: Oxford University Press.

Sudbury, Julia. 1998. *"Other Kinds of Dreams": Black Women's Organizations and the Politics of Transformation.* London and New York: Routledge.

Suen, Rachel Li Wai. 2000. "You Sure Know How to Pick 'Em: Human Rights and Migrant Farm Workers in Canada." *Georgetown Immigration Law Journal* 15, 199–227.

Sugiman, Pamela. 2001. "Privilege and Oppression: The Configuration of Race, Gender, and Class in Southern Ontario Auto Plants, 1939 to 1949." *Labour/Le Travail* 47:83–113.

Teelucksingh, Cheryl, and Grace-Edward Galabuzi. 2005. *Working Precariously: The Impact of Race and Immigrants Status on Employment Opportunities and Outcomes in Canada.* Toronto: Canadian Race Relations Foundation.

Thomas, Mark. 2002. "Regulating Flexibility: The Case of Employment Standards in Ontario." In *Rethinking Institutions for Work and Employment: Selected Papers from the Thirty-eighth Annual CIRA Conference,* eds. G. Murray, C. Bernier, D. Harrison, and T. Wagar, 123–36. Quebec: Canadian Industrial Relations Association.

– 2004. "Setting the Minimum: Ontario's Employment Standards in the Postwar Years, 1944–1968." *Labour/Le Travail: Journal of Canadian Labour Studies* 54:49–82.

– 2006. "Union Strategies to Re-Regulate Work Time." *Just Labour: A Canadian Journal of Work and Society* 9:1–15.

– 2007. "Toyotaism Meets the 60-Hour Work Week: Coercion, 'Consent' and the Regulation of Working Time." *Studies in Political Economy* 80:105–28.

Thompson, Paul. 1989. *The Nature of Work: An Introduction to Debates on the Labour Process.* 2d ed. London: Macmillan.

Thorpe, Vic. 1999. "Global Unionism: The Challenge." In *Labour Worldwide in the Era of Globalization: Alternative Union Models in the New World Order,* eds. R. Munck and P. Waterman, 218–28. New York: St Martin's Press.

Torobin, Allan J. 2000. "The Labour Program and the International Labour Organization: Looking Back, Looking Ahead." *Workplace Gazette: An Industrial Relations Quarterly* 3, no. 4: 85–91.

Tucker, Eric. 1988. "Making the Workplace 'Safe' in Capitalism: The Enforcement of Factory Legislation in Nineteenth-Century Ontario." *Labour/Le Travail* 21: 45–85.

Turk, James. 1997. "Days of Action: Challenging the Harris Corporate Agenda." In *Open for Business, Closed to People,* eds. D. Ralph, A. Regimbald, and N. St-Amand, 165–76. Halifax: Fernwood.

Union of Needletrades, Industrial and Textile Employees (UNITE). 2000. *UNITE!*

– *Ontario Council Submission to the Employment Standards Review Project.* Toronto: UNITE.

United Steelworkers of America (USWA). 2000. *Time for Change: Ontario's Employment Standards Legislation, Consultation Paper. Submission of the United Steelworkers of America.* Toronto: USWA.

Ursel, Jane. 1992. *Private Lives, Public Policy: 100 Years of State Intervention in the Family.* Toronto: Women's Press.

Vallee, Guylaine. 2005. *Towards Enhancing the Employment Conditions of Vulnerable Workers.* Ottawa: Canadian Policy Research Networks.

Verma, Veena. 2003. *The Mexican and Caribbean Seasonal Agricultural Workers Program: Regulatory and Policy Framework, Farm Industry Level Employment Practices, and the Future of the Program under Unionization.* Ottawa: North-South Institute.

Vosko, Leah F. 2000. *Temporary Work: The Gendered Rise of a Precarious Employment Relationship.* Toronto: University of Toronto Press.

Vosko, Leah F., Nancy Zukewich, and Cynthia Cranford. 2003. "Precarious Jobs: A New Typology of Employment." *Perspectives on Labour and Income* 4, no. 10: 6–26.

Watson, Steve. 1997. "Ontario Workers Take On the 'Common Sense Revolution.'" In *Open for Business, Closed to People,* eds. D. Ralph, A. Regimbald, and N. St.-Amand, 134–42. Halifax: Fernwood.

Wells, Don. 1995. "Origins of Canada's Wagner Model of Industrial Relations: The United Auto Workers in Canada and the Suppression of 'Rank and File' Unionism, 1936–1953." *Canadian Journal of Sociology* 20, no. 2: 193–224.

– 1998. "Fighting the Mexico Mantra: Labour's New Internationalism." *Our Times* 17, no. 6: 20–7.

– 2004. "How Credible Are Corporate Labour Codes? Monitoring Global Production Chains." In *Challenging the Market: The Struggle to Regulate Work and Income,* eds. J. Stanford and L.F. Vosko, 365–83. Montreal and Kingston: McGill-Queen's University Press.

– 2007. "Too Weak for the Job: Corporate Codes of Conduct, Non-Governmental Organizations and the Regulation of International Labour Standards." *Global Social Policy* 7, no. 1: 51–74.

White, Julie. 2002. "A New Look at Shorter Hours of Work in the Communications, Energy and Paperworkers Union." *Just Labour* 1: 41–9.

Whittingham, Frank. 1970. *Minimum Wages in Ontario: Analysis and Measurement Problems.* Kingston, ON: Queen's University Industrial Relations Centre.

Wilkinson, Frank, ed. 1981. *The Dynamics of Labour Market Segmentation.* London: Academic Press.

Winson, Anthony, and Belinda Leach. 2002. *Contingent Work, Disrupted Lives: Labour and Community in the New Rural Economy.* Toronto: University of Toronto Press.

Wood, Ellen. 1998. "Labor, Class, and State in Global Capitalism."
    In *Rising from the Ashes? Labor in the Age of "Global" Capitalism*, eds.
    E. Meiksins Wood, P. Meiksins, and M. Yates, 3–16. New York: Monthly
    Review Press.

Workers' Action Centre (WAC). 2007. *Working on the Edge*. Toronto: WAC.

Yalnizyan, Armine. 1993. "From the DEW Line: The Experience of
    Canadian Garment Workers." In *Women Challenging Unions: Feminism,
    Democracy and Militancy*, eds. L. Briskin and P. McDermott, 284, 303.
    Toronto: University of Toronto Press.

– 1998. *The Growing Gap: A Report on Growing Inequality Between the Rich
    and Poor in Canada*. Toronto: Centre for Social Justice.

– 2007. *The Rich and the Rest of Us: The Changing Face of Canada's Growing
    Gap*. Ottawa: Canadian Centre for Policy Alternatives.

Yanz, Linda, Bob Jeffcott, Deena Ladd, and Joan Atlin. 1999. *Policy
    Options to Improve Standards for Women Garment Workers in Canada and
    Internationally*. Ottawa: Status of Women Canada.

Yates, Michael. 2000. "Workers of All Countries Unite: Will This Include
    the U.S. Labour Movement?" *Monthly Review* 52, no. 3: 46–59.

Zeitinoglu, Isik Urla, and Jacinta Khasiala Muteshi. 2000. "Gender, Race
    and Class Dimensions of Nonstandard Work." *Relations Industrielles/
    Industrial Relations* 55, no. 1: 133–67.

Index